Anna-Katharina Hornidge, Christoph Antweiler (eds.)
Environmental Uncertainty and Local Knowledge

Anna-Katharina Hornidge, Christoph Antweiler (eds.)

Environmental Uncertainty and Local Knowledge

Southeast Asia as a Laboratory of Global Ecological Change

[transcript]

This book project was kindly supported and financed by the Southeast Asia Department, Institute for Oriental and Asian Studies and the Center for Development Research, Zentrum für Entwicklungsforschung (ZEF), University of Bonn.

Bibliographic information published by the Deutsche Nationalbibliothek
The Deutsche Nationalbibliothek lists this publication in the Deutsche Nationalbibliografie; detailed bibliographic data are available in the Internet at http://dnb.d-nb.de

Cover layout: Kordula Röckenhaus, Bielefeld
Cover illustration: Anna-Katharina Hornidge, West Timor, Indonesia, 2009
Proofread & typeset by Anna-Katharina Hornidge
Printed by Majuskel Medienproduktion GmbH, Wetzlar
ISBN 978-3-8376-1959-1

Table of Contents

Introduction

The Nexus of Agency, Knowledge, and Environmental Change in Southeast Asia

CHRISTOPH ANTWEILER AND ANNA-KATHARINA HORNIDGE

Headlines about Southeast Asia in the global media refer prominently to either economic miracles or to ecological disasters. Both of these images are not beyond the point, but they portray only parts of the reality of a notoriously complex region. What is more important is that these perspectives tend to focus on the pinnacles of change while concealing the continuous processes of socio-economic and environmental changes of which they are a part.[1] This book takes the opposite perspective by bringing together theory-guided empirical research, largely conducted in the rural areas of Southeast Asia, on the linkage between environmental change processes and human actions taken to live with these. Particular interest lies in the role of different types of knowledge, i.e. local, localized external, global-expert knowledge, and their mobilization and further development to match changes in nature – the basis of livelihood provision. The disciplinary approaches taken range from (environmental and knowledge) sociology, cultural anthropology, and Southeast Asian studies to human ecology and anthropologically-informed botany.

---

1   For a general orientation on change in Southeast Asia see the following anthologies, introductory monographs, and overview articles: on change in the region in general see Schmidt et al. (1997), Neher (2000); on economic change and development see Savage et al. (1998), Rigg (2001, 2002), McGregor (2008); on political change Vatikotis (1995), specifically on institutional change Sjöhölm & Tongzon (2004), Weller (2005), on identity change Slama (2009), on social and especially ethnic change see O'Connor (1995), Winzeler (2010) and Adams & Gillogly (2011).

AN AREA AS A LABORATORY OF GLOBAL CHANGE

Environmental changes as the consequences of ecosystem and natural resources exploitation, as well as changes in the global climate, are increasingly severe, worldwide in scale, and partially irreversible. It is for this reason that geologists and climatologists are debating whether our planet has entered a new geologic age, the era of the *Anthropocene* (Crutzen 2002, Crutzen/ Stoermer 2000, Zalasiewicz et al. 2010).

In Southeast Asia the impacts of economic activities on the natural environment have been observed since early colonial times. These effects were often large-scale and sometimes pertained to whole landscapes. Ecological change caused or mediated by human activity is thus an old theme in the sociological and anthropological study of the region (e.g. Geertz 1963, King 1998, Vayda 1983, 2006, Wallace 2005). More recent debates nevertheless increasingly distinguish between, and jointly address globally, climate change-induced as well as locally-induced environmental consequences.

On the global, climate change-induced consequences for Southeast Asia,[2] the Intergovernmental Panel on Climate Change (IPCC) projects a regional increase in temperature of about 2.5°C, thus matching the global average (IPCC 2007a: ch. 11). Rainfall is estimated to increase by 7 per cent, but will concentrate on certain regions. Due to the complex landscape in island Southeast Asia and the importance of the sea for the local climate, local developments can also strongly differ from regional trends. Indonesia, for example, is projected to be heavily affected by rising sea levels: with a rise of 1m, 2,000 islands and 400,000ha land will be lost (IPCC 2007b: 485). In addition, temperatures are likely to rise relatively more in the inner parts of the islands, leading to reduced rainfall and to longer dry seasons and droughts (Hulme/Sheard 1999). In the areas where rainfall increases, the tendency for heavy rainfall to arrive suddenly also increases (IPCC 2007a: 886), with erosion and flooding as consequences. Besides these globally-induced changes, locally-induced changes can be observed, prominent examples being the cutting down of rainforest for timber (Dauvergne 1997, 2001) and palm oil plantations (Pye 2010).

The effects of these locally- and globally-induced changes range from local consequences, such as seasonal flooding, droughts, or salinized soils, to regional

---

2   For geographic overviews see Potter et al. (1995) and Gupta (2005) on physical matters and Chia Lin Sien (2003) for a human geography textbook focused on change in the region. Vorlaufer (2011) masterfully combines physical and human geography and provides numerous cases, facts and data on current change. For a bibliography explicitly limited to area-overview publications see Antweiler (2004).

hazards, such as the regularly occurring haze in the Straits of Malacca. And similarly, measures taken to cope with and adapt span from the level of the acting individual to transboundary initiatives (Kasperson et al. 1995, Badenoch 2002, Nguitragoo 2011). The precise design and implementation of these measures is often influenced by a mix of globally influenced local conceptions of the environment and nature. Conceptions and perspectives become practically effective for action, e.g. for environmental education (Yenken et al. 2000). Among politically important concepts are images of entities such as the tropics, the jungle, water, rivers, tribes, peasants, preservation, and development.[3] All of those concepts express views of culture and society (Greenough/ Tsing 2003) and at the same time have an impact on land-use schemes, forest management, biological classification, water control strategies, and community-based conservation measures.

There are winners and losers in this struggle for resources and environment. Thus, there are also constant volatile tensions and conflicts, resulting in increasing environmental movements and campaigning since the 1980s (see Argyrou 2005). These movements tend to react to very concrete problems such as logging, the building of elite golf courses, or tourist development, so these activities normally have a local focus (Kalland/ Persoon 1998, Dupar/ Badenoch 2002), while often being linked with environmentalist activities in western countries. Others, such as the growing palm-oil industry, are also mediated by worldwide processes, but only link specific regions (here the EU, India, Pakistan) outside Southeast Asia and selected countries (here Malaysia and Singapore) within the region, thus being transnational without being truly global (Pye 2010).

Southeast Asia is consequently a site of contradictions between uneven economic growth, with severe environmental effects, on the one hand and a widely shared aim of environmental protection on the other. Different sections and groups motivated by different interests compete for shares in the resource base (see cases in Resosudarmo/ Jotzo 2009). Beyond that, they not only compete over resources but also battle over the very process of environmentally relevant decision-making. We are dealing with issues that form the core of political ecology.[4] Environmental issues are one of the most important foci of the coalescence

---

3   The effects of conceptions of the environment on landscape planning during colonial times has been studied by, amongst others, Boomgaard (2007), Boomgard et al. (1997, 2005), Grove et al. (1998), Colombijn (1997), Ingold (2000), Ellen/ Fukui (1996).

4   See e.g. Atkinson (1991), Blaikie (1999), Biersack (2006), Bryant (2001), Zimmerer/ Bassett (2003), Paulson (2004), Whitehead et al. (2007), Rangan/ Kull (2009), Robbins et al. (2010), Robbins (2012); especially pertaining global issues see Peet et al. (2011), regarding the knowledge interface see Croll/ Parkin (1992).

of social forces and of the building of alliances and strategic groups (cf. Hirsch & Warren 1998 Greenough & Tsing 2003). In consequence, conservationists and environmental movements cannot be understood in terms of protest against environmental destruction alone, but additionally as a form of political resistance or more generally an idiom of cultural critique (Kalland/ Persoon 1998). The environmental changes and uncertainties attached to them nevertheless impede on cash and food crop agriculture, and here especially those whose systems of livelihood provision directly depend on the environment, namely urban and even more so rural poor.

ECOLOGICAL UNCERTAINTY AND HUMAN INSECURITY

Research into environmental uncertainty is flawed by the fact that there is a lack of integration between studies into issues of uncertainty with research on insecurity. This seems to be a problem, since uncertainty and human existential insecurity are often linked, for instance as factors in human actions, especially in decision-making. Human well-being is a central concern of development policies and measures. A key element for allowing well-being is human security.

Since 9/11, security has been a buzzword of debates about globalization. Courses in 'Security Studies' are proliferating, especially in the US and Southeast Asia, so it is no wonder that security issues tend to be discussed only in relation to material aspects, economic issues, or physical security (Eriksen et al. 2010: 5-8). The aims are typically formulated along material or physical dimensions as "freedom from want" or "freedom from fear". The bulk of current work is policy-oriented and argues on the macro-level. Against all slogans of "Putting People First," local people are seldom placed first. Thus, most conventional accounts do not take non-material considerations of security and insecurity into account. Especially the experience-near dimensions of insecurity are often overlooked. Both the human condition of insecurity and a status of uncertainty are often directly linked to collective identity (Salemink 2010: 262f.).

Uncertainty and insecurity have to do with belonging and social cohesion, which are related to human scales and locales. Politicians and economists concerned with globalization constantly ask for flexibility, and they praise spatial freedom. The current stars of 'post'-theorizing in contemporary cultural studies, despite often being quite critical of globalization, are celebrating movement and flexibility as well. At the same time, social scientists all over the world observe people investing a lot of work and brains into developing their specific locales, establishing secure livelihoods, and gaining a little certainty.

Changes in seasonal timing, rainfall patterns, and temperature scales, as currently experienced by people across Southeast Asia, therefore lead to a constant increase in uncertainties, insecurities and a lack of safety, as discussed by Beck (2007, 1996): While 'uncertainties' result from the loss of belief in science and expert knowledge, 'insecurities' are a loss of social security due to the depletion of the social welfare system or, in the presently discussed context, the system of livelihood provision. A 'lack of safety' results from threats to health and life, such as poisoned food, violence, or life-threatening floods. Others, as for example the STEPS Center in Sussex (Hornidge, this volume), identify four types of incertitude, each characterized by different forms of incomplete knowledge, while others again (Walker et al. 2003 in Deswandi et al., this volume) point to the lack of a shared understanding of the concept of 'uncertainty' amongst scientists.

What is nevertheless of immediate relevance to this volume is that environmentally-based uncertainties are especially pressing, since environmental change fosters a high level of knowledge uncertainty, the not knowing of how different localities are affected, to what degree, how to cope with it as well as how to adapt to the changed conditions. This ignorance poses an immediate and constantly growing threat for agricultural production throughout Southeast Asia, and so it especially affects vulnerable communities with a low degree of resilience.

While this has been noted by many national decision-making bodies, international organizations, and development practitioners, the uncertain prognosis on which environmental changes will affect different localities – and how – poses an immense challenge to the local as well as the external formulation of responsive strategies. The realization of the effects of environmental changes due to climate change, as well as ecosystem exploitation and respective degradation, therefore structures thinking and guides action in Max Weber's understanding. Yet, uncertainty surrounding the precise effects of climate change on different localities and communities challenges systematic responses further, and locally embedded adaptations to the ongoing changes become even more pertinent than before. The abilities of local communities to innovate, to modify their existing stocks of knowledge, and to develop locally embedded coping, as well as adaptation strategies that enable local communities to stay rather than migrate, are challenged.

OVERVIEW OF THE BOOK

The chapters of this volume discuss issues of environmental change, increased feelings of uncertainties posing threats to everyday livelihood provision in

Southeast Asia, and local means of attaching sense and taking actions towards coping with and adapting to these changes. Especially (but not exclusively) rural areas and local responses come under focus. In our reading of the issue at hand, we look mainly at environmental change that fosters knowledge uncertainties. This issue regards questions such as how do local communities perceive environmental changes affecting their ecosystem? How do they deal, cope with, and adapt to them? What are the responses of the local knowledge and innovation systems in place to the challenges that lie ahead?

In Chapter 1, following this introduction, *Anna-Katharina Hornidge* critically reflects on the notion of 'knowledge' in development discourses of the past 20 to 30 years, by focusing on (a) ongoing debates on the construction of 'information' and 'knowledge societies'; (b) the notion of 'knowledge for development', as put forth by international donor organisations; (c) global initiatives for the bridging of 'the global digital divide' summarized under 'ICTs for development'; (d) the current turn towards 'innovations and 'innovation systems'; and (e) upcoming debates on the adaptive capacities of 'knowledge' for living with change processes. She links a social constructivist definition of knowledge as everything that is regarded as knowledge in and by society (Berger/ Luckmann 1966, 1984) with current discourses of 'knowledge' in development. Therefore, the potentially all-encompassing character of 'knowledge' is discussed along the line of a 'boundary concept' (Mollinga 2008, 2010) and thus heuristic space for conceptual exchange and practical cooperation. In development, nevertheless, these were largely filled by those already defining what was regarded as 'knowledge' in actual projects of development cooperation.

This overview and introduction into 'knowledge' in current development discourses is then followed, in Chapter 2, by a combination of generalizing theory and localizing methodology by *Christoph Antweiler*. The methodological part assesses local knowledge through the application of simplified and locally adapted methods taken from cognitive anthropology. The theory part of this paper presents a general model of local knowledge which outlines ten interrelated qualities of local knowledge. These are exemplified using ethnographic field research on the environmental and migration-related knowledge of urban citizens in Makassar, Indonesia. Based on this research, the paper discusses local knowledge as a specific form of knowing and rationality found in societies worldwide.

Chapter 3, by *Christian Reichel, Sofie Elena Martens* and *Arne Harms*, empirically remains in Indonesia, studying culturally mediated perceptions, forms of knowledge-specific and quotidian interactions and cognitions in living with environmental changes in the Taka Bonerate atoll and the Spermonde Archipelago in South Sulawesi. Both research sites are affected by similar environmental changes and their consequences (i.e. the destruction of coral reefs, significant losses in biodiversity, overfishing, etc.). And in consequence the frames of reference structuring how these environmental changes are experienced, understood, and acted upon (and thus the potential of violent conflict being employed) also vary significantly. As a window into these fluctuating relations, the authors concentrate on local environmental knowledge (LEK), emphasizing its constant reiteration, not only with regard to the material, environmental conditions but also equally within wider frames of reference.

The mobilization of varying knowledge reference systems also forms the focus of Chapter 4, by *Judith Ehlert*. Here, taking the Mekong Delta, Vietnam, as a case, the author studies the integration of traditional weather lore and scientific weather forecasting as a local strategy commonly applied by farmers and fishers, to adapt to changes in the natural environment. Actors are capable of drawing on plural modes of environmental knowledge with reference to flood and weather variability, in order to back up agricultural decision-making. This process of local knowledge hybridization, or 'local weather knowing' as termed by Ehlert, serves as an adaptive strategy used to encounter environmental changes. The empirical assessment of integrating both knowledge reference systems into everyday farming routines therefore further substantiates ongoing discussions on cultural-ecological pragmatism inherent in people's relationships with their natural environment.

Similarly, Chapter 5 by *Paul Sillitoe* and *Mahbub Alam*, studies local farmers' and fishers' assessments of, and practices of adaptation to, environmental changes. But, differently to earlier chapters, the authors concentrate on environmental changes resulting from the construction of flood defenses under the World Bank-funded Flood Action Plan (FAP) and their impacts on subsistence activities across the Bangladeshi floodplain. We included this example from South Asia, as it shows dynamics found also in parts of Southeast Asia. Here, the risks involved in implementing external 'solutions', without a full understanding of the local situation, are discussed and lessons formulated for future policy-making. One of the main lessons learned is the need to, even more so than already done, cultivate a mindset in international development cooperation by first learning from local views. Knowledge evolved over generations should be consulted before implementing external ideas, which is particularly true in a situation such as that seen in the Bay of Bengal, where people are well-equipped to handle the uncertainties of climate change, a region where floods, droughts, and cyclones have been features of everyday life for millennia. These lessons could be used for current development measures in Southeast Asia, e.g. in the Mekong Delta.

Living with ecological extremes that in themselves are not new, but in their occurrence and outreach increase, is also taken up by *Viola Bizard* in Chapter 6. Based on anthropological research carried out on the boundaries of the tropical peat swamp forest of Sebangau in Central Kalimantan, the chapter documents the stories and experiences of those living with recurrent fires. How do they explain, perceive, and manage the fires? The practices of fire management are discussed with regard to regulatory customary law (*adat*) and at the same time with reference to existing constraints in mitigating, coping with, and even gaining from fires. As such, the two case studies offer insights into the fire risks in Indonesia's peatlands and their emic evaluation as positive (i.e. potential of a successful swidden cycle), as well as negative (i.e. potential damage to personal property and thus social conflicts and political sanctions) to be considered in externally developed mitigation strategies.

Roy Ellen and *Hermien L. Soselisa*, in Chapter 7, discuss cassava (*Manihot esculenta*) diversity and the local practices of production and consumption in Nuaulu village on the island of Seram and Debut on the Kei archipelago, both in eastern Indonesia. Precisely, the authors study the role of cassava toxicity in agricultural production, nutrition, and change adaptation. Both cases suggest that cassava will gain additional importance in coping with changed environmental conditions. Yet, in Nuaulu it is likely to gain importance as a secondary 'fallback' crop, and the local ecology will allow the production of a narrow range of mostly sweet cassava only, while in the Kei islands the heavy reliance on bitter cassava as a strategy for ensuring food security is further enhanced by growing an increasingly diverse range of cassava folk varieties in response to farming uncertainty under changing conditions.

Local forms of coping with and adapting to environmental changes while assuring livelihood provision also represent the core of Chapter 8, by *Rio Deswandi, Marion Glaser* and *Sebastian Ferse*. Based on empirical research in Sungai Pisang, West Sumatra and the Spermonde Archipelago in eastern Indonesia, the authors particularly address institutional adaptability and thus the capacity to (re)allocate natural resource use rights in order to allow for the local employment of coping strategies for fishing households in the face of growing food insecurity. The authors argue that this institutional adaptability to ever-changing environments forms the basis of a resilient social system. Continuing fishing practices, part of prevalent local coping strategies, nevertheless threaten the sustainability of the ecological system and result in an imbalance between ecological and social resilience. The authors here point to the need for the local development of scientifically informed coping strategies and thus a stronger integration of scientific forms of knowledge into local coping and adaptation strategies. The book closes with an afterthought by *Fabian Scholtes*. As the in-house expert of an aid agency, and at the same time an academic who has worked intensively on the topics at hand, he discusses the orchestra of chapters with regard to their contributions to ongoing academic debates on knowledge in change adaptation, as well as their potential practical value. His critical and constructive remarks on the contributions encourage the editors and authors – as well as you, our readers – to explore further the interlinkage of environmental changes, uncertainties, and knowledge in shaping change processes. It is in the nexus of environmental change and local ways of making sense of, coping with, and adapting to them that the interdisciplinary and empirically-based case studies presented here offer exemplary insights into Southeast Asia as a laboratory of global change.

REFERENCES

Adams, K. M./Gillogly, K. A. (eds.) (2011): Everyday Life in Southeast Asia. Bloomington & Indianapolis: Indiana University Press.

Antweiler, Ch. (2004): Southeast Asia: A Bibliography on Societies and Cultures. Münster: Lit Verlag/Singapore: Institute of Southeast Asian Studies (ISEAS).

Argyrou, V. (2005): The Logic of Environmentalism: Anthropology, Ecology, and Postcoloniality. London/New York: Routledge.

Atkinson, A. (1991): Principles of Political Ecology. London: Belhaven Press.

Badenoch, N. (2002): Transboundary Environmental Governance: Principles and Practice in Southeast Asia. Washington, D.C.: World Resources Institute.

Beck, U. (1996): Das Zeitalter der Nebenfolgen und die Politisierung der Moderne. In: Beck, U./Giddens, A. (eds.): Reflexive Modernisierung: Eine Kontroverse. Frankfurt/Main: Suhrkamp. 19-112.

Beck, U. (2007): Weltrisikogesellschaft. Frankfurt/Main: Suhrkamp.

Berger, P./Luckmann, T. (1966): The Social Construction of Reality. Garden City, New York: Anchor Books.

Berger, P./Luckmann, T. (1984): Die Gesellschaftliche Konstruktion der Wirklichkeit: Eine Theorie der Wissenssoziologie. Frankfurt/Main: Fischer Taschenbuch Verlag.

Biersack, A. (2006): Reimagining Political Ecology: Culture, Power, History, Nature. In: Biesack, A./Greenberg, J. P. (eds.): Reimaging Political Ecology.

Durham & London: Duke University Press (New Ecologies for the Twenty-First Century). 3-40.

Blaikie, P. (1999): A Review of Political Ecology: Issues, Epistemology and Analytical Narratives. Zeitschrift für Wirtschaftsgeographie 43(3-4). 131-147.

Boomgaard, P. (ed.) (2007): A World of Water: Rain, Rivers and Seas in Southeast Asian Histories. Leiden: LITLV Press.

Boomgaard, P./Colombijn, F./Henley, D. (eds.) (1997): Paper Landscapes: Explorations in the Environmental History of Indonesia. Leiden: KITLV Press.

Boomgaard, P./Henley, D./Osseweijer, M. (eds.) (2005): Muddied Waters: Historical and Contemporary Perspectives on Management of Forests and Fisheries in Island Southeast Asia. Leiden: KITLV Press.

Bryant, R. L. (2001): Political Ecology: A Critical Agenda For Change? In: Castree, N./Braun, B. (eds.): Social Nature: Theory Practice, and Politics. Malden/Oxford: Blackwell Publishers. 151-169.

Chia, L. S. (ed.) (2003): Southeast Asia Transformed: A Geography of Change. Singapore: Institute of Southeast Asian Studies (ISEAS) (Environment and Development Issues, 7).

Colombijn, F. (1997): The Ecological Sustainability of Frontier societies in Eastern Sumatra. In: Boomgaard, P./Colombijn, F./Henley, D. (eds.): Paper Landscapes: Explorations in the Environmental History of Indonesia. Leiden: KITLV Press. 309-339.

Croll, E./Parkin, D. (eds.) (1992): Bush Base, Forest Farm: Culture, Environment and Development. London/New York: Routledge (EIDOS; European Inter-University Development Opportunities Study Group).

Crutzen, P. J. (2002): Geology of Mankind. Nature 415. 23.

Crutzen, P. J./Stoermer, E. F. (2000): The 'Anthropocene'. Global Change Newsletter 41. 17–18.

Dauvergne, P. (1997): Shadows in the Forest: Japan and the Politics of Timber in Southeast Asia. Cambridge: The MIT Press (Politics, Science & the Environment).

Dauvergne, P. (2001): Loggers and Degradation in the Asia-Pacific: Corporations and Environmental Management. Cambridge: Cambridge University Press (Cambridge Asia-Pacific Studies).

Dupar, M. K./ Badenoch, N. (2002): Environment, Livelihoods and Local Institutions: Decentralization in Mainland Southeast Asia. Washington, D.C.: World Resources Institute.

Ellen, R. F./Fukui, K. (eds.) (1996): Redefining Nature: Ecology, Culture and Domestication. Oxford/Washington, D.C.: Berg (Explorations in Anthropology).

Eriksen, T. H. (2010): Human Security and Social Anthropology. In: Eriksen, T. H./ Bal, E./Salemink, O. (eds.): A World of Insecurity: Anthropological Perspectives on Insecurity. London/New York: Pluto Press (Anthropology, Culture & Society). 1-19.

Geertz, C. J. (1963): Agricultural Involution: The Processes of Ecological Change in Indonesia. Berkeley: University of California Press.

Greenough, P. R./Lowenhaupt Tsing, A. (eds.) (2003): Nature in the Global South: Environmental Projects in South and Southeast Asia. Durham/London: Duke University Press.

Grove, R. H./Damodaran, V./Sangwan, S. (eds.) (1998): Nature and the Orient: The Environmental History of South and Southeast Asia. Oxford: Oxford University Press.

Gupta, A. (ed.) (2005): The Physical Geography of Southeast Asia. New York: Oxford University Press.

Hirsch, P./Warren, C. (eds.) (1998): The Politics of Environment in Southeast Asia: Resources and Resistance. London/New York: Routledge.

Hulme, M./Sheard, N. (1999): Climate Change Scenarios for Indonesia. Norwich: Climate Research Unit.

Ingold, T. (2000): The Perception of the Environment: Essays on Livelihood, Dwelling and Skill. London/New York: Routledge.

IPCC (2007a): Climate Change 2007: The Physical Science Basis. Contribution of working group I to the fourth assessment Report of the Intergovernmental Panel on Climate Change. Cambridge/New York: Cambridge University Press. Available at: www.ipcc.ch/ipccreports/ar4-wg1.htm

IPCC (2007b): Climate Change 2007: Impacts, Adaptation and Vulnerability. Contribution of Working Group II to the Fourth Assessment Report of the IPCC. Cambridge/New York: Cambridge University Press. Available at: www.ipcc.ch/ipccreports/ar4-wg2.htm

Kalland, A./Persoon, G. (1998): An Anthropological Perspective on Environmental Movements. In: Kalland, A./ Persoon, G. (eds.): Environmental Movements in Asia. Richmond: Curzon Press (Nordic Institute of Asian Studies, Man & Nature in Asia Series, 4). 1-43.

Kasperson, J. X./Kasperson, J. E./Turner, B. L. (eds.) (1995): Regions at Risk: Comparisons of Threatened Environments. Tokyo et. al.: United Nations University Press.

McGregor, A. (2008): Southeast Asian Development. London/New York: Routledge (Routledge Perspectives on Development).

Mollinga, P. (2008): The Rational Organisation of Dissent. Bonn: ZEF Working Paper Series, Center for Development Research, University of Bonn, 33.

Mollinga, P. (2010): Boundary Work and the Complexity of Natural Resources Management. In: Crop Science, 50. 1–9.

Nguitragoo, P. (2011): Environmental Cooperation in Southeast Asia: ASEAN's Regime for Transboundary Haze Pollution. London/New York: Routledge (Routledge Contemporary Southeast Asia Series, 29).

O´Connor, R. (1995): Agricultural Change and Ethnic Succession in Southeast Asian States: A Case for Regional Anthropology. In: Journal of Asian Studies 54. 968-996.

Paulson, S./Gezon, L. L. (eds.) (2004): Political Ecology Across Spaces, Scales and Social Groups. New Brunswick: Rutgers University Press.

Peet, R./Robbins, P./Watts, M. J. (eds.) (2011): Global Political Ecology. London/New York: Routledge.

Potter, L./Brookfield, H./Byron, Y. (1995): The Eastern Sundaland Region of South-East Asia. In: Kasperson, J. X./Kasperson, J. E./Turner, B. L. (eds.) (1995): Regions at Risk: Comparisons of Threatened Environments. Tokyo et. al.: United Nations Uni-versity Press. 460-507.

Pye, O. (2010): The Biofuel Connection: Transnational Activism and the Palm Oil Boom. In: Journal of Peasant Studies 37(4). 851–874.

Rangan, H./Kull, C. A. (2009): What Makes Ecology 'Political'? Rethinking "Scale" in Political Ecology. Progress in Human Geography 33(1). 28-45.

Resosudarmo, B. P. /Jotzo, F. (eds.) (2009): Working with Nature against Poverty: Development, Resources and the Environment in Eastern Indonesia. Singapore: Institute of Southeast Asian Studies (Indonesia Project, the Australian Natinal University).

Rigg, J (2001): More than the Soil: Rural Change in Southeast Asia. Harlow: Prentice Hall, Pearson Education.

Rigg, J. (2002): Southeast Asia: The Human Landscape of Modernisation and Development. London/New York: Routledge.

Robbins, P. (2012): Political Ecology: A Critical Introduction. London: Wiley Blackwell (Critical Introductions to Geography).

Robbins, P. J. / Hintz, J. /Moore, S. A. (2010): Environment and Society: A Critical Introduction. London: Wiley Blackwell (Critical Introductions to Geography).

Salemink, O. (2010): Ritual Efficacy, Spiritual Security and Human Security: Spirit Mediumism in Contemporary Vietnam. In: Eriksen, T. H./Bal,

E./Salemink, O. (eds.): A World of Insecurity: Anthropological Perspectives on Insecurity. London/New York: Pluto Press (Anthropology, Culture & Society). 262-289.

Savage, V. R./Kong, L./Neville, W. (1998): The Naga Awakens: Growth and Change in Southeast Asia. Singapore: Times Academic Press.

Schmidt, J./Dragsbaek, J. H./Fold, N. (eds.) (1997): Social Change in Southeast Asia. Harlow: Longman.

Sjohölm, F./Tongzon, J. (eds.) (2004): Institutional Change in Southeast Asia. Richmond: RoutledgeCurzon (European Institute of Japanese Studies, East Asian Economics and Business Series).

Slama, M. (ed.) (2009): Konflikte, Mächte, Identitäten: Beiträge zur Sozialanthropologe Südostasiens. Wien: Verlag der Österreichischen Akademie der Wissenschaften (Österreichische Akademie der Wissenschaften, Philosophisch-Historische Klasse, Sitzungsberichte, 785).

Vatikotis, M. R. J. (1995): Political Change in South-East Asia: Trimming the Banyan Tree. London/New York: Routledge (Routledge in Asia).

Vayda, A. P. (1983): Progressive contextualization: Methods for research in human ecology. In: Human Ecology 11(3). 265-281.

Vayda, A. P. (2006): Causal Explanation of Indonesian Forest Fires: Concepts, Applications and Research Priorities. Human Ecology 34. 615-635.

Vorlaufer, K. (2011): Südostasien: Brunei, Indonesien, Kambodscha, Laos, Malaysia, Myanmar, Osttimor, Philippinen, Singapur, Thailand, Vietnam. Darmstadt: WBG (Wissenschaftliche Länderkunden).

Walker, W. E./Harremoës, P./Rotmans, J./van der Sluijs, J. P./van Asselt, M. B. A./Janssen, P./von Krauss, M. P. K. (eds.) (2003): Defining Uncertainty: A Conceptual Basis for Uncertainty Management in Model-Based Decision Support. In: Integrated Assessment 4/1. 5-17.

Wallace, B. J. (2005): The Changing Village Environment in Southeast Asia: Applied Anthropology and Environmental Reclamation in the Northern Philippines. London/New York: Routledge Chapman & Hall (Modern Anthropology of South-East Asia).

Weller, R. P. (2005): Civil Life, Globalization and Political Change in Asia: Organizing Between Family and State. London/New York: Routledge.

Whitehead, M./Jones, R./ Jones, M. (2007): The Nature of the State: Excavating the Political Ecologies of the Modern State. Oxford: Oxford University Press (Oxford Geographical and Environmental Studies).

Winzeler, R. L. (2010): The Peoples of Southeast Asia Today: Ethnography, Ethnology, and Change in a Complex Region. Lanham: Altamira Press.

Yenken, D./Fien, J./Skes, H. (eds.) (2000): Environment, Education and Society in the Asia-Pacific: Local Traditions and Global Discourses. London/New York: Routledge (Routledge Advances in Asia-Pacific Studies, 1).

Zalasiewicz, J./Williams, M./Steffen, W./Crutzen, P. (2010): The New World of the Anthropocene. In: Environmental Science & Technology 44 (7). 2228-2231.

Zimmerer, K. S./Bassett, T. J. (eds.) (2003): Political Ecology: An Integrative Approach to Geography and Environment-Development Studies. New York: Guilford Press.

'Knowledge' in Development Discourse

A Critical Review

Anna-Katharina Hornidge

INTRODUCTION

The idea of the mutual influence of 'knowledge' and 'development' can be traced back to 19th-century theories of social technology, emphasizing the role of knowledge for social change. In the mid-20th century, this conviction of "social interventions based on expert knowledge (possessed by a privileged group that acts as a trustee for the common good) [being] necessary to achieve positive social change" (Ziai 2011: 3; cf. Cowen/Shenton 1996) was taken up in international development discourse[1]. Especially the expert knowledge-based development paradigm of the 1950s to 1970s, with its revivalism in the "top-down, donor-conditionality-driven and outside-expert-led" (Gore 2000: 975) implementation approach of the *Washington Consensus* in the 1990s, was based on and heavily subscribed to the idea of 'development' being a linear process that universally follows a certain pattern. In order to trigger this "societal and economy-wide transition from a 'traditional' (rural, backward, agricultural) society to a 'modern' (urban, advanced, industrial) society" (2000: 794), mainly tangible, perceived as superior, forms of expert knowledge, i.e. innovations and technologies, stood at the core of large-scale development projects.

This assumed "sequence of stages of growth" (2000: 794), as well as an imbalance in the nature of 'cooperation' between the largely western 'experts' and

---

1   In the following I use the singular or plural of 'development discourse(s)' depending on whether the respective section refers to 'development discourse' in general and seen as the sum of multiple sub-discourses contributing to it, or explicitly to several sub-discourses of it.

'to-be developed' societies from the 1980s onwards, created a fertile ground for (a) substantial scholarly thought on forms of knowledge other than 'expert knowledge' in development (i.e. local, traditional, indigenous, tacit knowledge)[2] and (b) influential alternative development theories (i.e. dependency theory such as Cardoso/Faletto 1979; sustainable development and participation, i.e. WCED 1987; Doyle 1998; Cleaver 1999; gender, i.e. Chowdhury 1995; and post-development, i.e. Escobar 1985).[3]

Despite these opposing and, in their implementation, continuously contested development paradigms, the idea that 'knowledge' is crucial for change and change inherent to development has prevailed. Thus, the increasingly debated question is not so much whether 'knowledge' is of crucial importance for development, but rather which types of knowledge are activated by whom, how, and for what purpose. The topics discussed under the notion of 'knowledge' in development therefore range from culture- and religion-specific concepts of (national) identity to science policymaking, the construction of knowledge societies, the building of economic zones, science parks ('knowledge hubs' and 'clusters'), and information and communication technology networks, as well as the design of educational curricula. In these topic- and sector-specific debates, the broadness of the notion of 'knowledge' in many cases supports its heuristic role in facilitating conceptual exchange and practical cooperation. As such, and here pointing to the positive, the notion takes on the character of a boundary concept, which Mollinga defines with reference to Löwy and Star/Griesemer (Löwy 1992) by stressing:

"[...] boundary concepts are words that operate as concepts in different disciplines or perspectives, refer to the same object, phenomenon, process or quality of these, but carry (sometimes very) different meanings in those different disciplines or perspectives. In other words, they are different abstractions of the same 'thing'." (Mollinga 2008: 24)

---

2 Contributors include amongst others Polanyi (1966), Richards (1985), Geertz (1983), Banuri (1990), Apffel Marglin (1990), Appadurai (1990), Nonaka/Takeuchi (1995), Marglin (1996), Antweiler (1998, 2004), Sillitoe (1998a, 1998b), Ellen et al. (2000, 2002), Marchand (2003), Gerke/Evers (2006), Sillitoe/Marzano (2009), El-Berr (2009), Gerke/Ehlert (2011).

3 For critical reviews of development critiques, please see, amongst others, Pieterse (1998) and Blaikie (2000).

The notion of 'knowledge' as a boundary concept in development cooperation thus provides space for its creative exploration and acts as a platform for different actor groups communicating and contesting its diverse conceptualizations.[4]

These spaces for creative exploration also mean that "those who name the world," to use Spender's words (2000), are the ones who, with relatively more outreach and impact, break down the notion of 'knowledge' in development discourses and define and instrumentalize it in their (rather than opponents' or simply 'those who do not name the world') own terms.[5] In full, the quote reads as follows: "Those who name the world have the privilege of highlighting their own experiences – and thereby identify what they consider important. Thus, groups that have a marginal status are denied the vocabulary to define (and express) their own experiences" (Spender 2000: 195). While Spender refers in her work to gender-specific imbalances in existing power constellations, rather than the notion of 'knowledge' in development cooperation, the underlying imbalance between those who have the means to define futures and step towards these futures and those who do not also refers to the context at hand. This of course is exacerbated further if the 'spaces for explorative creativity' provided by the terminological and conceptual 'fuzziness' of a notion such as 'knowledge' in development are foremost filled by donor organizations and development agencies of the West, and less so by the representatives of 'to-be developed' societies or communities. Spender's quote continues by stating: "Naming is the means whereby we attempt to order and structure the chaos and flux of existence which would otherwise be an undifferentiated mass. By assigning names we impose a pattern [...] which allows us to manipulate the world" (Spender 2000: 195).

Studying the adoption, conceptualization, and "translation into practical action" of the notion of 'knowledge' in development discourses suggests a slight modification to this assessment. Here, the fuzziness of the notion of 'knowledge' in development (a) provided conceptual, physical, and virtual spaces for interaction for a wide range of definitions and consecutive actions taken, each with partly overlapping but diverging foci. The two UN-World Summits on the Information Society (WSIS), held in Geneva in 2003 and Tunis in 2005, can be mentioned as examples providing physical as well as virtual spaces of interaction. Yet, as some of the defining and acting donor organizations, government bodies, and private and public sector collective actors were more influential in

---

4 For an assessment of 'creative industries' as boundary concepts in the interaction between UNESCO and Singapore, see Hornidge 2011a.

5 Ziai goes even further and, despite the positive connotation of 'development' as forward directed change, regards the notion of 'development' as an "empty signifier that can be filled with almost any content but constrains its form" (2009: 183).

communicating their definitions than others, (b) these spaces allowed for and were filled by an imbalanced level of competition between more and less influential definitions of 'knowledge' in development. Amongst the more influential definitions can be found largely technocratic concepts with a strong technology focus and which are useful in the (short-term) planning and implementation of projects, but often not useful in the actual fostering of long-term sustainability.[6] The following foci can be mentioned as examples: the construction of 'information societies' and 'knowledge-based economies' by focusing on high-level investments in the building of 'science parks' and 'knowledge hubs', i.e. cluster developments, with a focus on research institutes, universities, and research conducting industries, and investing in research and development[7], constructing information and communication infrastructures – 'ICT for development', as well as investing in the development of agricultural technologies and innovation diffusion processes[8]. The sheer fact that the conceptual space for diversely defining 'knowledge' existed and was in general open to all nevertheless (c) acted as a legitimation for the definitions to come. Those largely technocratic definitions that 'won the race' gained legitimacy through the possibility of referring to the open space(s) in which (theoretically) every actor or actor group could participate and communicate their definition of 'knowledge' in development.

Consequently, the second part of Spender's quote above underlines only one aspect of naming while forgetting another: Naming is not merely an attempt to order, structure, and guide action, but instead 'fuzzy naming', the installment of broad, possibly widely definable terms and phrases such as 'knowledge' in development is, besides acting positively as a boundary concept, a means whereby ordering and structuring are left to those actors who are in a position to define it in more detail and legitimize action based on their ability to compete successful-

---

6   In consolidating and communicating these technocratic conceptualizations of 'knowledge', the UN-World Summits on the Information Society, with the International Telecommunication Union (ITU) as lead organizer, again played a crucial role (WSIS 2003, 2005, UNESCO 2009, Hornidge 2004).

7   For a review of respective activities along the Straits of Malacca, as well as the USA, Europe, Japan, and Germany, please see Evers/Hornidge 2008, Hornidge 2007a & b, 2010, 2011b.

8   Besides international funding foci within, for example, the CGIAR system, larger-scale development research projects under for example the program line of Integrated Water Resources Management (IWRM) of the Federal Ministry of Education and Research (BMBF), Germany can also be mentioned as examples. One example of German science policy implementation with regard to land- and water-related innovation development processes can be found in Hornidge et al. (2011a).

ly with others and their respectively opposing definitions over the power to define and move through action towards the realization of the defined. This then suggests that we should ask, whether, by assigning 'fuzzy' names and concepts, we actually create spaces in which those who already manipulate the world can further strengthen their power position, and then impose (or reaffirm) a pattern which allows them to continue manipulating the world, but now in an even more 'legitimate' manner?

With this question in mind, it is the aim of this chapter to shed further light on the notion of 'knowledge' in development discourses by assessing the positives and negatives of the notion's fuzziness. In doing so, I critically retrace 'knowledge' in development in five related discourses: (a) ongoing debates on the construction of 'information' and 'knowledge societies'; (b) as put forth as the development agenda of international donor organizations, summarized under 'knowledge for development'; (c) global initiatives for the bridging of 'the global digital divide' summarized under 'ICTs for development'; (d) the current trends of 'innovations' and 'innovation systems'; and (e) upcoming debates on the adaptive capacities of 'knowledge' for the living with change processes, ranging from climatic and environmental changes to socioeconomic and political transformation processes. Finally, the chapter ends with a concluding discussion.

A GLOBAL 'KNOWLEDGE' OR 'INFORMATION' SOCIETY?

From the late 1960s and early 1970s onwards, scholars from mainly Japan, the USA, and Europe assessed the increasing importance of different types of knowledge for the development of economies and societies and conceptualized the assessed subjects under terms such as 'knowledge society' and 'information society'.[9] International organizations such as the OECD closely followed, by

---

9   Amongst others, the following scholars can be mentioned as primary contributors: Machlup (1962); Umesao (1963); Lane (1966); Drucker (1969, 1993a, 1993b); Touraine (1969); Bell (1973, 1987); Porat (1976); Nora and Minc (1979); Böhme and Stehr (1986); Kreibich (1986); Castells (1989, 1996,1997, 1998); Gibbons et al (1994); Stehr (1994); and Willke (1998). Their works were then scrutinized and developed further in a secondary phase of construction by scholars such as Kumar (1978); Gershuny (1978); Collins (1981); Lyon (1988, 1996); Dordick and Wang (1993); Stehr (1994, 1999, 2001a, 2001b); Webster (1995); Willke (1998, 1999); Maasen (1999); Dunning (2000); Evers (2000a, 200b, 2002a, 2002b, 2003, 2005); Evers et al (2000); Hofmann (2001); Steinbicker (2001); David and Foray (2002); Lloyd and Payne (2002); Evers and Menkhoff (2004); Mattelart (2003); Evers and Gerke (2005);

sharpening economic focus on the ongoing debate and arguing for the development of 'knowledge-based economies'.[10] From there – although far from complete – all three concepts entered the national policymaking of many countries with the aim of constructing 'knowledge societies' for economic growth and future prosperity (Hornidge 2007a, 2010, 2011b). From the 1990s onwards, this drive towards 'knowledge societies' took on the form of global hype, leading in some countries to enormous investments in the building of (technology-focused) science parks and economic zones (i.e. Multimedia-Super-Corridor Malaysia, Biopolis Singapore, Nusantara 21 Indonesia)[11], the re-evaluation of applied versus basic research, and the development and widening of the portfolio of specially funded scientific disciplines in research and teaching, ranging from natural sciences and engineering to economics, social sciences, the arts, and 'creative industries'.[12]

The large majority of these government and (donor) organizations' activities in the construction of 'knowledge societies' broke down the vision into the technology-'information society' or the economy-'knowledge-based economy', both of which appeared more realizable to policymakers.[13] In the USA, for example, the idea of the preferred 'information society' gained significant ground in public debates in early 1992 and as part of the presidential campaign of Governor Bill Clinton and Senator Al Gore, which focused on the extension of the 'infor-

---

Knoblauch (2005); Kübler (2005); Tänzler, Knoblauch and Soeffner (2006) and Hornidge (2007a) to name a few.

10 Please see OECD (1996a, b), Stiglitz (1999) and APEC (1998, 2000).

11 Bunnell speaks of a "particularly high-tech strand of developmental utopianism" with regard to Malaysia (2002: 267). For a historic review of the emergence and planned construction of knowledge hubs along the Straits of Malacca, see Evers/Hornidge (2008).

12 For an assessment of these changes in the conceptualization of knowledge as captured under the notion of the 'knowledge society', see Hornidge (2007b). For an explicit focus on the rise of the concept of 'creative industries', see Hornidge (2011a).

13 Interview data from government representatives in Germany and Singapore on employing the terms 'information society' (in Germany) and 'knowledge-based economy' (in Singapore), rather than 'knowledge society' in government programs and action plans, cite two main reasons: the emphasis on (a) steps towards improved technological and economic/market infrastructures, i.e. the propagation of broadband or the linking up of companies, which are achievable in one election period, and (b) the economic value and tradable character of information and knowledge as resources for economic growth (Hornidge 2007: 169-192).

mation infrastructure' facilitating the growth of the Internet.[14] This technological focus underlined the tangibles of a future 'knowledge society' and found expression in the terminological preference for 'information society'. In Japan and the European Union, the terminological preference was 'information society' over 'knowledge society' in government programs and action plans. Yet, while Japan legitimized its actions by pointing to the need for research- and knowledge-based inspiration for its manufacturing industry, the European initiative has to be understood as a reaction to the pressures of global competition and increasing unemployment rates. Singapore identified the 'knowledge-based economy' as a path to economic survival and socio-political stability (Hornidge 2007, 2011a, 2011b). As such, the image of the 'knowledge-based economy' continues to be regularly frequented in government speeches and acts as a "guiding lamp" (Hornidge 2010: 812-814) and focal point of collective identity for Singapore's society.

In each of the four countries, adopting the image of a 'knowledge' or 'information society' as a future phase of societal development was thus based on the countries' internal and economic situations and as such answered the governments' searches for the legitimization of largely economy- and technology-government action and policymaking.

Nevertheless, at the same time the idea of 'knowledge' becoming increasingly key to economic and social development, and forming the basis for the development of 'knowledge societies' as the development stage following the industrial society, also entered the national science policymaking of developing countries hoping to accelerate their own economic development. At the beginning of the 1990s, for example, Malaysia[15] and Indonesia[16], as two developing nations with the ambition of following Singapore's path in developing into a fully industrialized society within three decades, also adopted the aim to develop local knowledge hubs that would form the basis for further development into 'knowledge societies'. Both countries, irrespective of their actual comparative

---

14 For a detailed overview over the conceptual development as well as the steps taken by the USA, Japan, EU and Singapore towards the actual construction of 'knowledge societies', see Hornidge (2011b), as well as amongst others Kubicek (1997), Read/Youtie (1995), Morris-Suzuki (1996), Tuomi (2001), Mattelart (2003), Bangemann (1994), Vogel (2000).

15 For details on Malaysia's path towards a 'knowledge society', please see amongst others Mahathir (28.02.1991), Bunnell (2002), Evers et al. (2010), Khor (2000), Taylor (2003), Fatimah (2009).

16 For details on Indonesia's path towards a 'knowledge society', please see amongst others Evers (2003), Rahardjo (2002), Pannen (2003).

advantages, and advised by McKinsey, the World Bank and the International Monetary Fund (Khor 2000, Pannen 2003), as earlier done by the USA, Japan, and the EU, identified information and communication technologies (ICTs) and new media, bio- and lifesciences, nanotechnologies, biotechnologies and creative industries (including arts and media content production) as key sectors for future development. Local comparative advantages, existing for example with regard to natural and synthetic rubber production or in the field of traditional medicine (*Jamu*), were less considered. Despite immense investment in the development of ICT and biotechnology sectors in Malaysia, today, 12 years later, Malaysia performs mainly supporting tasks for ICT and biotechnology R&D centers elsewhere (Evers et al. 2010).

The idea of 'knowledge' becoming increasingly important to social and economic development spread from the level of global 'knowledge society' discourse to development discourses, as discussed in the following. In both discourses, 'knowledge' as captured under notions of 'knowledge society' and 'information society', as well as 'knowledge' as discussed in development cooperation and measures of poverty alleviation, the broad concept of 'knowledge' (a) in its fuzziness allowed for its creative exploration by different actor groups and for the contestation of different conceptualizations, resulting in both cases in (b) that 'those who name the world' successfully competed with 'those who do not' over breaking the potentially emancipating, all-encompassing, and integrative notion of 'knowledge' down into applicable, largely technology categories and based on this defining new knowledge-centered constructs that guide action.

'KNOWLEDGE FOR DEVELOPMENT'

In 1996, the World Bank President, James Wolfensohn, rebranded the bank from a 'lending bank' into 'the knowledge bank' (King/McGrath 2004). In 1997, and with reference to the G-7 Global Information Society meeting in Brussels in 1995, as well as the Information Society and Development Conference in South Africa in 1996, the Global Knowledge Partnership then organized the first Global Knowledge Conference in Toronto, Canada (GKP 1997a). The conference brought together the global development and donor community, government and planning officials from developing countries, non-governmental organizations, and the private sector with the aim of discussing "the role of the 'information revolution' in the development process" (GKP 1997b).

Inspired by these predecessors, the idea of 'knowledge' being a key element of successful development cooperation and poverty alleviation culminated in 1999 in the publishing of the World Bank report entitled *Knowledge for Devel-*

opment. Envisioning a future saturated with knowledge and knowledge application, the report states: "Knowledge is like light. Weightless and intangible, it can easily travel the world, enlighten the lives of people everywhere" (WB 1999: 1). With this report, the notion of 'knowledge' as a driver of development, and a topic of debate for centuries, reached the summit of global (donor-driven) development discourse. From there it globally triggered further development interventions framed around the issue of 'knowledge for development'.

The report focuses, as stated explicitly on Page 1, on two sorts of knowledge and two types of problems, perceived as "critical to developing countries" by the bank. These are 'knowledge about technology', also referred to as 'technical knowledge' or 'know-how' and 'knowledge about attributes', such as "the quality of a product, the diligence of a worker or the creditworthiness of a firm," and incomplete knowledge about attributes, referred to as 'information problems' (WB 1999: 1). As such, the report adopts a technology-focused and highly applied definition of knowledge, based on a clearly stated assumption (1999: 1) that the employment of these two types of knowledge, as well as their delivery when they are missed by international institutions and developing-country governments, will further enable donor organizations' activities, projects, and programs in bringing about 'development'. The report consequently adopts a conceptualization of 'knowledge' that, at that time and up to the present day, also forms the core of envisioned future societies, replacing the development stage of the 'modern society', namely 'knowledge societies'.

Earlier research underlining the crucial role of indigenous, traditional, and local tacit knowledge for the development of communities,[17] basically standing in opposition to the 'expert knowledge'-focused development paradigm of the 1950s to 1970s, were acknowledged in the report (Chapters 1 & 9)[18.] The focus on 'knowledge about technology' and 'knowledge about attributes', both types of knowledge relatively more in the possession of industrialized countries, until today generally the countries of origin of these technologies, nevertheless renewed the former focus on 'expert knowledge' from the North.[19] Past experiences with sustainability issues involved in large-scale technology transfer were incorporated into a strong focus on institutional and system-level capacity building (getting the policy frameworks right), knowledge communication strategies, and the diffusion and out-scaling of technologies and their 'social attributes'.

---

17 For references please see footnote 2.

18 The term 'local knowledge' is used 11 times in the report, 'traditional knowledge' three and 'indigenous knowledge' also three times.

19 And this, despite the fact that the term 'expert knowledge' is only used once in the report, 'technical knowledge' eight times and 'technological knowledge' twice.

Similar to the World Bank, and further influenced by the bank's report, the United Nations Educational, Scientific and Cultural Organization (UNESCO) joined the global 'knowledge' for 'knowledge societies' and 'development' bandwagon and identified in its medium-term strategy 2002-2007 as "the contribution of information and communication technologies to education, science, culture, and information and the building of knowledge societies" as one of two cross-cutting themes which must be intrinsic to all UNESCO activities in the given time span (*UNESCO* 2002: 1).[20] Different to the World Bank, nevertheless, UNESCO does not adopt technology-(expert) knowledge conceptualization, but instead – in line with its overall mandate – emphasizes an open, integrating, and different conceptualization of knowledge in regard to its definition. As such, it identifies as three strategic thrusts: "(a) developing and promoting of universal principles and norms based on shared values; (b) promoting pluralism through recognition and safeguarding of diversity, together with the observance of human rights; and (c) promoting empowerment and participation in the emerging knowledge society through equitable access, capacity-building and knowledge-sharing" (2002: 2). This open, integrating conceptualization of knowledge 'for development' and 'in a knowledge society', which was outlined in detail in UNESCO's *World Report Towards Knowledge Societies*, published in 2005, forms a clear contrast to the one propagated in the World Bank report *Knowledge for Development* (WB 1999). At the same time, though, it also poses an example of a competing conceptualization that was largely overheard[21], as the increased turn to no longer 'knowledge for development' but explicitly 'ICTs for development' in the global discourses of knowledge of the early 2000s illustrates.

Interestingly, in Germany, the Federal Ministry for Economic Cooperation and Development (BMZ) only in May 2009, several years after the global pinnacle of the catch phrase 'knowledge for development', took it up again and published a position paper entitled accordingly. Here, the ministry emphasizes tertiary education and science production, less 'ICTs for development', as crucial areas of German development policy in times of a 'global knowledge society' (BMZ 2009). It thus lays the groundwork for an increased interest in tertiary

---

20 The second cross-cutting theme was "the eradication of poverty, especially extreme poverty" (UNESCO 2002: 1).

21 A rough Google search for 'World Bank Knowledge' and 'UNESCO Knowledge' offers a similar picture. While the former counts 130,000,000 entries, the latter produces only 28,500,000. The discrepancy is even larger when searching for 'World Bank Knowledge for Development' pointing to 54,900,000 entries and 'UNESCO Medium-Term Strategy 2002-2007' to 152,000 (conducted 01.11.2011).

education and science policymaking in German development policy under liberal leadership from October 2009 onwards. In the context of what we assess here, though, it can be regarded as an example for how the fuzziness of the notion 'knowledge for development' (a) allows for a diverse range of definitions in program planning and (b) how definitions that seemed to have 'won the race', as was the case with the conceptualization captured under 'ICTs for development' and discussed below, are evenly likely to be repeatedly contested (and possibly the strong positions of their supporters re-legitimized and re-affirmed by this repeated act of contestation) in the future.

'INFORMATION AND COMMUNICATION TECHNOLOGIES (ICT) FOR DEVELOPMENT'

The *Millennium Declaration* of the United Nations, published in 2000, does not point to 'knowledge for development', but instead regards the provision of 'access to information' as crucial (UN 2000, Millennium Development Goal (MDG) 23). Furthermore, the declaration underlines the adoption of this applied concept of knowledge by pointing to the importance of information and communication technologies (MDG 18):

"We [the heads of State and Government] also resolve, to ensure that the benefits of new technologies, especially information and communication technologies, in conformity with recommendations contained in the Economic and Social Council (ECOSOC) 2000 Ministerial Declaration, are available to all."

In the same year, and framed around the concern to close the 'digital divide', the *Okinawa Charter on the Global Information Society* (ADB 2000) emphasizes the role of investing in the building of ICT infrastructure. The charter's focus legitimates itself by pointing to the aim to foster 'development' in less developed and potentially, in the future, even more left behind regions, due to insufficient ICT access in times of a 'global information society'.

In September 2001, the General Assembly of the United Nations in its 'Road Map towards the Implementation of the United Nations Millennium Declaration' pointed to its newly found Information and Communication Technologies Task Force, which would "take steps to begin the bridging of the digital divide" (UN 2001: 3).

As such, 'knowledge' in development, and here especially also in the MDGs, is increasingly framed around 'information' and 'technologies'.[22] A focus also taken up by the World Bank in its *ICT Sector Strategy Paper*, approved by the board of the bank in 2001 and published in 2002 under the title *Information and Communication Technologies – A World Bank Group Strategy* (WB 2002b), was followed up with reference to the MDGs in December 2003 under the title *ICT and MDGs – A World Bank Group Perspective* (WB 2003). The four strategic areas identified by the bank under 'ICT for development' initiatives comprise information and communication infrastructure sector reforms, improving ICT access, ICT applications for e-business and e-government, and ICT-related human capacity building. Additionally, the bank increasingly legitimizes activities in the field of tertiary education with reference to the global 'knowledge society' discourse, touched on above (WB 2002a, Collins/Rhoads 2010).

In December 2001, the General Assembly of the United Nations once more underlined the importance of information and communication technologies for achieving the millennium development goals and welcomed the organization of a UN World Summit for the Information Society, sponsored by the UN, with the key objective of contributing to the narrowing of the digital divide, increasingly separating developed and less developed countries from one another, by providing access to information and information and communication technologies worldwide (UN 2002, Hornidge 2004). The 'lead managerial role' in organizing the summit was given to the International Telecommunication Union (ITU)[23], the council which had already endorsed this proposal by the ITU's Secretary-General in 1998 and 2001 (ITU 1998, UN 2002). Besides the ITU, numerous UN organizations, such as UNDP, UNESCO, UNICEF and WHO, international financial institutions, such as the World Bank and the IMF, as well as more than 50 heads of state contributed to the organization. As announced in the UN resolution, the summit was held in two phases and "at the highest possible level" (UN 2002: 2), with the first in Geneva 2003 and the second in Tunis 2005. Both parts of the summit were prepared in numerous preparatory conferences and meetings all over the world,[24] eventually bringing together 14,000 participants from 170 countries for the first phase held December 10 to 12, 2003 in Geneva

---

22 In Germany, the Federal Government pursues ICTs for development in its action program for 2015: Poverty Alleviation – a Global Task (BMZ 2001).

23 With regard to the cooperation with developing countries, the Telecommunication Development Sector of ITU (ITU-D) is especially active with regard to the development of the respective telecommunication sectors.

24 With the first one taking place in July 2002 and the last in September 2005. Please check www.itu.int/wsis for details.

(WSIS I) and 19,401 participants from 174 countries for the second phase held November 15 to 18, 2005 in Tunis (WSIS II). The most controversially discussed topics in Geneva were 'Internet governance', in the hands of the US-based Internet Corporation for Assigned Names and Numbers (ICANN), as well as the proposal by Senegal to consider the creation of a 'digital solidarity fund' as a financial instrument for the future targeting of the digital divide. At the end of WSIS I a 'Declaration of Principles' (WSIS 2003a) and a 'Plan of Action' (WSIS 2003b) were signed and a Digital Solidarity Fund (DSF) established as an "innovative financial mechanism of a voluntary nature open to interested stakeholders with the objective of transforming the digital divide into digital opportunities for the developing world" (WSIS 2003a: §28). The topic 'Internet governance' nevertheless was postponed to WSIS II, where the proposal by the European Union to relinquish US control over ICANN, and thus Internet-related policymaking, finally was not resolved. As such, WSIS II merely led to the formulation of a *Tunis Commitment* (WSIS 2005a) and a *Tunis Agenda for the Information Society* (WSIS 2005b).

Overall, both summit phases were highly successful in positioning the topic of 'ICTs for development' and the 'closing' of a global digital divide in global development discourse, as well as the main organizers as key actors in the field.[25] As such, the strategic narrowing down of the former 'knowledge for development' to 'ICTs for development', a process possibly also nurturing the interests of the ICT industries of mainly developed countries, and thus supporting an 'expert knowledge'-focused approach in development cooperation, ultimately still led to the contestation of the assumed superiority or inferiority of different types of knowledge and power structures. Even by focusing on the highly applied notion of 'knowledge', namely ICTs used for the bridging of digital divides and the building of 'information societies' and in the realm of a technology-dominated (*ITU*) UN world summit, questions after which types of knowledge, activated by who, how and for what purpose emerged as key points of contestation. The example of 'ICTs for development' therefore once more underlines that even technocratically organized debates on the most applied forms of knowledge (here 'information' and 'technology') cannot avoid questions on its governance. To make this point through Foucault (1974, 1988), the

---

25 Continued platforms for multi-stakeholder discussions on i.e. ICTs for Development and questions of Internet governance comprise amongst others of the United Nations Group on the Information Society (UNGIS), which in May 2011, has started a review process of the implementation of the Summit outcomes by 2015, the 'WSIS community' (www.wsis-community.org), facilitated by the ITU maintained WSIS Stocktaking Platform.

power/knowledge nexus prevails, even in the most depoliticized environment and on the most depoliticized form of knowledge.

'INNOVATIONS' AND 'INNOVATION SYSTEMS'

With the focus on 'knowledge about technology' or 'technical knowledge' and 'know-how', as well as 'knowledge about attributes', as postulated in the *World Bank Report 1998/99*, and the explicit focus on ICTs in the Millennium Development Goals, the prioritizing emphasis was once more placed on technology-related expert knowledge. Yet, different from before, technologies' 'social attributes', basically their institutional, socioeconomic, and cultural embedding and the required capacity development on the individual, institutional, and system level (Alaerts 2009), and thus also the localization of 'expert' knowledge, are increasingly recognized. As such, the former explicit focus on 'technologies' is increasingly replaced by stressing the need for 'innovations' and the creation of conducive environments for their development and further diffusion, hence the development of (national) 'innovation systems'. The term 'innovation' depicts social, institutional, financial, or technological innovations, which are no longer developed merely in the ivory towers of academia but increasingly in 'real-life' situations, with 'local stakeholders' or 'problem owners' (Hornidge et al. 2009; Hornidge et al. 2011a).

While the term 'national innovation system' was originally coined by Christopher Freeman in the late 1980s, with regard to Japanese institutional networks linking public and private sector activities for technology development (Freeman 1987), the idea of assessing the innovative capacities of societies rather than merely their current economic situation increasingly also enters development discourse. As such, in 2010, UNESCO published its UNESCO Science Report 2010 (UNESCO 2010a)[26] as well as its World Social Science Report 2010 (UNESCO 2010b),[27] drawing attention to knowledge production in the developing and developed worlds.[28] It becomes obvious here that even when applying Science, Technology and Innovation (STI) indicators originally developed by the

---

26 The term 'science' is used 2,386 times throughout the report, 'technology' 1,345 times, 'innovation' 903 times, 'innovation system' 59 times, 'knowledge' 380, and 'ICTs' 73 times.

27 The term 'science' is used 2,140 times throughout the report, 'knowledge' 653 times, 'technology' 166 times, 'innovation' 115 times, 'innovation system' not at all, and 'ICTs' two times.

28 Together, the two reports offer a comprehensive and highly useful overview of knowledge producing entities, science, and innovation systems worldwide.

OECD for OECD countries (UNESCO 2010a: 14, Freeman and Soete 2009, Tijssen and Hollanders 2006), knowledge production in the developing world is growing and increasingly gains the attention of developing countries' governments (UNESCO 2010a, 2010b).

The recent World Bank publication *Igniting Innovations* furthermore underlines this focus on 'innovations' and 'innovation systems' for the development of countries, but it holds on to a largely economically-oriented definition of 'innovation', here focusing on the role of governments in spurring high-technology innovation development and diffusion in emerging Europe and Central Asia. The report regards innovations as:

"[...] the development and commercialization of products and processes that are new to the firm, new to the market, or new to the world. The activities involved range from identifying problems and generating new ideas and solutions, to implementing new solutions and diffusing new technologies." (Goldberg et al. 2011: 5)

This linking of linear development and innovation diffusion thinking goes back to the expert knowledge-focused development paradigm seen between the 1950s and 1970s, as well as the innovation theory of the 1940s to 1980s. As examples, the pioneering works of diffusion theory by Ryan and Gross (1943), as well as the later Transfer of Technology approach by Chambers and Jiggins (1986), can be mentioned. Similar to 'development' in development theory of that time, this 'linear model' applied to innovation diffusion (Kline/Rosenberg 1986) postulates that introducing a new idea, technology/technique, or method – an innovation, in a 'recommendation domain' – can lead to a wave of adoption along an S-shaped 'diffusion curve': the diffusion process starts slowly, then gathers momentum, and finally peters out when all users for whom it is feasible have adopted the innovation (Rogers 2003; Röling 2005). Similar to the assumed superiority of (western/donor) expert knowledge in development, scientific knowledge implicitly is regarded consequently as superior to problem owners' knowledge and independent of context (Robertson/McGee 2003, Douthwaite et al. 2001).

This thesis, from the 1980s onwards, was answered by a wide range of criticism, pointing to the 'lack of fit' of externally developed technologies with problem owners' needs, due to an undervaluing of their knowledge of their own situation (e.g. Biggs 1978, 1980, Rhoades/Booth 1982, Richards 1985, Marglin 1996). Consequently, and together with participatory approaches increasingly influencing development discourse and practice, innovation and diffusion theory also turned to joint experimentation and transdisciplinary approaches to innovation development – in itself, again, not without problems (Chambers et al. 1989;

Jiggins/Zeeuw 1992; Hornidge et al. 2011a). Here, the importance of innovations being deployed each time in a specific social, political, and cultural context, and by the problem owners themselves to get them to work, is especially underlined. By stressing the socially constructed character of innovations, innovations' social embeddedness is emphasized as a determinant of their diffusion.[29]

Building on these decades of contested approaches to the linkage between 'innovations' and 'development', the STEPS[30] Center at the University of Sussex, England, forty years after the original Sussex Manifesto, prepared for the UN-Report *Science and Technology for Development: Proposals for the Second United Nations Development Decade* and rejected by the UN in 1970 (The Sussex Group 1970), published a new version under the title *Innovation, Sustainability, Development: A New Manifesto* (STEPS 2010). The group turns against the linear technology-focused development model of the UN's second development decade and instead proposes a combination of constructivist and positivist approaches to innovation development and diffusion within a globalizing and an ever-faster changing world (Leach et al. 2007). It furthermore emphasizes the need for more integrative and open innovation conceptualizations, fostering the integration of much wider stocks than the narrow technology focus reaffirmed above. The manifesto states on its opening page:

"By innovation, we mean new ways of doing things. This includes not only science and technology, but – crucially – the related array of new ideas, institutions, practices, behaviors and social relations that shape scientific and technological patterns, purposes, applications and outcomes. Central to this is a move away from progress defined simply by the scale or rate of change – about who is 'ahead' or 'behind' in some presumed one-track race." (STEPS 2010: 1)[31]

As such, the contestation of 'knowledge' in development, as captured under the term 'innovation', continues. Along the lines of a 'boundary concept', 'knowledge' in development creates conceptual, physical, and virtual spaces for

---

29 Amongst others, please see MacKenzie/Wajcman (1985), Bijker et al. (1987), Bijker/Law (1997), Oudshoorn/Pinch (2003), Duncan/Barnett (2005), Rath/Barnett (2006), Hall (2007).

30 STEPS - Social, Technological and Environmental Pathways to Sustainability.

31 And concludes by envisioning: "The result will be a flourishing of a more vibrant and creative diversity of pathways – scientific, technological, organizational and social. It is only in such ways that human ingenuity may truly rise to the imperatives of poverty alleviation, social justice and environmental sustainability" (2010: 24).

explorative interaction. Nonetheless, the above also suggests that each of the actors (and acting organizations) is determined by its legacies, path dependencies, and, of course, strategic interests. Spaces for the creative exploration of 'knowledge' in development are therefore quickly filled by the already existing and only minimally adjusted definitions of 'knowledge' for actual, long-term-oriented, emancipating social change.

Given the speed and magnitude of different processes of change increasingly inflicted on societies worldwide, the question arises as to whether these open but simultaneously repeatedly filled spaces by 'those who already name the world' and their agendas become increasingly irrelevant for 'manipulating' the world. This is discussed in the following by examining the increasing importance of 'knowledge' for coping with and adapting to change.

'KNOWLEDGE' AND '(CLIMATE) CHANGE ADAPTATION'

The achieved, and at the same time continued to be contested, learning of the past four decades of development cooperation on (a) 'development' not being as a linear process as we still often like to believe and (b) technologies only not being the 'magic bullets' of development, is today challenged by increasingly more prevalent processes of change and their consequences for local livelihood provision in the developing world. They range from environmental and climatic changes (currently felt especially along the equator) to socioeconomic transformation processes (i.e. in the countries of post-Soviet Central Asia), and the challenges they pose for the field of development cooperation are largely twofold: First, these processes of change significantly increase the speed at which change in some developing and transformation countries is taking place. On the one hand this opens up great opportunities to influence these change processes, but on the other hand it also means that the 'to-be-changed' is already changing at such a rapid pace that planned interventions from in- or outside are likely to be outdated by the time they are actually implemented. Second, and this is mainly true for climate change processes, we look at change processes caused largely by the actions and behaviorisms of developed countries (the North), but with the most immediate consequences in developing countries (the South). This 'justice gap' increases the pressure on international donor agencies and the sector of development cooperation to assist in coping with and adapting to these consequences of climate change.

Amongst the most pressing consequences of these different change processes are the rapid increases in different types of risk. Beck defines three types of risk that relate to three different dimensions of life (Beck 1996: 20f.). 'Uncertainties' result from the loss of belief in science and expert knowledge. 'Insecurities' are a loss of social security, for instance due to the depletion of the social welfare system. A 'lack of safety' results from threats to health and life, such as poisoned food, violence, or the like.[32] The STEPS Center in Sussex speaks of four types of 'incertitude', each characterized by different forms of incomplete knowledge. As such, the center identifies (Leach et al. 2007: 3):

"Some involve risk, where the range of possible outcomes and probabilities amongst them are known. Others involve uncertainty, where the possible outcomes are known but there is no basis for assigning probabilities, and judgment must prevail. Others still involve ambiguity, where there is disagreement over the nature of the outcomes, or different groups prioritize concerns that are incommensurable. Finally, some social, technological and ecological dynamics involve ignorance, where we don't know what we don't know, and the possibility of surprise is ever-present."

In situations characterized by constant change, all four forms of incomplete knowledge gain prevalence in everyday life. To cope with these in the short term, and to adapt to them in the long term, challenges existing knowledge stocks, basically the ability to mobilize different forms of knowledge in order to think creatively of ways to live with the changed situation at hand. Generally, and especially when the pace of ongoing changes is quite high, the need to find answers quickly – and matching very particular locally specific situations – determines that these 'solutions' have to be developed primarily by the problem owners themselves. Externally-funded activities can merely assist in these processes.[33] Consequently, the issue of the so-called 'lack of fit' often associated with expert knowledge from outside becomes increasingly relevant, while local capacities, and thus individual, institutional, and system level capacity development for knowledge and innovation development, gain importance.[34] Local

---

32 For an empirical assessment of living with environmental- and climatic change-induced risks in West Timor, Indonesia, as well as the activation of different stocks of knowledge for adaptation to these events, please see Hornidge/Scholtes (2012 forthcoming).

33 For a study on the linkages between climate change and poverty alleviation, please see Scholtes/Hornidge (2009, 2010).

34 This also has been acknowledged by the Federal Ministry of Education and Research (BMBF) of Germany, which increasingly stresses multi-level capacity development activities in all larger international and natural resource use focused research projects (i.e. BMBF program line on Integrated Water Resources Management). For an account of tightly state-defined spaces for local innovativeness in the agricultural sector

knowledge and its dynamic and creative potential (see Bizard, Sillitoe/Alam and Ellen/Soselisa in this volume) for coping and adapting to ongoing changes therefore increasingly moves into the center of sustained livelihood provision.

This argues for horizontally organized knowledge systems, allowing for the decentralized and independent (uncontrolled or censored/copyrighted) production and sharing of knowledge, and thus the free development of the individual's and society's creative potential, with a crucial determinant being legally ascertained freedom of speech. Nevertheless, it also argues for enabled societies, and thus education systems, fostering independently and critically thinking, self-reflective minds, rather than functional elites and high degrees of self-censorship.

As such, the issue of 'knowledge' for living with change, strengthening change resilience (see Deswandi et al. and Reichel et al. in this volume), and building adaptive capacities becomes a question of political will and the (long-term) (re)distribution of power within local communities, nation states, and measurements of development cooperation.

Interestingly these change-induced urgencies to cope and to enable/allow for coping with the consequences of change increasingly result in a situation in which 'those who name the world' are no longer able to manipulate (or merely control) the triggered change processes. Instead, those affected are forced to cope with and adapt to the changes, and in consequence they challenge their own (often limited) spaces of decision-making and innovative capacities. By doing so, these locally specific types of 'knowledge' for change adaptation (with the aim to sustain the already thin basis of livelihood provision) im- or explicitly contest existing systems of knowledge governance, as can currently be observed in Uzbekistan (Hornidge et al. submitted). They stand in direct competition with the above outlined expert and technological knowledge focused conceptualizations of 'knowledge' in development (Hornidge/Scholtes 2012 forthcoming), but gain prominence due to their immediate urgency in relation to coping with change consequences.

Whether such diversity-focused conceptualizations of 'knowledge' for change adaptation will nevertheless prominently enter global development discourse, potentially altering longstanding power imbalances, remains to be seen.

---

of Uzbekistan, and its impediments to changes with regard to water and land management, please see Hornidge et al. (2011b).

CONCLUSION

With the aim of critically reflecting on the notion of 'knowledge' in development discourses of the past 20 to 30 years, the above retraced changing framings and conceptualizations over time, namely 'knowledge' as captured under various sub-concepts of 'knowledge society', 'knowledge for development', 'ICTs for development', 'innovations', and 'innovation systems', as well as 'knowledge' and 'change adaptation'. Each of these conceptualizations has been constructed in and through discourse while at the same time, in line with Berger and Luckmann (1966/1984), has been communicated further as an action guiding construct in itself. The underlying idea of all these sub-discourses is that different types of knowledge are of crucial importance to development. Yet, which types of knowledge especially, and for what type of development, remains an open and ongoing contested question. However, by looking at the different sub-discourses of 'knowledge' in development, it becomes clear that some conceptualizations of knowledge, i.e. those emphasizing applied types of knowledge and information, as well as technological innovation packages (and as such expert knowledge largely from outside the developing countries themselves), prevail in so far all of these sub-discourses (with 'knowledge' and 'change adaptation' forming an exception). It consequently raises the questions underlying any research into knowledge systems, as to who decides which knowledge is regarded as crucial, is produced and shared, for what purpose and in whose interest? The above suggests a path dependency with regard to expert knowledge-focused approaches in development, further supported by existing structures of (short-term) project implementation, prevailing beliefs in development as a linear process, and the strategic (economic and political) interests of developed nations in emphasizing types of knowledge largely originating from the North, rather than the South. As such, the above also illustrates the close linkage between knowledge governance and power already stressed by Foucault (1974, 1984). The notion of 'knowledge' in its potentially all-encompassing character offers, along the line of a 'boundary concept' (Mollinga 2008, 2010), heuristic spaces for conceptual exchange and practical cooperation. However, when assessing how these conceptual, physical, and virtual spaces with a focus on 'knowledge' in development were largely filled in development discourses of the past 20 to 30 years, the role and potential of a 'boundary concept' not merely creating these spaces of interaction, but for this interaction to actually change existing power imbalances and knowledge conceptualizations (both mutually determining each other), seems rather limited. Instead, these conceptual, physical, and virtual spaces become arenas in and through which 'those who already name the world' successfully compete with 'those who do not'. The gained legitimacy reaffirms the position of the former, while the latter is merely left with the chance to continue contesting.

Nevertheless, is this a too simplistic and negative account of 'knowledge' in development? Looking at the wide range of types of 'knowledge' discussed with regard to change adaptation, and the sheer urgency to cope and let cope with the immediate as well as the longer term consequences of change (i.e. increases in incertitude), suggests a degree of patient interest. Technologies and expert knowledge developed outside of the affected regions do not meet the needs of immediate answers to immediate consequences that make sense locally. Additionally, the basis of the legitimacy of existing power imbalances is questioned by the so-called 'justice gap' between the main causers and the mainly affected regions. Consequently, the dominant conceptualizations of 'knowledge' and their embeddedness in power relations are questioned. However, whether change processes, their global reach, and the role of 'knowledge' in dealing with them reach the extent that prevailing power relations and the conceptualizations of 'knowledge' in development shaped by them will be modified, remains to be seen.

REFERENCES

Alaerts, G. J. (2009): Knowledge and capacity development (KCD) as tool for institutional strengthening and change. In: Alaerts, G.J./Dickinson, N (Eds.) Water for a changing world - Developing local knowledge and capacity. Delft.

Antweiler, Ch. (1998): Local Knowledge and Local Knowing. In: Anthropos 93(4-6). 469-494.

Antweiler, Ch. (2004): Local Knowledge Theory and Methods: An Urban Model from Indonesia. In: Bicker, Alan/Sillitoe, Paul/Pottier, Johan (eds.): Investigating Local Knowledge. Aldershot: Ashgate. 1-34.

APEC Economic Committee (1998): Towards an Information Society: Developments in Apec. Singapore: APEC Secretariat.

APEC Economic Committee (2000): Towards Knowledge-Based Economies in Apec - Framework and Summary. Singapore: APEC Secretariat.

Appadurai, A. (1990): Technology and the Reproduction of values in rural western India. In: Appfel Marglin, F./Marglin S.A. (eds.): Dominating Knowledge. Development, Culture and Resistance. Oxford: Clarendon Press. 185-216.

Appfel Marglin, F. (1990): Smallpox in Two Systems of Knowledge. In: Appfel Marglin, F./Marglin S.A. (eds.): Dominating Knowledge. Development, Culture and Resistance. Oxford: Clarendon Press. 102-144.

Asian Development Bank (ADB) (2000): Okinawa Charter on the Global Information Society. Asian Development Outlook 2000 Update. Box 1, 59. Manila.

Banuri, T. (1990): Modernization and its Discontents: A Cultural Perspective on Theories of Development. In: Appfel Marglin, F./Marglin S.A. (eds.): Dominating Knowledge. Development, Culture and Resistance. Oxford: Clarendon Press. 73-101.

Bangemann, M. (1994): Bangemann-Bericht: Europa Und Die Globale Informationsgesellschaft. Empfehlungen Für Den Europäischen Rat. Brüssel: Kommission der Europäischen Union.

Beck, U. (1992): Risk Society. Towards a New Modernity, London: Sage.

Beck, U. (2007): Weltrisikogesellschaft. Frankfurt a.M.: Suhrkamp.

Bell, D. (1973): The Coming of Post-Industrial Society. New York: Basic Books Inc.

Bell, D. (1987): The Post-Industrial Society: A Conceptual Schema. Evolution of an Information Society. London: Aslib.

Berger, P./Luckmann, T. (1966): The Social Construction of Reality. Garden City, New York: Anchor Books.

Berger, P./Luckmann, T. (1984): Die Gesellschaftliche Konstruktion der Wirklichkeit – Eine Theorie der Wissenssoziologie. Frankfurt/Main: Fischer Taschenbuch Verlag.

Biggs, S. D. (1980): Informal Research and Development. Ceres 13 (4): 23-26.

Biggs, S. D. (1978): Planning Rural Technologies in the Context of Social Structures and Reward Systems. Journal of Agricultural Economics 29 (3): 257-277.

Bijker, W./Hughes, T. P./Pinch, T. (eds.) (1987): The Social Construction of Technological Systems: New Directions in the Sociology and History of Technology. Cambridge: MIT Press.

Bijker, W./Law, J. (eds.) (1997): Shaping Technology / Building Society: Studies in Sociotechnical Change. Cambridge: MIT Press.

Blaikie, P. (2000): Development, post-, anti-, and populist: a critical review. Environment and Planning, 32, 1033-1055.

Böhme, G./Stehr, N.(eds.) (1986): The Knowledge Society. The Growing Impact of Scientific Knowledge on Social Relations. Boston: D. Reidel Publishing Company.

Bundesministerium für wirtschaftliche Zusammenarbeit und Entwicklung (BMZ) (2001): Armutsbekämpfung – eine globale Aufgabe, Bonn: BMZ.

Bundesministerium für wirtschaftliche Zusammenarbeit und Entwicklung (BMZ) (2009): Wissen für Entwicklung: Hochschulbildung und Wissenschaft in der deutschen Entwicklungspolitik. Ein Positionspapier des BMZ, BMZ Spezial 161, Bonn: BMZ.

Bunnell, T. (2002): Multimedia Utopia? A Geographical Critique of High-Tech Development in Malaysia's Multimedia Super Corridor, Antipode, Blackwell Publishers.

Cardoso, F. H./Faletto, E. (1979): Dependency and development in Latin América. University of California Press.

Castells, M. (1989): The Informational City - Information Technology, Economic Restructuring, and the Urban-Regional Process. Oxford: Basil Blackwell.

Castells, M. (1996): The Information Age: Economy, Society, and Culture, Volume 1: The Rise of the Network Society. Oxford, Malden: Blackwell Publishers.

Castells, M. (1997): The Information Age: Economy, Society, and Culture, Volume 2: The Power of Identity. Oxford, Malden: Blackwell Publishers.

Castells, M. (1998): The Information Age: Economy, Society, and Culture, Volume 3: End of Millenium, Oxford, Malden: Blackwell Publishers

Chambers, R./Pacey, A./Thrupp, L. A. (1989): Farmers First/ Farmer Innovation and Agricultural Research. London: Intermediate Technology Publications.

Chambers, R./Jiggins, J. (1986): Agricultural Research for Resource-Poor Farmers: A Parsimonious Paradigm. IDS Discussion Paper 220. Brighton (Sussex): IDS.

Chowdhry, G. (1995): Engendering development? Women in Development (WID) in international development regimes, In: Marchand, M./Parpart, J. (eds.): Feminism/Postmodernism/Development. London: Routledge, 26-41.

Cleaver, F. (1999): Paradoxes of Participation: Questioning Participatory Approaches to Development, in: Journal of International Development 11, 597-612.

Collins, R. (1981): Postindustrialism and Technocracy. In: Collins, Randall: Sociology since Midcentury. Essays in Theory Cumulation. New York: Academic Press. 305-308.

Collins, C. S./Rhoads, R. A. (2010): The World Bank. Support for universities, and asymmetrical power relations in international development. In: Higher Education 59. 181-205.

Cowen, M. P./Shenton, R. W. (1996): Doctrines of Development. London: Routledge.

David, P. A./Foray, D. (2002): An Introduction to the Economy of the Knowledge Society. Oxford: Blackwell Publishers.

Dordick, H. S./Wang, G. (1993): The Information Society: A Retrospective View. Newbury Park: SAGE Publications.

Douthwaite, B./de Haan, N. C./Manyong, V./Keatinge, D. (2001): Blending "hard" and "soft" Science: the "follow-the-technology" Approach to Catalyzing and Evaluating Technology Change. Ecology and Society 5(2).

Doyle, T. (1998): Sustainable Development and Agenda 21: the secular bible of global free markets and pluralist democracy. Third World Quarterly 19(4), 771-786.

Drucker, P. F. (1969): The Age of Discontinuity. Guidelines to Our Changing Society. London: Heinemann.

Drucker, P. F. (1993a): Die Postkapitalistische Gesellschaft. Düsseldorf: Econ Verlag.

Drucker, P. F. (1993b): The Rise of the Knowledge Society. The Wilson Quarterly 17(2). 52-72.

Duncan, A./Barnett, A. (2005): How Can Research-based Development Interventions be more Effective at Influencing Policy and Practice?, Workshop organized by the Making Market Systems Work Better for the Poor (M4P) program, October 31st- November 4th, 2005. Hanoi: The Policy Practice.

Dunning, J. H. (2000): Regions, Globalization, and the Knowledge-Based Economy. Oxford: Oxford University Press.

El-Berr, S. (2009): Wer sind hier die Experten? Lokales Wissen und interkulturelle Kommunikation in Entwicklungsprojekten mit Indigenen Ecuadors. Bonn: University of Bonn.

Ellen, R. F./Parkes. P./Bicker, A. (eds.) (2000): Indigenous environmental knowledge and its transformations: critical anthropological perspectives. Amsterdam: Harwood Academic Publishers.

Ellen, R. F. (2002): Déja vu, all over again', again: reinvention and progress in applying local knowledge to development. In: Sillitoe, P./Bicker, A./Pottier, J. (eds.) Participating in development: approaches to indigenous knowledge, [ASA Monogr. 39] London and New York: Routledge, pp. 235-258.

Escobar, A. (1985): Discourse and Power in Development: Michel Foucault and the relevance of his work to the Third World. Alternatives, 10 (3), 377-400.

Evers, H.-D. (2000a): Die Globalisierung Der Epistemischen Kulturen: Entwicklungstheorie Und Wissensgesellschaft. In: Menzel, U. (ed.): Vom Ewigen Frieden Und Dem Wohlstand Der Nationen. Frankfurt/Main: Suhrkamp. 396-417.

Evers, H.-D. (2000b): Knowledge Societies: An Overview of Issues and Theories. Singapore: National University of Singapore.

Evers, H.-D. (2002a): Southeast Asian Knowledge Societies. Bonn: University of Bonn.

Evers, H.-D. (2002b): Malaysian Knowledge Society and the Global Knowledge Gap. Bonn: University of Bonn.

Evers, H.-D. (2003): Transition Towards a Knowledge Society: Malaysia and Indonesia in Comparative Perspective. Comparative Sociology 2(2). 355-373.

Evers, H.-D. (2005): Global Knowledge: The Expistemic Culture of Development. In: Hassan, R. (ed.): Local and Global: Social Transformation in Southeast Asia. Leiden and Boston: Brill. 3-179.

Evers, H.-D./Menkhoff, Th. (2004): The Role of Expert Knowledge and Consultants in an Emerging Knowledge-Based Economy. Human Systems Management 23(2). 123-135.

Evers, H.-D./Gerke, S. (2005): Closing the Digital Divide: Southeast Asia's Path towards a Knowledge Society. ZEF Working Paper No. 1. Bonn: Center for Development Research.

Evers, H.-D./Hornidge, A.-K. (2007): Knowledge Hubs along the Straits of Malacca. Asia Europe Journal 5(3). 417-433.

Evers, H.-D./Nordin, R,/Nienkemper, P. (2010): Knowledge Cluster Formation in Peninsular Malaysia: The Emergence of an Epistemic Landscape, Center for Development Research (ZEF), Working Paper Series, No. 62.

Fatimah, M. A. (2009): The Agriculture Development Path in Malaysia: Experiences and Challenges for the Future. In: Abdul Razak Baginda (ed.) Malaysia at 50 & Beyond, Kuala Lumpur: Malaysian Strategic Research Centre, pp. 39-100.

Foucault, M. (1974): Die Ordnung der Dinge. Eine Archäologie der Humanwissenschaften. Frankfurt/Main: Suhrkamp.

Foucault, M. (1988): Archäologie des Wissens. Frankfurt/Main: Suhrkamp.

Freeman, C. (1987): Technology Policy and Economic Performance: Lessons from Japan. Frances Pinter, London.

Freeman, C./Soete, L. (2009): Developing science, technology and innovation indicators: What we can learn from the past. Research Policy 38 (4), pp. 583-589.

Geertz, C. (1983): Local Knowledge: Fact and Law in Comparative Perspective. In: Geertz, Clifford: Local Knowledge further essays in interpretive anthropology. New York: Basic Books. 167-236.

Gerke, S./Evers, H.-D./Hornidge, A.-K. (eds.) (2008): The Straits of Malacca - Knowledge and Diversity. Munster, Penang: Lit Verlag,Straits G.T..

Gerke, S./Evers, H.-D. (2006): Globalizing Local Knowledge: Social Science Research on Southeast Asia, 1970-2000. Sojourn: Journal of Social Issues in Southeast Asia - Volume 21, Number 1, April 2006, pp. 1-21.

Gerke, S./Ehlert, J. (2011): Local Knowledge as a Strategic Resource: Fisheries in the Seasonal Floodplains of the Mekong Delta, Vietnam. In: Menkhoff, T., H.-D. Evers, Y.W. Chay, and E. F. Pang (eds.): Beyond the Knowledge Trap: Developing Asia's Knowledge-Based Economies. Singapore etc.: World Scientific, 383-410.

Gershuny, J. (1978): Die Ökonomie Der Nachindustriellen Gesellschaft. Produktion und Verbrauch Von Dienstleistungen. Frankfurt/Main, New York: Campus.

Gibbons, M./Limoges, C./Nowotny, H./Schwarzman, S./Scott, P./Trow, M. (1994): The New Production of Knowledge. Dynamics of Science and Research in Contemporary Societies. London: SAGE Publications

Global Knowledge Partnership (GKP) (1997): GK7 – A Storyline. Available at http://gkpcms.com/gkp/images/docs/GK97/Storyline.pdf (Date of access: 01 November 2011).

Global Knowledge Partnership (GKP) (1997): GK7 –Conference Evaluation. Executive Summary. Available at: http://www.gkpcms.com/gkp/images/docs%5CGK97/97%20Exec%20summ.pdf (Date of access: 01 November 2011).

Goldberg, I./Goddard, J. G./Kurioakose, S./Racine, J.-L. (2011): Igniting Innovation – Rethinking the Role of Government in Emerging Europe and Central Asia. Washington: The World Bank.

Gore, Ch. (2000): The Rise and Fall of the Washington Consensus as a Paradigm for Developing Countries. World Development 28.5, 789-804.

Hall, A. (2007): Challenges to Strengthening Agriculture Innovation Systems: Where Do We Go From Here? Maastricht, The Netherlands, United Nations University; UNU_MERIT.

Hofmann, J. (2001): Digitale Unterwanderungen: Der Wandel Im Innern Des Wissens. Aus Politik und Zeitgeschichte 36. 3-6.

Hornidge, A.-K. (2004, unpublished): Follow-up des Weltgipfels zur Informationsgesellschaft für InWEnt. Internal Consultancy Report. Bonn: InWEnt Ggmbh.

Hornidge, A.-K. (2007a): Knowledge Society. Vision & Social Construction of Reality in Germany & Singapore. Münster: Lit-Verlag.

Hornidge, A.-K. (2007b): Re-Inventing Society – State Concepts of Knowledge in Germany and Singapore. Journal of Social Issues in Southeast Asia 22(2). 202-229.

Hornidge, A.-K. (2008): From Trading Goods to Trading Knowledge: Singapore's development into a knowledge hub. In: Gerke/Evers/Hornidge (2008). 63-84.

Hornidge, A.-K. (2010): An Uncertain Future – Singapore's Search for a New Focal Point of Collective Identity and its Drive towards 'Knowledge Society'. Asian Journal of Social Sciences 38(5). 785-818.

Hornidge, A.-K. (2011a): Creative Industries – Economic Program and Boundary Concept. Journal of Southeast Asian Studies 42(2). 253-279.

Hornidge, A.-K. (2011b): 'Knowledge Society' as Academic Concept and Stage of Development - A Conceptual and Historical Review. In: Menkhoff, Th./Evers, H.-D./Wah, Ch. Y./Pang, E. F. (eds.): Beyond the Knowledge Trap: Developing Asia's Knowledge-Based Economies. Singapore etc.: World Scientific. 87-128.

Hornidge, A.-K./Oberkircher, L./Kudryavtseva, A. (re-submitted): Boundary Management and the Discursive Sphere – Negotiating 'Realities' in Khorezm, Uzbekistan, submitted to Geoforum.

Hornidge, A.-K./Ul-Hassan, M./Mollinga, P. P. (2011a): Transdisciplinary Innovation Research in Uzbekistan – 1 year of 'Following The Innovation'. Development in Practice 21(6). 825-838.

Hornidge, A.-K./Oberkircher, L./Tischbein, B./Schorcht, G./Bhaduri, A./Awan, U.K./Manschadi, A.M. (2011b): Reconceptualising Water Management in Khorezm, Uzbekistan. Natural Resources Forum, 35: 4, pp. 251-348.

Hornidge, A.-K./Scholtes, F. (2011): "Climate Change Implications on everyday life in Toineke Village / West Timor – Knowledge, Uncertainty and Adaptation," Sociologus – Zeitschrift für empirische Ethnosoziologie und Ethnopsychologie / Journal for Empirical Social Anthropology, 2, 151-175.

International Telecommunication Union (ITU) (1998): ITU Resolution 73 atken at Minneapolis Plenipotentiary Conference 1998 (Res. 1158, Res 1179), Geneva: ITU.

Jiggins, J./de Zeeuw, H. (1992): Participatory Technology Development in practice: process and methods. Chapter 8, In: Reijntjes, C./Haverkort, B./Waters-Bayer, A. (eds.) Farming for the Future. An Introduction to Low- External-Input and Sustainable Agriculture. London: MacMillan and ETC/ILEIA, pp. 135-162.

Khor, M. (2000): Globalization and the South – Some Critical Issues. United Nations Conference on Trade and Development, April 2000, Discussion pa-

per. Available at http://unpan1.un.org/intradoc/groups/public/documents/A
PCITY/UNPAN002428.pdf (date of access: May 13, 2011).

King, K./McGrath, S. A. (2004): Knowledge for development?: comparing British, Japanese, Swedish and World Bank aid, Capetown: HSRC & London, New York: ZED Books.

Kline, S./Rosenberg, N. (1986): An overview of Innovation. In: Landau, R./Rosenberg, N. (eds.) The Positive sum strategy. Harnessing technology for economic growth. Washington DC: National Academic Press, pp. 275-306.

Knoblauch, H. (2005): Wissenssoziologie. Konstanz: Universitätsverlag Konstanz.

Kreibich, R. (1986): Die Wissenschaftsgesellschaft - Von Galilei Zur High-Tech-Revolution. Frankfurt/Main: Suhrkamp.

Kubicek, H./Dutton, W.H./Williams, R. (eds.) (1997): The Social Shaping of Information Superhighways. European and American Roads to the Information Society. Frankfurt/Main: Campus Verlag.

Kübler, H.-D. (2005): Mythos Wissensgesellschaft – Gesellschaftlicher Wandel Zwischen Information, Medien Und Wissen. Eine Einführung. Wiesbaden: VS Verlag für Sozialwissenschaften.

Kumar, K. (1978): Prophecy and Progress: The Sociology of Industrial and Post-Industrial Society. New York: Penguin Books.

Lane, R. E. (1966): The Decline of Politics and Ideology in a Knowledgeable Society. In: American Sociological Review 31(5). 649-662.

Leach, M./Scoones, I./Stirling, A. (2007): Pathways to Sustainabilitiy: an overview of the STEPS Centre approach. STEPS Approach Paper. Brighton: STEPS Centre.

Lloyd, C./Payne, J. (2002): In Search of the High Skill Society: Some Reflections on Current Visions. Warwick: ESRC Research Centre on Skills, Knowledge and Organizational Performance (SKOPE).

Löwy, I. (1992): The Strength of Loose Concepts – Boundary Concepts, Federative Experimental Strategies and Disciplinary Growth: The Case of Immunology, In: History of Science, 30, pp. 371-96.

Lyon, D. (1988): The Information Society: Issues and Illusions. Cambridge: Polity Press.

Lyon, D. (1996): The Roots of the Information Society Idea. In: Heap, N./Thomas, R./Einon, G./Mason, R./Mackay, H. (eds.): Information Technology and Society. 54-73.

Maasen, S. (1999): Wissenssoziologie. Bielefeld: Transcript Verlag.

Machlup, F. (1962): The Production and Distribution of Knowledge in the United States. Princeton: Princeton University Press.

MacKenzie, D./Wajcman J. (eds.) (1985): The Social Shaping of Technology. Maidenhead: Open University Press.

Mahathir bin Mohammad. (28.02.1991):Malaysia: The Way Forward. Public Speech by Prime Minister of Malaysia Dato' Seri Dr. Mahathir bin Mohamad.

Marchand, T. H. J. (2003): A possible explanation for the lack of explanation. Or, 'why the master builder can't explain what he knows': Introducing informational atomism against a 'definitional' definition of concepts. In: Pottier, J./Bicker, A./Sillitoe, P. (eds.): Negotiating Local Knowledge. Power and Identity in Development. London, Sterling: Pluto Press. 30-50.

Marglin, S. A. (1996): Farmers, Seedsmen, and Scientists: Systems of Agriculture and Systems of Knowledge. In: Appfel Marglin, F./Marglin S.A. (eds.): Decolonizing Knowledge. From Development to Dialogue. Oxford: Clarendon Press. 185-248.

Mattelart, A. (2003): Kleine Geschichte Der Informationsgesellschaft. Berlin: Avinus Verlag.

Mollinga, P. (2008): The Rational Organization of Dissent, ZEF Working Paper Series, Center for Development Research, University of Bonn, 33.

Mollinga, P. (2010): Boundary Work and the Complexity of Natural Resources Management, Crop Science, 50 pp. 1-9.

Morris-Suzuki, T. (1996): The Technological Transformation of Japan. Cambridge: Cambridge University Press.

Nonaka, I./Takeuchi, H. (1995): The Knowledge-Creating Company: How Japanese Companies Create the Dynamics of Innovation. New York: Oxford University Press.

Nora, S./Minc, A. (1979): Die Informatisierung der Gesellschaft. Frankfurt, New York: Campus Verlag.

Organization for Economic Cooperation and Development (OECD) (1996a): The Knowledge-Based Economy in 1996: Science, Technology and Industry Outlook. Paris: OECD.

Organization for Economic Cooperation and Development (OECD) (1996b): The Knowledge-Based Economy. Paris: OECD.

Oudshoorn, N./Pinch, T. eds. (2003): How Users Matter: The Co-Construction of Users and Technology. Cambridge: MIT Press.

Pannen, P. (2003): Distance education public policy and practice in the higher education: the Case of Indonesia. Revista Barasileira de Aprendizagem Aberta e a Distancia, Sao Paulo, Setembro, 2003.

Pieterse, J. N. (1998): My Paradigm or Yours? Alternative Development, Post-Development, Reflexive Development, Development and Change 29, 343-373.

Porat, M. (1976): The Information Economy. Stanford: University of Stanford.

Polanyi, M. (1966): The tacit Dimension. New York: Doubleday and Co.

Rahardjo, B. (2002): A Story of Bandung High-Technology Valley. Paper presented at 'Seminar Nasional Industry Berbasis Teknologi Informasi dan Telekomunikasi,' Aula Barat, ITB, Bandung, 11 May 2002.

Rath, A./Barnett, A. (2006): Innovation Systems, Concepts, Approaches and Lessons from RNRRS, RNRSS Synthesis Study Number 10.The Policy Practice.

Read, W. H./Youtie, J. L. (1995): Policy Strategies Along the Information Superhighway. Policy Studies Review 14.1/2: 99-106.

Rhoades, R. E./Booth. R. H. (1982): 'Farmer-back-to-farmer: A Model for Generating Acceptable Agricultural Technology' Agricultural Administration 11: 127-137.

Richards, P. (1985): Indigenous Agricultural Revolution: Ecology and Food-Production in West Africa. London: Hutchinson.

Robertson, H. A./McGee, T. K. (2003): 'Applying local knowledge: The contribution of oral history to wetland rehabilitation at Kanyapella Basin, Australia', Journal of Environmental Management, 69: 275-287.

Rogers, E. M. (2003): Diffusion of Innovations (5th ed.). New York: The Free Press.

Röling, N. (2005): Gateway to the Global Garden: Beta/Gamma Science for Dealing with Ecological Rationality. In: Pretty, J., The Earthscan Reader in Sustainable Agriculture. London: Earthscan.

Ryan, B./Gross, N. (1943): 'The Diffusion of Hybrid Seed Corn in two Lowa Communities' Rural Sociology 8: 15-24.

Scholtes, F./Hornidge, A.-K. (Fallstudie Indonesien) (2009): Warten bis das Wasser kommt? Armutsbekämpfung in Zeiten des Klimawandels. Bonn: Care International Germany-Luxembourg e.V., Center for Development Research.

Scholtes, F./Hornidge, A.-K. (Case Study Indonesia) (2010): Waiting for the Water to come? – Poverty Reduction in Times of Climate Change. Bonn: Care International Germany-Luxembourg e.V., Center for Development Research.

Sillitoe, P. (1998a): The Development of Indigenous Knowledge. In: Current Anthropology 39(2). 223-252.

Sillitoe, P. (1998b): What, know natives? Local knowledge in development. Social Anthropology 6(2). 203-220.

Sillitoe, P./Marzano, M. (2009): Future of indigenous knowledge research in development. Futures 41(1). 13-23.

Spender, D. (2000): The politics of naming, in M. Curtis (ed), The Composition of Ourselves, Dubuque, IA: Kendall/Hunt, 195-200.

Stehr, N. (1994): Knowledge Societies. London: SAGE Publications.

Stehr, N. (1999): Wissensgesellschaften Oder Die Zerbrechlickeit Moderner Gesellschaften. In: Konrad, Wilfried/Schumm, Wilhelm (eds.): Wissen Und Arbeit - Neue Konturen Der Wissensarbeit. Münster: Verlag Westfälisches Dampfboot. 13-23.

Stehr, N. (2001a): Moderne Wissensgesellschaften. In: Aus Politik und Zeitgeschichte 36. 7-13.

Stehr, N. (2001b): A World Made of Knowledge. In: Society 39(1). 89-92

Steinbicker, J. (2001) Zur Theorie Der Informationsgesellschaft. Ein Vergleich Der Ansätze Von Peter Drucker, Daniel Bell Und Manuel Castells. Opladen: Leske + Budrich.

STEPS Centre, The (2010): Innovation, Sustainability, Development: A New Manifesto, Brighton: STEPS Centre.

Stiglitz, J. E. (1999): Public Policy for a Knowledge Economy. London: Center for Economic Policy Research.

Sussex Group, The (1970): The Sussex Manifesto: Science and Technology to Developing Countries during the Second Development Decade. Sussex: Institute of Development Studies, University of Sussex, Brighton, England.

Tänzler, D./Knoblauch, H./Soeffner, H.-G. (2006): Zur Kritik Der Wissensgesellschaft. Konstanz: UVK.

Taylor, R. D. (2003): The Malaysia Experience: The Multimedia Super Corridor. In: Jussawalla, M./Taylor, R.D. (eds.), Information Technology Parks of the Asia Pacific – Lessons for the Regional Digital Divide, New York: M.E. Sharpe.

Tijssen, R./Hollanders, H. (2006): Using science and technology indicators to support knowledge-based economies. United Nations University Policy Brief 11.

Touraine, A. (1969): La Société Post-Industrielle. Paris: Denoël.

Tuomi, I. (2001): From Periphery to Centre: Emerging Research Topics on Knowledge Society. Helsinki: TEKES.

Umesao, T. (1963): Information Industry Theory: Dawn of the Coming Era of the Ectodermal Industry. Hoso Asahi, Jan. 1963. 4-17

United Nations General Assembly (2000): Millennium Declaration of the United Nations (A/res/55/2), Washington: United Nations.

United Nations General Assembly (2001): Road map towards the implementation of the United Nations Millennium Declaration (A/56/326), Washington: United Nations.

United Nations General Assembly (2002): Resolution adopted by the General Assembly - World Summit on the Information Society (A/Res/56/183), Washington: United Nations.

United Nations Educational, Scientific and Cultural Organization (UNESCO) (2002): Medium-Term Strategy 2002-2007 Contributing to peace and human development in an era of globalization through education, the sciences, culture and communication. Paris: UNESCO.

United Nations Educational, Scientific and Cultural Organization (UNESCO) (2005): Towards Knowledge Societies. UNESCO World Report. Paris: UNESCO.

United Nations Educational, Scientific and Cultural Organization (UNESCO) (2009): Fostering Information and Communication Technologies for Development – UNESCO's Follow-up to the World Summit on the Information Society. Paris: UNESCO.

United Nations Educational, Scientific and Cultural Organization (UNESCO) (2010a): UNESCO Science Report 2010. Paris: UNESCO.

United Nations Educational, Scientific and Cultural Organization (UNESCO) (2010b) World Social Science Report 2010. Paris: UNESCO.

Vogel, C. (2000): Deutschland Im Internationalen Technologiewettlauf - Bedeutung Der Forschungs- Und Technologiepolitik Für Die Technologische Wettbewerbsfähigkeit. Berlin: Duncker und Humblot GmbH.

Webster, F. (1995): Theories of the Information Society. London: Routledge.

Willke, H. (1998): Organisierte Wissensarbeit. In: Zeitschrift für Soziologie 27. 161-177.

Willke, H. (1999): Die Wissensgesellschaft - Wissen Ist Der Schlüssel Zur Gesellschaft. In Welcher Gesellschaft Leben Wir Eigentliche? In: Pongs, Armin (ed.): Gesellschaftskonzepte Im Vergleich.Vol. 1. München: Dilemma Verlag. 261-279.

World Bank, The (2002a): Constructing Knowledge Societies: New Challenges for Tertiary Education, Washington: WB.

World Bank, The (1999): World Development Report Knowledge for Development 1998/1999, New York: Oxford University Press.

World Bank, The (2002b): Information and Communication Technologies – A World Bank Group Strategy, Washington: WB.

World Bank, The (2003): ICT and MDGS – A World Bank Group Perspective, Washington: WB.

World Commission on Environment and Development (1987): Report of the World Commission on Environment and Development: Our Common Future, Washington: United Nations.

World Summit on the Information Society (WSIS) (2003a): Declaration of Principles – Building the Information Society: a global challenge in the new Millennium, Geneva: ITU.

World Summit on the Information Society (WSIS) (2003b): Plan of Action, Geneva: ITU.

World Summit on the Information Society (WSIS) (2005a): Tunis Commitment, Geneva: ITU.

World Summit on the Information Society (WSIS) (2005b): Tunis Agenda for the Information Society, Geneva: ITU.

Ziai, A. (2011): Some Reflections on the Concept of 'Development'. ZEF Working Paper Series, No. 81, Bonn: Center for Development Research, University of Bonn.

Ziai, A. (2009): 'Development': Projects, Power, and a Poststructuralist Perspective. Alternatives 34. 183-201.

Urban Environmental Knowledge as Citizens' Science

Theoretical Issues and Methods from Indonesia

CHRISTOPH ANTWEILER

INTRODUCTION

Local knowledge, by definition, has a certain basis in localized cultural contexts and its distribution is thus limited spatially. Nevertheless, this knowledge is not necessarily confined to one locality or a specific ethnic group. Local knowledge is gained usually through long-term experience and consists primarily of cognitive capabilities related to the performance of action. Knowledge is power, not so much political power but more in Francis Bacon's sense as an action power, a capacity to get things moving (Stehr 2001: 9). No wonder then that the discussion on knowledge in the social sciences is influenced by current societal issues and global interests. Whereas the general social science debate currently is heavily biased towards discussing a knowledge society (for an overview cf. Engelhardt/ Kajetzke 2010, Hornidge 2011), debates about local knowledge are biased towards issues connected with its potential uses for development or biodiversity conservation. Especially since the 1990s, its status as a special form of intellectual property has been at the center of debates (Greaves 1994; Brush/Stabinsky 1996; Posey/Dutfield 1996; Agrawal 1998; Schareika/Bierschenk 2004; Anderson 2009; Krikorian & Kapczynski 2010; cf. Hornidge, this volume).

User- or policy-oriented discussions tend to sidestep basic phenomenaligal aspects of local knowledge by way of simplifying assumptions. As regards the relation of local knowledge to science, there is a strong tendency to (a) oppose local knowledge to scientific knowledge, often with the assumption they will be incompatible, and then as a consequence (b) homogenize or essentialize both, and (c) regard one as more valuable than the other. In an all too idealized view, local knowledge tends to be associated falsely with sustainable actions, purity, naturalness, social equality, equity, political justness, outsiders, powerless or otherwise marginal people, or subaltern interests (e.g. Lyotard 1986). First of all it is important not to conflate knowledge with information. As Einstein said, knowledge is not information but experience. Knowledge in general, not only local knowledge, is action-oriented and often not explicit (or codified) but tacit. Knowledge may be conceived as the purposeful coordination of action (Zeleny 2010: 24-28). This chapter asks whether local knowledge might have some general structural aspects despite its tremendous diversity. It is proposed that local knowledge should neither be equalized with scientific knowledge (e.g. as ethnoscience) nor contrasted in an essential way with science (e.g. as wisdom or counter-science). Furthermore, local knowledge should not be associated automatically with indigenous groups or indigeneity, hence my use of the term "local knowledge," which is also somewhat problematic but less so than "indigenous knowledge."

Local knowledge shares some attributes with empirical scientific knowledge. The question is whether some of these qualities are lost if local knowledge is formalized and de-localized. A general model of local knowledge is presented which outlines ten interrelated qualities of local knowledge, and this is then exemplified using an ethnographic case drawn from fieldwork in Indonesia. The examples relate to environmental- and migration-related knowledge of urban people. The paper asks if local knowledge might be a specific form of knowing and rationality found in societies worldwide.

KNOWLEDGE, KNOWING AND IGNORANCE: AN ATTEMPT AT SYSTEMATIZING

Despite often being called a 'knowledge system' (especially among cognitive anthropologists), local knowledge in general does not necessarily present itself as a comprehensive system. Mostly what we find empirically is a patchy form of detailed and systematic knowledge in certain topical areas and sketchy knowledge in others. Local knowledge is not only cognitive but also entails emotive and corporeal aspects, and it is situated in the current way of life and in the historically accumulated experience. Thus, local knowledge may be best understood as a 'cultural product' or 'social product' (Antweiler 1998, 2009). Furthermore, it encompasses knowledge in the strict sense of shared information and 'ways of 'knowing', 'ontology', 'framing reality', 'being acquainted with', and 'bodily knowledge', which transcend the purely cognitive realm (Siverts

1991: 308; D'Andrade/Strauss 1992; Borowsky 1994; Harrison 1995; Kronenfeld 1996:14-19; Strauss/Quinn 1997; Nygren 1999: 278; Friedberg 1999:6-10; Farnell 1999).

Drawing on local knowledge for understanding development and for solutions should not be restricted to the elicitation of cognitive content seen as the state of information. What is especially relevant to development measures is an understanding of knowledge processes (Brokhensha et al. 1980; Honerla/Schröder 1995; Arce/Long 2000; Lölke 2002; Pottier et al. 2003; Miehlau/ Wickl 2007; Hornidge 2007; Sillitoe 2009; Hornidge, this volume). Local knowledge should not be seen simply in dichotomous contrast or as a countermodel to western science (e.g. Agrawal 1996). Contrary to popular views, activities informed by local knowledge are not necessarily sustainable or socially just (Murdoch/Clark 1994; Hauck/Kößler 2004: 51ff.). Local knowledge is frequently geared to real-life practices and may only be understood with reference to the situation in which it is to be applied, known as referential transparency (Quinn/Holland 1987), which is important in selecting research methods. Knowledge relating to practices and situations may be called 'situated knowledge' (Lave 1993, 1996: 90; Nygren 1999: 277; Antweiler 2008). Hobart (1993: 4, 17) speaks of 'situated practices' and 'knowledge as practice', but local knowledge should not be reduced to practical, mundane, everyday, or routine knowledge.

Empirical data on urban knowledge collected in the city of Makassar (Sulawsei Selatan, Indonesia) show that local knowledge may comprise on the one hand fixed and structured 'knowledge' which can be articulated, or on the other hand may, by virtue of its combination with the performance of actions, involve a more fluid process of 'knowing' (Antweiler 2002). Furthermore, there is a distinction to be made between knowledge in the sense of that which is known and knowing in the sense of how something is known (cf. Hobart 1993: 19; Borowsky 1994: 335-339; Barth 1995). Local knowledge should not be contrasted with science but may be conceived on a continuum between formal science and everyday rationality (Sillitoe 2000; Antweiler 2007; cf. Hornidge, this volume).

Local knowledge comprises not only technological and environmental knowledge, but also covers the social environment. In the final analysis, it is possible to speak in a comprehensive way about 'knowledge of social systems' (von Cranach 1995). Thus, local knowledge in the broadest sense also includes the social management of information, learning and teaching as well as decision-making routines, particularly given that human beings exist in a continuous flux of experiences and practices. Local knowledge can involve knowing about group peers and their interrelations, which is known as social cognition in social psychology (Fiske/Taylor 1991; Augoustinos/Walker 1995; Pennington 2000) and may include the wider social environment (e.g. neighboring communities, cf. Stokols/Altman 1987). Social cognition in this sense, despite its importance in human societies in general, is mostly skipped in debates on local knowledge. An aspect of local social cognition would be what people of one cultural group know about the network of experts in their own and neighboring collectives. Social cognition is especially important for development measures (Boggs 1990; Quarles van Ufford 1993). Other fields worthy of mention include organizational and management knowledge and legal knowledge, for instance pertaining to non-formal organizations (Blackburn/Andersson 1993; Marsden 1994). Local knowledge of development projects would also fall into this category – an as-yet almost unstudied field[1]. Alongside this there is also more individual, less collective knowledge, for instance on how to mobilize joint interests in an action group (if there is no suitable organizational form in the local case).

---

1   Many underpaid academics in Southeast Asian countries, for example, have an intricate knowledge about the ideals and procedures of northern, non-governmental organizations. They use this to acquire money from them or to establish their own NGOs (LSM, Lembaga Swadaya Masyarakat in Bahasa Indonesia), often as an income-generating device.

Table 1: Forms and levels of local knowledge

Levels and forms of knowledge	Examples
1 Declarative knowledge	
1.1 Recognition and naming knowledge	Attribution of entities to terms, discreet entities and diversity
1.2 Factual knowledge	Traits of animals, plants, temperature, social status, prices, salaries, administrative levels
1.3 Categorical knowledge	Orderings of organisms, colors, kinship, development project types
2 Procedural knowledge	
2.1 General processes, rules	Farming calendar, religious calendar, environmental crises, household cycle, development project cycle
2.2 Specific processes (scripts, schemas, action plans)	Everyday routines, e.g. greetings and farewells, natural resource management, ritual sequences, project request schema, and non-routines
3 Complex knowledge (concepts, belief systems)	Cosmology, model of whole society, models of "honor", of "marriage", of "justice," cropping systems, therapies, decision-making procedures

Source: Antweiler 1998, 2007, combined.

Knowing the local legal system and conflict management is another field of political relevance, as this knowledge is important for actors when someone asks: 'How do I assert a claim?' and may require information on unwritten rules and locally appropriate ways of arguing one's case (cf. Hutchins' 1980 cognitive study of Trobriand land use conflicts, as well as Hutchins 1996). These examples illustrate the overlaps between various fields of knowledge. Empirical studies suggest three levels of thought in any form of knowledge: (1) recognition and the naming of discreet entities; (2) ordering discontinuity and diversity; and (3) the unity of ensembles of living beings, including one's own society. Distinguishing these levels may be important for eliciting parallels between scientific and local representations and establishing a dialogue between them. The chances are good for an exchange regarding the first two levels, but there are problems with the third (Friedberg 1999: 14).

If we read closely through the many examples of local knowledge published since the 1970s, we can figure out several general levels of local knowledge (Fig. 1). The examples given are taken from both 'traditional' fields as well as modern contexts, such as development, to illustrate that local knowledge is not only a traditional or rural or 'other' form of knowledge, but also may imply a universal capacity (Malinowski 1948:196; Salmond 1982; Barth 1995; Nader 1996: 7; Scott 1998: 331; cf. Jones 1999: 559-566; Hauck/Kößler 2004; Antweiler 2007). This approach challenges the supposed contrast between 'knowledge of a different kind' ('non-western knowledge' or 'non-western wisdom') as opposed to 'western' or 'scientific' knowledge. In real-life situations, for example in development exchanges, there are usually more than two parties and two sets of knowledge.

Local knowledge of a declarative nature is knowledge of discreet entities relating to the natural and social environment, facts relating to neighboring groups or, for example, details on development organizations. But local knowledge may involve categories and classifications, such as of plants, animals or relatives. The practical value of such classifications, known to anthropologists for decades, has only become evident in development in recent years. Ongoing debates revolve around the internal coherence and similarity to western classifications. The underlying causes of these classifications are also disputed: The question is to what degree it represents (a) pan-human perception and intellect acting on natural discontinuities; (b) utilitarian concerns; or (c) reflections of cultural relations (cf. Crick 1982: 293-298; Hunn 1982: 839-844; Berlin 1992; Ellen 1993: 3; Nazarea 1999: 4; Sillitoe 1998c).

Local knowledge may relate to processes, which might comprise knowledge of rapid changes in the natural environment, in market prices for goods, or in experiences of development projects. Analytically we can distinguish between knowledge pertaining to general and specific processes. An example of the former would be a religious calendar, in which specific knowledge includes knowledge of the precise sequence of steps involved in processes (e.g. in rituals or everyday activities). There also exist prototypical, idealized process models whereby normal human beings, like stage performers, follow a sequence of schematically prescribed steps ('scripts', Schank/Abelson 1977; Quinn 2005). A classic example of such an 'everyday script' is the sequence of actions performed on entering a restaurant: Open door – look for unoccupied table – occupy table – look for cloakroom or hand over coat(s) – sit down – pick up menu list –

order drinks, etc. These 'scripts', although not fixed in writing anywhere, constitute cultural rules or sequences of steps. They are not necessarily taught, but are learned by individuals themselves through frequent performance and frequent observation. Consequently, this procedural knowledge usually remains unconscious or at least unspoken. Nevertheless, even minor errors in the sequence of actions can cause confusion among actors, or can lead to failure. If, for instance, I were to enter a restaurant in the United States and follow the customary European script of looking for a table myself, we would be breaking the rule of 'waiting to be seated'. Conversely, applying the American script in a European restaurant (unless it was an American Steakhouse or an upscale restaurant) would as a rule mean waiting at the entrance, to no avail.

In many cases local knowledge seems to be considerably more complex than these scripts suggest. It may include knowledge of complex systems, e.g. about ways of farming crops or treating environmentally induced diseases (cf. Kalland 2003), including explicit causal knowledge, and it may also relate to relationships in everyday life or information on relationships within the cosmos, or the aetiology of diseases, the creation of humankind, or the origin of a community. This systemic knowledge informs action and should be considered a crucial dimension in development (cf. Warren et al. 1995). Such complex knowledge constructs may be termed 'belief systems' and knowledge systems/systems of meaning (cf. van der Ploeg 1989). The word 'system' indicates that these constructs are not simply aggregates of isolated concepts, but comprise interlinked concepts and their constituent elements. Religious worldviews are an example of this point because, within such systems, cosmologies and prototypical concepts play a major role. These are termed 'cultural models' or 'schemas', and models of this kind, which may for instance center around ideas such as 'honor and shame', 'the self-made man' or the 'typical American marriage' are usually shared by the majority.

Although these schemes or models constitute only loose patterns of association, they are thematically organized and are highly stable in both individual and historical terms (Quinn/Holland 1987: 24; Rogoff/Lave 1984; Strauss/Quinn 1997, 2005). Cultural models structure knowledge processing, as they link affects and motives with accumulated experiences. They are also linked to linguistic metonymies (pars pro toto), analogies, or visual metaphors. A self-reflexive case in point is the conceptions of knowledge in modern talk about science, which often revolve around the metaphor of physical landscape. Knowledge is a territory and scientific activity is a journey, thus science has a destination, scientists try to understand the world, to see reality, the mind is a container, and language is a conduit transmitting knowledge (Salmond 1982: 67-74).

A GENERAL MODEL OF LOCAL KNOWLEDGE

Local knowledge always has a history and is synchronically dynamic. The kernel of local knowledge consists of skills and acquired intelligence responding to constantly changing social and natural environments. Scott describes this masterfully with reference to the ancient Greek concept of mêtis, translatable as a sort of cunning intelligence, but one specifically responding to constant dynamics (Scott 1998: 311[2]). Local knowledge, considering its diversity and dynamics, needs to be understood and embedded in the larger cultural system. There are various types of 'public' regarding knowledge distribution – some information is made manifest to all, whilst other information may remain concealed from the majority. Some things are known only to women or to men, and only a few specialists may possess in-depth knowledge in a particular field, for instance medical or cropping expertise. Certain individuals, or either sex, may be excluded in principle from certain fields or topics of knowledge on cultural grounds, and even some agricultural knowledge may be categorized as secret (Pottier 1993: 30-32).

The ability to know something about certain themes (knowledgeability, cf. Lave 1993: 13, 17) is different for the different members of a culture, and it changes, as it is itself a social product. Expertise may be conceived as socially sanctioned coordination of action (Zeleny 2010: 28). An individual's knowledge changes through time with the situation (Borowsky 1994: 334), and there may be different or even rival items or forms of knowledge, different 'versions of the world'. As regards its content, practical relevance, and centrality, knowledge is often differentially distributed between the young and the old, a process which may even lead to virtual parallel knowledge systems (Mersmann 1993). In times of rapid change, one knowledge system may be morally significant, yet without practical value: "It is in the nature of interactions within and between 'knowledge systems' to make manifest certain sorts of information and to keep other sorts hidden" (Marsden 1994: 33). Knowledge is power. Thrift (1996: 99-100) differentiates between five kinds of unknown knowledge:

- Knowledge that is unknown, because it is spatially or historically unavailable;
- Knowledge not understood, i.e. outside a frame of meaning;
- Knowledge not discussed and perhaps taken for granted;
- Actively and consciously concealed knowledge; and
- Distorted knowledge.

---

2   Some of the conceptions of knowledge in general exclude pure routine capacities and thus already come near to this aspect of local knowledge (e.g. Stehr 2001: 8-11).

It is possible to draw a broad distinction between local specialist knowledge and local everyday knowledge (knowledge of 'just plain folks'; Lave 1996: 87). Studies in the sociology of knowledge and network anthropology have demonstrated that differential knowledge distribution concerns not only specialist knowledge, but also everyday knowledge. It is therefore necessary to determine empirically who, within a population at any time, has what type of knowledge. The most intriguing issue is the attitude to their concepts held by the people themselves and the extent to which they adhere to them. What, for instance, constitutes 'factual knowledge' for the people in contrast to "what can only be credibly claimed" for them (Sperber 1989: 98-103; Flick 1995: 56-59)?

Moreover, to what extent can we understand a particular local knowledge realm as representing a 'body of knowledge'? The fields of the sociology of knowledge (cf. Hornidge, this volume) and of social psychology provide some useful definitions of knowledge. They characterize knowledge, for example, as "stored information which refers to important structures, processes and functions of the system producing it [...] and which therefore generates evaluative processes" (von Cranach 1995: 25) and as "any and every set of ideas and acts accepted by one or another social group or society of people – ideas and acts pertaining to what they accept as real for them and for others" (McCarthy 1996: 23; cf. Maasen 2007).

Table 2: A general model of local knowledge: ten interrelated qualities

Key Characteristic	Aspects
1. Knowledge *plus* skills	• combination of specific factual knowledge and practice all action-oriented skills
2. Adaptation to situational dynamics and variability	• keyed to common, but never precisely identical, features of a particular place; thus adapted to ambiguous, mutable, stochastic and thus in-determinant issues
3. Empirical local basis and experiential saturation	• based on local observation, low cost /-risk trial and error and natural experiments, proven by coping over a prolonged period in the "laboratory of life"
4. Redundancy and holism	• represented parallel in several cultural domains; embeddedness; holistic orientation through systemic relations with other aspects of culture
5. Tacit nature of knowledge	• often implicit, uncodified, intuitive, corporeal-embodied, less verbalized, less susceptible to verbal or written communication, non-disciplinary
6. Informal learning	• oral transmission, decentralized and piecemeal learning, learning by imitation, demonstration and apprenticeship more than by instruction
7. Scientific character	• (partially) systematic, methodical, parsimonous, empirical-hypothetical, comprehensive and generating causal theory
8. Optimal ignorance	• information only as detailed and accurate as it needs to address the problem; no more and no less
9. Evaluation criterion, test basis	• practical efficacy as the yardstick vs. e.g. theoretical consistency, parsimony, elegance, etc. (but see 4)
10. Resulting actions and problem solutions	• solutions familiar and thus broadly accepted by local peoples, oriented towards "satisficing" and optimizing (vs. maximizing) and the use of local resources

Source: Antweiler 2008, modified.

If we consult recent studies of local knowledge (few of which attempt explicit generalization[3]) and read them closely with a comparative view in mind, a number of general features and patterns can be found (Antweiler 2008). This may be taken as a basis for building a general model of local knowledge, stressing both its universal capability and specific situational character (Table 2), which emphasizes the practical relevance and social significance of knowledge. Local knowledge has both a practical and social dimension, in that it is not knowledge isolated and abstracted from everyday life. It consists not only of information, or factual knowledge as a resource, but also of capabilities and skills. The knowledge utilized for the use of skills remains implicit, as it is usually acquired through a process of learning by doing. With all human beings, capabilities and skills tend to be less conscious than factual and formalized knowledge. Without much comment, experienced persons demonstrate to their students how to perform actions, instead of providing detailed verbal instruction.

Complex actions performed may depend on procedural knowledge, which is only partially conscious. This applies especially to actions involving knowledge embodied in movements (Farnell 1999), rituals (Tambiah 1990), and decision-making (Prattis 1973; Fjellman 1976; Gladwin 1989; Antweiler 2000). Procedural knowledge is less verbalized. A topical example would be asking a colleague to help with a computer problem that he or she solves after several trials but is afterwards unable to explain the steps followed. The question today is less about how specific items of information find their way into people's minds and more about how individuals comprise communities of knowing by participating in their knowledge (Karamoy/Dias 1982). Furthermore, local knowledge is linked to some common views of the future, which may comprise 'best worlds', ontologically-based theories of 'the good life', or 'endogenous development' goals.

Being a both result of universal cognitive capacities and localized respectively situated performance, local knowledge may cause some apparent contradictions, if it is systematized in the global arena. As such, what are the consequences of local knowledge being isolated, simplified, documented, stored, repackaged, codified, transferred, and commodified (Agrawal 1995; Ellen/Harris 2000: 17; Sillitoe 2009; Menkhoff et al. 2010)? These transformations imply de-

---

3   The following works from different disciplinary backgrounds have informed my understanding of the general characteristics of local knowledge the most: Malinowski, 1948; Lindblom, 1959; Crick, 1982; Tambiah, 1990; Lave, 1993; DeWalt 1994; Barth, 1995; Harrison, 1995; Lambek, 1993; Lave, 1996; Nader 1996; Strauss & Quinn, 1997; Pasquale et al. 1998,; Sillitoe, 1998a, 1998b; Scott, 1998; Friedberg, 1999; Nazarea, 1999; Nygren, 1999; Ellen & Harris, 2000 and Schareika 2004.

localization, de-contextualization, and de-personalization that may be possible for general know-how, specific expertise, and some skills. These aspects are especially relevant for nations aiming at a transition into a knowledge society, as attempted by several countries in the South, especially in Southeast Asia (Evers 2010). On the other hand, along other dimensions such as locale and environmental context, cultural embeddedness and socially situated character (sometimes featuring specified topographical information) cannot be discarded without distortion. We need culturally sensitive methods while at the same time approaches that are systematic and allow comparative analysis.

METHODS: SYSTEMATIC ANTHROPOLOGICAL TECHNIQUES

Standard elicitation procedures vs. quick-and-dirty methods

Current techniques for eliciting local knowledge are torn between two opposing poles. On the one hand, there are standard ethnographic methods, such as structured interviewing of cognitive anthropology (Spradley 1980; Werner/Fenton 1970; Werner/Schoepfle 1987; Strauss 1987; Quinn 2005), which are often very formal and time-consuming. On the other hand, we have the simple tools of rapid and/or participatory appraisal and learning methods (cf. Chambers 1991; Schönhuth/Kievelitz 1995; Sillitoe et al. 2005). Both approaches have drawbacks. Cognitive anthropological methods usually only enquire in-depth into specific cultural domains (e.g. the classification of animals or soils) and tend to forget people's understanding and practical use of concepts. Furthermore, often based on talking to knowledgeable specialists, intracultural cognitive variability remains largely unexplored (Sankoff 1971; Nygren 1999: 277; Sillitoe 1998c: 190). Participatory methods are rapid, cheap and generally more inclusive than survey methods, but they present problems if one tries to upscale them and they are laden with (often hidden) political agendas and generally all too often are blind to the larger cultural context.

Simplifying systematic elicitation procedures

Participatory methods have their strengths, but as a result of tinkering are often theoretically ungrounded. This paper argues for systematic, systemic, and multi-focal approaches (cf. Vayda 1983; Ellen 1996: 459). Specifically, I argue that we need comparative yet culturally sensitive methods for larger samples. Methods like Rapid Rural Appraisal (RRA), Participatory Rapid Appraisal (PRA) and

Participatory Learning Approaches (PLA) should be complemented with procedures originating from cognitive anthropology and clinical psychology. The problem with cognitive methods is that while there are many works on the data processing procedures, there are few on data gathering techniques in cross-cultural contexts. Anthropological experience shows that the systematic elicitation of data may be very problematic in a cultural context different from that of the researchers. There are guidebooks for methods such as systematic interviewing, systematic data collection, or systematic elicitation techniques (e.g. Weller/Romney 1988; Werner/Schoepfle 1987), but the assumption in these books is that the methods may be universally applied.

Critics maintain that these methods are overly formal, too complicated, and inapplicable to real-life, non-western settings. Cognitive anthropologists who use these methods claim to be able to reveal the insider view (the emic perspective). These methods are based largely on US-American experiences with people who are accustomed to formal tests and whose cultural background is already well known. Reported experiences with such methods in the context of anthropological fieldwork in non-western settings are varied. Some colleagues report that informants found them funny and interesting, while others regarded them as childish and instead proposed having a coffee, an ouzo, or a kretek cigarette. As an illustration of the gap between bold textbook claims and fieldwork experiences, compare Weller/Romney (1988: 9) with Barnes (1991: 290):

"[…]the interviewing and data collection tasks contained in this volume are as appropriate for use in such exotic settings as the highlands of New Guinea as they are in the corporate offices on Wall Street."

"(the informants) quickly got stuck, re-sorting the cards as each new name was added, before stopping and declaring the task to be impossible."

Table 3: Methods for the elicitation of local knowledge

Method	Themes, aspects (in examples)
1. Listening, talking to people	• terminology, local cultural themes
2. Systematic/structured interviewing, formal elicitation techniques	
• free listing; question-answer-frame	• domains, themes, propositions
• card/pile sorting; slip sorting	• dictionary, basic cognitive structure
• triadic comparison; triad test	• similarity comparisons, taxonomy
• rating, rating scale	• evaluative comparisons
• ranking, rank ordering	• hierarchy of values, coherence vs. diversity
• sentence frame format, frame elicitation	• logical relationships, causes & effects
• combination of the above (e.g. repertory grid method)	• environmental perception, personal constructs
• graphic methods (visualization, drawing trees, cognitive maps)	• concepts; hierarchies; spatial concepts
3. Observation	
• non-participant, time allocation	• practices, routines, products
• participant observation	• procedural knowledge, knowing
4. Documentation and study of documents	
• photos, films, video	• knowledge products (texts, objects)
• mapping	• knowledge distribution
• recording of narrative texts ("orature")	• nature and mode of knowledge, knowledge transfer
• recording of natural discourse	• themes, forms of discourse, implicit knowledge
5. Combinations of the above methods	
• natural decision-making	• procedural knowledge, rules, cultural models
• apprenticeship, teacher-pupil interaction	• implicit knowledge, scripts
• action research	• knowledge acquisition, creativity, implicit knowledge
• participatory methods (e.g. PRA, RRA, PLA)	• participation in gathering, dissemination and utilization of knowledge

Source: Author's compilation, 2011.

What are the ways of handling these issues? Well, we may respond to these problems in three ways. Firstly, we can continue to use the methods of the established participatory approaches, regardless of the problems, although we should remain aware of the limitations of the methods and the fuzziness of the term 'participation'. Secondly, we can drop systematic elicitation and resort to less formal, systematic ways of collecting local knowledge data. This is the option often followed by anthropologists, collecting normal discourse, e.g. rumors and gossip; however, it foregoes control over data collection and results are difficult to compare. Thirdly, we can adapt and simplify the methods of cognitive anthropology. Criticisms of cognitive anthropology mentioned above apply to older, often very formal procedures (e.g. Metzger/Williams 1966). Some modern methods (cf. Weller/Romney 1988: ch.2; Antweiler 1993; Bernard 2006), such as listings, are simple and suitable if we want to know from the outset themes, criteria, and problems relevant to people. Accordingly, they are already used in some participatory approaches and can elicit informants' knowledge as well as evaluations and sentiments. In addition, they allow for intracultural variation, e.g. as a consequence of age, gender, network position, or social rank.

Figure 1: Street life in Rappocini neighborhood, Makassar (formerly Ujung Pandang), Sulawesi Selatan

Source: Antweiler 2006

MAKASSAR KNOWLEDGE: LOCALIZING A COGNITIVE APPROACH

Residential knowledge in a provincial metropolis

I conducted a detailed study on decision-making about housing and intra-urban residential moves (Antweiler 2000, 2009). Within this research context-specific questions arose concerning knowledge and the sentiments pertaining to residential relocation and the subjective relevance of the built environment (*residential cognition*; cf. Tognoli 1987; Saegert/Winkel 1990; Aitken 1990; Jansen et al. 2011). The main research questions were: What do people know of the area (*knowledge*)? How do they know it and what are the ways in which they represent streets cognitively (*knowing*)? What are their evaluations and the meanings of the built environment? What are the evaluations of neighborhoods or places as potential residential locations?

Urban geographers and environmental psychologists interested in perception often use techniques of cognitive or mental mapping to understand such issues. Months of living with people in Makassar and exchanges with a research assistant showed that ordinary people are not accustomed to using maps, so any results would have been quite artificial. Consequently, I turned to the Repertory Grid Method (also called the Repgrid technique) that elicits cognitive and emotive data via language to reveal so-called 'constructs' (Scheer 1993: 25-36; Fransella et al. 2003). The method was developed by George Kelly (1955; cf. Fransella 1995) and is classically used in clinical psychology to reveal so-called 'subjective theories' (Catina/Schmitt 1993; Jankowicz 2003). Guides to the method include Scheer/Catina (1993) and Fromm (1995). It is also used by environmental psychologists and urban geographers interested in neighborhood evaluation and residential choice (e.g. Aitken 1984, 1987, 1990; Anderson 1990; Preston/Taylor 1981; Tanner/Foppa 1996). The method is barely known in knowledge research and seldom used in the field of development (for exceptions see Barker 1980: 300; Richards 1980: 187; Seur 1992: 124-127).

Humans order their world cognitively by using dual polarities, which constitutes the basic and simple assumption of constructive psychologists using this method. Referring to everyday decisions, the supposition is that individuals 'construe' several aspects within the diversity of their experiences according to similarities and dissimilarities (Catina/Schmitt 1993). The main assumptions of the Repertory Grid Technique are:

- Humans do not merely react to events but are in charge of their actions;
- People think in dichotomies of diverse content;
- Personal constructs consist of psychic polarities. Each pole is only relevant to its counterpart, but they need not be logical poles or contradictions; they need not to be rational or precise;
- Personal repertoires are rooted in the biographic framework of earlier experiences and anticipation of the future;
- A person has a repertoire of several such constructs;
- Individuals select between several of their constructs according to the given situation;
- Individuals can rebuild their constructs. Alternative views are present anytime, which is important in everyday decision-making.

Every person uses many polarities and these differ intra- as well as inter-culturally, which conflicts with the principal dualism assumed by structuralists in anthropology.

A simple tool for mental mapping: procedure and advantages of the Repertory Grid Method

Technically, the Repertory Grid Method consists of two steps (cf. Scheer 1993; Jankowicz 2003): (1) an elicitation of constructs via a comparison of two or three items (dyads, triads) and (2) an evaluation of (other) items according to the constructs elicited in a scaling procedure. Step 1 is the 'construct question', in which two or three items called 'elements' are compared by the person being interviewed. These elements might be words or short sentences on cards, photographs or concrete objects, such as a plant or an animal specimen. The interviewer asks the subject to discriminate on the basis of similarity (dyad comparison, triad comparison), without any other inputs, which reveals certain stated characteristics, for example 'these two are similar because they are both clean' or 'this one is different because it is dangerous'. Thus, an 'initial construct pole' emerges. Asking for the reverse of the stated trait – if not obvious – reveals pairs of contrasts (e.g. 'clean/dirty', 'dangerous/secure'), which are known as 'polarities' or 'personal constructs'. It is possible to elicit several constructs per dyad or triad.

Step 2 uses the constructs elicited as poles on a scale for ordering other items presented to the interview partner. New items are evaluated by ranking or rating them on a scale established by the interviewee, not the ethnographer. Only the items for comparison come from the interviewer, which differentiates this method from semantic differential or polarity profile procedures, where given items are rated or ranked. A matrix, which is formed by arranging constructs (from step 1) horizontally and rating values (from step 2) vertically, represents the person's cognitive and emotive repertoire regarding a specific theme or domain. The semantic space consisting of elements and constructs is called the person's repertory grid.

Here I present the method in the form of a recipe adapted to the Makassar fieldwork setting. Subsequently, I explain the adaptation to the local setting, which is an important step often not mentioned in cognitive anthropology methods texts and RRA, PRA, and PLA handbooks.

Step One: Elicitation of constructs via triad comparison:

1. Present three elements (houses, lanes, neighborhoods) A, B, C as photos;
2. Ask: 'Which of these two are similar or which one is specific in any respect?'
3. Ask: 'Why this one/these ones?' Note response as one pole on a ten-point scale;
4. Ask: 'What would be the reverse of that?' Note reply as other polarity;
5. Ask: 'Which one would you prefer of these two qualities?' Note preference with a symbol;
6. Repeat several triads with the same procedure to obtain several constructs.

Step Two: Assessment of urban areas with the constructs elicited in step 1:

1. Ranking of eight plastic slips with the names of residential areas or streets within the poles of the first polarity profile;
2. Repeat this ranking of the eight slips within the other constructs elicited in step one.

Repertory grids have several advantages compared either to survey-like methods or open interviews. The method involves qualitative and quantitative aspects. In the media used there are similarities to participatory methods (e.g. PRA), except that the method is more rigorous although not less participatory because (1) it elicits emic data systematic from a sample (same stimuli for everyone) and is thus both qualitative and quantitative; (2) we gain emic cognitive results for individuals (not generalized ones) and can document intracultural variation; (3) the researcher gives only stimuli instead of a prearranged polarity profile, thus allowing for local perspectives (e.g. local classifications or sentiments); (4) photos are used as stimuli instead of words, thus allowing for more control of stimuli; (5) the items are presented parsimoniously instead of via an elaborate procedure and are thus applicable to real life; (6) notation is easy and simple and thus transparent for the interview partners, which is also an ethical issue; and (7) the interview procedure is short and thus open for further dialogue on emic-related topics.

I can think of a number of ways to modify this method. For example, one could ask people to sort or rank items according to desired future states of their residential environment (Aitken 1990: 253). The method elicits subjective theories, but being oriented towards comparative methods it may be used to understand intersubjective emic theories.

Figure 2: Set of interview materials for repertory grid interview

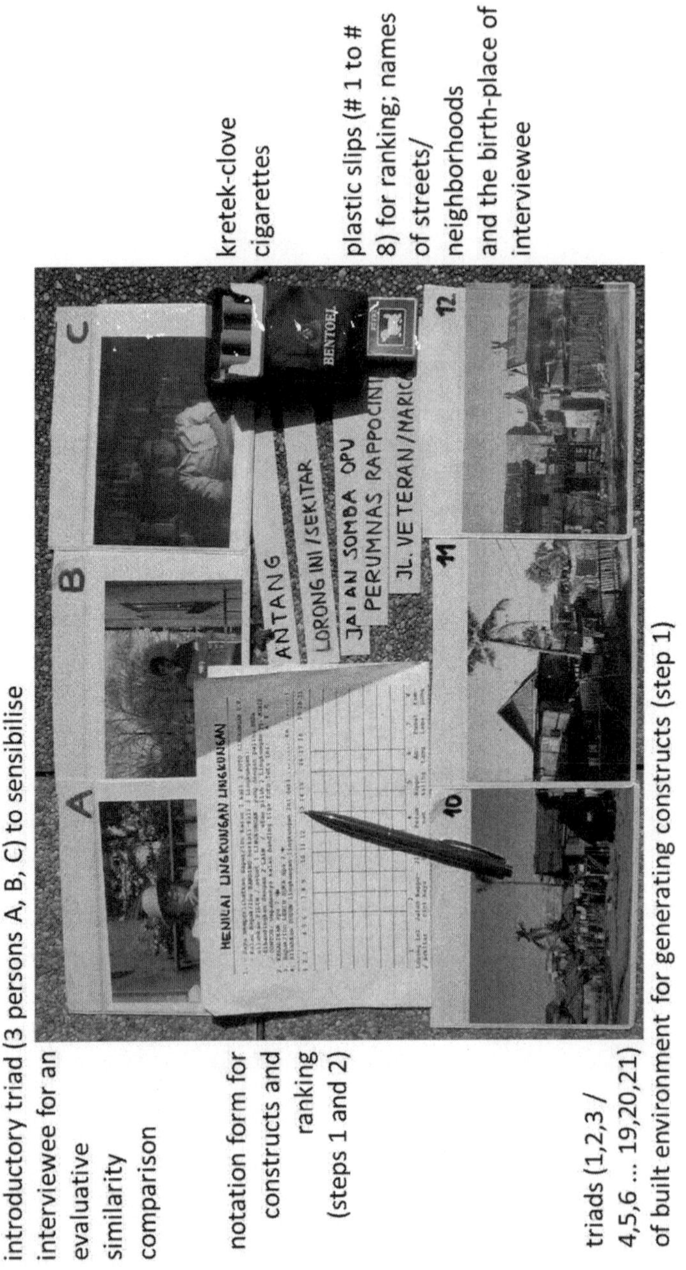
introductory triad (3 persons A, B, C) to sensibilise interviewee for an evaluative similarity comparison
notation form for constructs and ranking (steps 1 and 2)
triads (1,2,3 / 4,5,6 ... 19,20,21) of built environment for generating constructs (step 1)
kretek-clove cigarettes
plastic slips (# 1 to # 8) for ranking; names of streets/ neighborhoods and the birth-place of interviewee
A
B
C
10
11
12
ANTANG
LORONG INI /SEKITAR
PERUMNAS RAPPOCINI
BENTOEL

Source: Author's compilation

Often forgotten: using culturally relevant themes and media

Textbook methods demand considerable modifications if we are really aiming at participation of our partners in the field. The challenge is to simplify and adapt the methodology without localizing it so much as to prevent comparison and generalization. The localization aspect is often forgotten in applying PRA methods because it needs time and some ethnographic grounding, as I will show in the following. I resorted to this method after having been in the field for five months and trying different approaches, for example cognitive maps. I interviewed a random sample of house owners (30 per cent; n = 21) from the neighborhood. My respondents determined the interview locations. Often we talked in their small guest rooms (*ruang tamu*), on the terrace, or in front of the dwelling at the edge of the small lane. Interviews lasted between ½ and 1½ hours depending on the age and education of the interviewees, as well as situational factors such as their mood and the presence of neighbors.

Triads usually motivate people to think and evaluate far more than dyads, which are often too obviously similar or different. For any triad I selected photographs that showed relatively similar situations to make the comparison interesting, but I also tried to maximize the variance of living situations through the triads. One triad showed three poor houses while in another the interviewee saw three well-organized middle class neighborhoods. I used photographs (Figure 2) for step one, the elicitation of the constructs, because I found during the first few months of my stay that people like to talk about photographs; they keep albums of family pictures and almost every household displays photos. As such, it is relatively easy to present the same stimuli to every person interviewed using photos. Furthermore, photographs are suitable for exploring urban environmental knowledge because they reveal details of living spaces that people can compare.

The selection of suitable photographs was important. The color photographs I used showed typical residential areas in Makassar. I did not use photos of the area where the interviewees lived, because in step one I wanted to elicit general value orientations based on observable traits and not the evaluation of a known area (Nasar 1998). Likewise, I did not use photos of well-known places, streets, buildings, or advertising hoardings. Instead, I selected from hundreds of photos that I had taken during the first five months of fieldwork, to document the city and to cover the diversity of living situations and residential areas. Pragmatic as well as ethical considerations prompted me to show only outdoor situations. Firstly, indoor photos too obviously reflect residents' social status and thus would not be very productive. Secondly, I could only take indoor photos when I knew the people well. Using indoor photos of households personally known to the interviewees would have been dubious in a society where living conditions are a common theme of everyday gossip. Further practical considerations regarding photographs included using the locally common 10 x 15cm print format and numbering the photos for easy identification. This also facilitated notation and was transparent to interview partners, a significant consideration for a participatory citizen science methodology.

The comparative evaluation of urban areas within the constructs (step 2) also needed some preparation based on my fieldwork experiences. For the stimuli, I presented eight urban areas using their names (not photographs). The neighborhood names were written clearly on plastic slips, which were easy to handle if there was only dim light within a house or in the evening, and they didn't get dirty if the interview had to be conducted outside in front of a house or during rain in the monsoon season. I selected six areas, an interviewee's present neighborhood, and his or her birthplace. The reasoning behind the inclusion of the last two areas was to connect the ranking with the person's biographical experience. During my fieldwork about residential decision-making it had become apparent that previous country-city migration experiences are a key factor in selecting areas for intra-urban residential moves. Awareness was to be guided towards general evaluations, images, and prejudices, not specific traits. Ranking was used instead of rating because it is less laborious and implies a comparison of elements.

Culturally adequate knowledge elicitation

As might be expected, people from an ethnically and economically mixed neighborhood reacted differently to this method. Most of them were interested or amused, but to some it was strange. Having been in the field for five months, I had visited all interviewees several times before the repertory grid interview. I had had informal discussions and conducted a household census and residential history interview with all of them, so they knew me and knew my overall research topic was intra-urban residential mobility.

When introducing this specific interview I stressed that I was not seeking 'correct' answers but that I was interested in their personal perceptions and evaluations. This was important, as my trials with this formal procedure revealed that some people associated it with intelligence tests. In a city with many schools, universities, and offices, many people have had experiences with such tests. After some conversation and a few obligatory kretek clove cigarettes I showed the people three outdoor photographs: one of myself, one of my brother, and one of my mother. I used my family because people are very keen on seeing photos of western people and of families. I then asked the triad question and answered it by grouping according to sex: my brother and myself versus my mother. Then I pointed out that we could also group in the same way but for other reasons. My mother was improperly (kurang cocok) dressed for women, whereas my brother and I were properly dressed. The aim was to demonstrate the method to the interviewee using an everyday topic, and I used gender roles to make them aware of an evaluative comparison in the interview. In addition, I deliberately used a very simple notation form. I used big letters because of my poor handwriting and dim light. The notation was facilitated by the numbering of the photographs (step 1) and the plastic slips (step 2).

The repertory grid method presented here is simple regarding the theoretical assumptions and procedures followed, but using it requires reasoning and some preparation. Time is needed, as most of this preparatory work has to be done in the field. The conclusions drawn from the repertory grid interview in my specific case are as follows:

- One problem of cognitive textbook methods is that they often require many interviews with the same person;
- Even 'simple' cognitive textbook methods are complicated and time consuming;
- A short interview is the better option in most instances;
- Increase transparency by using simple notation, allowing for visual sharing;

- Restrict the number of personal constructs elicited;
- Ensure that items presented are culturally appropriate;
- Photographs are often suitable, as people are interested in them;
- Plan time to prepare suitable photos and pre-test them;
- Ask what the locally relevant themes of discourse are;
- Prepare the interview partners with another locally relevant topic using the same method.

Figure 3: Selected concepts about residential areas: emic vs. the official idiom

Everyday concepts		Official idiom (e.g. in maps, planning documents)	
pole 1	*pole 2*		
(being) alone (sendiri)	populated (bermasyarakat)		
like village (sama kampung)	urban (kota)		
still like kampung (masih kampung)	already urban (sudah kota)		
plain, simple (sederhana)	luxurious (mewah)		
orderly (rapi)	not (yet) orderly (belum rapi)		
dense (population) (padat)	distantly spaced (renggang)		
dense (population) (padat)	good ventilation (udara bagus)		
dense (population) (padat)	still empty (masih kosong)		
calm (tenang, sunyi)	ado, duss, gossip (cencong)		
calm (sunyi)	full of life (ramai)		
secure (aman)	disturbed, unsafe (rawan)		
secure, clear (tenang)	insecure (kacau)	same as everyday concept	
orderly planned (teratur)	not orderly (tidak teratur)	same as everyday concept	
the rich (yang kaya)	ordinary people (orang biasa)	rich (orang kaya)	poor (miskin)
modern (maju)	not (yet) modern (belum maju)	modern (maju)	traditional (tradisional)
dirty (kotor)	clean (bersih)	dirty area (kawasan kumuh)	
		economically strong (economi kuat)	economically weak (economi lemah)
		upper people	lower people

	(masyarakat ting-gi)	(masyarakat rendah)

Source: Author's compilation, 2011. Empty fields: no complement observed.

CITIZENS' KNOWING AND UNIVERSAL KNOWLEDGE

We have seen that the repertory grid method yields various results, ranging from simple qualitative data about cases to detailed quantitative sample data. The results may be employed in several ways:

- Simple graphic representation to allow visual sharing, which is a good basis for direct further discussion and reveals proposals for as-yet unrecognized evaluation criteria;
- Analysis through simple sorting by hand (cf. Raethel 1993: 47-49);
- Using software analysis, e.g. Anthropac (Borgatti 1989); and
- Use of specific quantitative and graphic data processing for which there is software available (cf. Raethel 1993: 53-67).

In this case, there were striking differences between the perceptions of local residents on the one hand and the language and concepts employed in official urban planning brochures on the other (Figure 3). Formal but simple cognitive methods have some potential in development research, as demonstrated using local urban knowledge to achieve more humanized and effective urban planning. Regarding methods, the universality of cognitive approaches can be maintained provided that informants are either accustomed to formal questioning or textbook versions are adapted to the local cultural setting. The latter requires a certain ethnographic grounding in local culture, which is not normally available in development projects.

As presented here the 'Repertory Grid Method' is an approach which allows the elicitation of information regarding local cognition and emotion in a systematic yet sensitive way. In urban situations, besides knowledge about dwellings, space, and mobility options, knowledge of prices, unwritten rules of the public sphere, and of bureaucracy are particularly important (cf. Irwin 1995; Cresswell 1996; Burgess et al. 1997; 2000; Knorr-Siedow/Gandelsonas 2004; regarding Indonesia: Nas 1995). Such knowledge could be used both to counter dominant official regulations and to enrich expert knowledge. If local knowledge research was less idealistic, hurried, more systematic, multi-focal, and context-sensitive, this would make development and specifically urban planning more effective and participatory, with the aim toward community enablement.

Methods derived from cognitive anthropology are applicable provided that textbook versions are considerably simplified and adapted to the local cultural setting. Participatory methods often used in development currently are useful but are frequently too quick and mostly lack theoretical grounding. Local knowledge research is mostly done in the realm of development, which means that it is problem-oriented. Nevertheless, even such applied research needs well-defined methodologies, which require a clear theoretical understanding of the phenomenon of local knowledge. The kernel of local knowledge should be seen in a form of knowledge and performance found in all societies, comprising skills and acquired intelligence, which are action-oriented, culturally situated, and responding to constantly changing social and natural environments.

Given that the general properties of local knowledge, as outlined in the general model presented here (or a variant thereof), will pass more empirical cross-cultural tests, local knowledge might emerge as a human universal (for details cf. Antweiler 2007). People may live differently in this world, but they do not live in different worlds.

REFERENCES

Agrawal, A. (1995): Dismantling the divide between indigenous and scientific knowledge. Development and Change, 26, 413-439.

Agrawal, A. (1998): Geistiges Eigentum und 'indigenes Wissen': Weder Gans noch goldene Eier. In: Flitner, M./Görg,C./Heins V. (eds.), Konfliktfeld Natur. Biologische Ressourcen und globale Politik: 193-214). Opladen: Leske und Budrich.

Aitken, S. C. (1984): Normative views and ordering the urban milieu. East Lakes Geographer, 14, 1-16.

Aitken, S. C. (1987): Households moving within the rental sector: mental schemata and search spaces. Environment and Planning A 19, 369-383.

Aitken, S. C. (1990): Local evaluations of neighborhood change. Annals of the American Association of Geographers, 80, 247-267.

Anderson. J. E. (2009): Law, Knowledge, Culture. The Production of Indigenous Knowledge in Intellectual Property Law. Aldershot: Edward Elgar Publications.

Anderson, T. J. (1990): Personal construct theory, residential decision-making and the behavioral environment. In F. W. Boal/ D.N. Livingstone (eds.) The behavioral environment. Essays in reflection, application and re-evaluation: 133-162. London / New York: Routledge.

Antweiler, Ch. (1993): Universelle Erhebungsmethoden und lokale Kognition am Beispiel urbaner Umweltkognition in Süd-Sulawesi/Indonesien. Zeitschrift für Ethnologie, 118, 251-287.

Antweiler, Ch. (1998): Local knowledge and local knowing: an anthropological analysis of contested 'cultural products' in the context of development. Anthropos, 93, 469-494.

Antweiler, Ch. (2000): Urbane Rationalität: eine stadtethnologische Studie zu Ujung Pandang (Makassar), Indonesien (Urban rationality. An urban anthropological study on Ujung Pandang (Makassar), Indonesia). Berlin: Dietrich Reimer Verlag (Kölner Ethnologische Mitteilungen, 12).

Antweiler, Ch. (2002): Rationalities in Makassar. Cognition and Mobility in a Regional Metropolis in the Indonesian Periphery. In P. Nas (Ed.), The Indonesian Town Revisited: 232-261). Münster etc.: Lit Verlag und Singapore: ISEAS (Southeast Asian Dynamics, 1).

Antweiler, Ch. (2004): Local Knowledge Theory and Methods. An Urban Model from Indonesia. In: Bicker, A./Sillitoe, P./Pottier/ J. (eds.): Investigating Local Knowledge. New Directions, New Approaches: 1-34. Aldershot/ Burlington: Ashgate Publishing.

Antweiler, Ch. (2007): Wissenschaft quer durch die Kulturen: Wissenschaft und lokales Wissen als Formen universaler Rationalität. In H. R. Yousefi, K. Fischer, R. Lüthe / P. Gerdsen (eds.), Wege zur Wissenschaft. Eine interkulturelle Perspektive. Grundlagen, Differenzen, Interdisziplinäre Dimensionen: 67-94). Nordhausen: Verlag Traugott Bautz.

Antweiler, Ch. (2008): Kognitive Methoden. In: Beer, B. (ed.): Methoden ethnologischer Feldforschung: 233-254). Berlin: Dietrich Reimer Verlag (Ethnologische Paperbacks).

Antweiler, Ch. (2009): Kognitive Anthropologie. Kulturelle Rationalität und lokales Wissen. In: Wagner, A. (ed.): Anthropologische Aufbrüche. Alttestamentliche und interdisziplinäre Zugänge zur historischen Anthropologie: 45-67. Göttingen: Vandenhoeck/ Ruprecht (Forschungen zur Religion und Literatur des Alten und Neuen Testaments, 232).

Antweiler, Ch. (2011): Interkulturalität in Südostasien – Migration als Motor der Genese von Kulturräumen. In: Barmeyer, Ch./Genkova, P./ Scheffer, J. (eds.): Interkulturelle Kommunikation und Kulturwissenschaft. Grundbegriffe, Wissenschaftsdisziplinen, Kulturräume. Passau: Verlag Karl Stutz: 499-517.

Arce, A./Long, N. (eds.) (2000): Anthropology, development and modernities. Exploring discourses, counter-tendencies and violence. London/ New York: Routledge.

Augoustinos, M./Walker, I. (1995): Social cognition: an integrated introduction. London etc.: Sage Publications.

Barker, D. (1980): Appropriate technology: an example using a traditional African board game to measure farmers' attitudes and environmental images. In Brokhensha et al. (eds.), Indigenous knowledge systems and development: 297-302). Washington, D.C.: University Press of America (The International Library of Development and Indigenous Knowledge).

Barnes, R. H. (1991): Review of Röttger-Rössler 1989 Zeitschrift für Ethnologie, 115, 289-291.

Barth, F. (1995): Other knowledge and other ways of knowing. Journal of Anthropological Research, 50, 65-68.

Berlin, B. (1992): Ethnobiological classification: principles of categorization of plants and animals in traditional societies. Princeton: Princeton University Press.

Bernard, H. R. (2006): Research Methods in Anthropology. Qualitative and Quantitative Approaches. Thousand Oaks etc.: Sage Publications (11998).

Boggs, J. P. (1990): The Use of Anthropological Knowledge under NEPA. Human Organization, 49, 217-226.

Borgatti, S. P. (1989): Provisional documentation Anthropac 2.6. Manuscript. No place given; n.y.

Borowsky, R. (1994): On the knowledge and knowing of cultural activities. In R. Borowsky (Ed.). Assessing Cultural Anthropology: 331-347). New York: McGraw-Hill.

Brokhensha, D.D./Warren, D.M./Werner, O. (eds.) (1980): Indigenous knowledge systems and development. Washington, D.C.: University Press of America (The International Library of Development and Indigenous Knowledge).

Brush, S. B./Strabinsky, D. (eds) (1996): Valuing local knowledge: indigenous people and intellectual Property Rights. Washington, D.C.: Island Press.

Burgess, R./Carmona, M./Kolstee, T. (1997): Contemporary policies for enablement and participation: a critical review. In. M. Burgess, Carmona, M./Kolstee, T. (eds.), The challenge of sustainable cities: neoliberalism and urban strategies in developing countries: 139-162). London: Zed Books.

Catina, A./Schmitt, G.M. (1993): Die Theorie der Persönlichen Konstrukte. In Scheer, J. W./A. Catina (eds.), Einführung in die Repertory Grid-Technik. Band 1: Grundlagen und Methoden:11-23. Bern: Verlag Hans Huber.

Chambers, R. (1991): Shortcut and participatory methods for gaining social information for projects. In M. M. Cernea (Ed.), Putting people first: sociological variables in rural development: 515-637). Oxford: Oxford University Press (for the World Bank).

Cresswell, T. (1996): Participatory approaches in the UK urban health sector: keeping faith with perceived needs. Development in Practice, 6, 16-24.

Crick, M. R. (1982): Anthropology of knowledge. Annual Review of Anthropology, 11, 287-313.

D'Andrade, R. G./Strauss, C. (eds.) (1992): Human motives and cultural models. Cambridge: Cambridge University Press.

DeWalt, B. R. (1994): Using indigenous knowledge to improve agriculture and natural resource management. Human Organization, 53, 123-131.

Ellen, R. F. (1993): Nuaulu ethnozoology: a systematic inventory. Canterbury: University of Kent at Canterbury; Center for Social Anthropology and Computing in Cooperation with the Center of South-East Asian Studies.

Ellen, R. F. (1996): Putting plants in their place: anthropological approaches to understanding the ethnobotanical knowledge of rainforest populations. In D. S. Edwards et al. (eds.), Tropical Rainforest Research-Current Issues. Dordrecht: Kluwer Academic Publishers.

Ellen, R. F./Harris, H. (2000): Introduction. In: R. F. Ellen/P. Parkes/A. Bicker (eds.) Indigenous environmental knowledge and its transformations: critical anthropological perspectives. Amsterdam: Harwood Academic Publishers, p. 1-33.

Engelhardt, A./Kajetzke, L. (eds.) (2010): Handbuch Wissensgesellschaft. Theorien, Themen und Probleme. Bielefeld: Transcript (Transcript Sozialtheorie).

Evers, H.-D. (2010): Local and global knowledge: Social science research on Southeast Asia. In Th. Menkhoff et al. (eds.), Governing and managing knowledge in Asia: 79-92). Singapore etc. World Scientific (Series on Innovation and Knowledge Management, 9).

Fransella, F. (1995): George Kelly. London, New York: Sage (Key Figures in Counselling and Psychotherapy).

Fransella, F./Bell, R./Bannister, D. (2003): A Manual for Repertory Grid Technique: New York: John Wiley/ Sons.

Farnell, B. (1999). Moving bodies, acting selves. Annual Review of Anthropology, 28,341-373.

Fiske, S. T./Taylor, S. E. (1991): Social cognition. London: Addison-Wesley.

Fjellman, S. (1976): Natural and unnatural decision-making: a critique of decision theory. Ethos 4, 73-94.

Flick, U. (1995): Psychologie des Sozialen: Repräsentationen in Wissen und Sprache. Reinbek bei Hamburg: Rowohlt Taschenbuch Verlag.

Friedberg, C. (1999): Diversity, order, unity: different levels in folk knowledge about the living. Social Anthropology, 7, 1-16.

Fromm, M. (1995): Repertory Grid Methodik. Ein Lehrbuch. Weinheim: Deutscher Studien Verlag.

Gladwin, Ch. H. (1989): Ethnographic decision tree modeling. Newbury Park, Ca./ London: Sage Publications (Qualitative Research Methods 19).

Greaves, T. (ed.) (1994): Intellectual rights for indigenous peoples: a source book. Oklahoma City: Society for Applied Anthropology.

Harrison, S. (1995): Anthropological perspectives on the management of knowledge. Anthropology Today, 11, 10-14.

Hauck, G./Kößler, R. (2004): Universalität der Vernunft und lokales Wissen – nicht nur epistemologische Überlegungen. In: N. Schareika/Bierschenk, Th. (eds.), Lokales Wissen – Sozialwissenschaftliche Perspektiven: 9-39). Münster: Lit Verlag (Mainzer Beiträge zur Afrika-Forschung, 11).

Hobart, M. (1993): Introduction: The growth of ignorance. In M. Hobart (ed.) An anthropological critique of development. The growth of ignorance: 1-30). London, New York: Routledge.

Honerla, S./Schröder, S.: (eds.) (1995): Lokales Wissen und Entwicklung.. Saarbrücken: Verlag für Entwicklungspolitik (Entwicklungsethnologie; special issue).

Hornidge, A.-K. (2007): Re-Inventing Society - State Concepts of Knowledge in Germany and Singapore. In: Journal of Social Issues in Southeast Asia, 22(2): 202-229.

Hornidge, A.-K. (2011) 'Knowledge Society' as Academic Concept and Stage of Development – A Conceptual and Historical Review. In: Menkhoff, Th./Evers, H.-D./Wah, Ch. Y./Pang, E. F. (eds.): Beyond the Knowledge Trap: Developing Asia's Knowledge-Based Economies. New Jersey, London, Singapore, Beijing: World Scientific. 87-128.

Hunn, E. (1982): The utilitarian factor in folk biological classification. American Anthropologist , 84, 930-847.

Hutchins, E. (1980): Culture and inference: a Trobriand case study. Cambridge, Mass./London: Harvard University Press.

Hutchins, E. (1996): Cognition in the wild. Cambridge, Mass.: The MIT Press.

Irwin, A. (1995): Citizen science: a study of people, expertise and sustainable development. London etc.: Routledge (Environment and Society).

Jankowicz, D. (2003): An Easy Guide to Repertory Grids. New York: Wiley.

Jansen, S. J. T./Coolen, H. C. C. H. /Goetgeluk, R. W. (eds.) (2011): The Measurement and Analysis of Housing Preference and Choice. Theory, Practice and Examples. The Hague: Springer Netherlands.

Jones, D. (1999): Evolutionary psychology. Annual Reviews of Anthropology, 28, 553-575.

Karamoy, A./Dias, G. (eds.) (1982): Participatory urban services in Indonesia: people participation and the impact of government social services programs on the kampung communities: a case study in Jakarta and Ujung Pandang. Jakarta: Lembaga Penelitian, Pendidikan dan Penerangan Ekonomi dan Sosial (LPIIIES).

Kalland, A. (2003): Environmentalism and Images of the Other. In Selin, H. (Ed.), Nature across Cultures. Views of Nature and the Environment in Non-Western Cultures (Science Across Cultures, 4): 1-17). Dordrecht, Amsterdam: Kluwer Academic.

Kelly, G. A. (1955): The Psychology of personal constructs (2 vols.). New York: W. W. Norton/ Company.

Knorr-Siedow, Th./Gandelsonas, C. (2004): Lokales Wissen in der Stadtpolitik und Quartiersentwicklung. In U. Matthiesen (Ed.), Stadtregion und Wissen. Analyzen und Plädoyers für eine wissensbasierte Stadtpolitik: 293-307). Wiesbaden: VS Verlag für Sozialwissenschaften.

Krikorian, G./Kapczynski, A. (eds.) (2010): Access to Knowledge in the Age of Intellectual Property. Brooklyn, N.Y.: Zed Books.

Kronenfeld, D. B. (1996). Plastic glasses and church fathers: semantic extension from the ethnoscience tradition. Oxford etc.: Oxford University Press (Oxford Studies in Anthropological Linguistics).

Lakoff, G./Johnson, M. (1980): Metaphors we Live By. Chicago: The University of Chicago Press (1980).

Lave, J. (1993): The practice of learning. In: J. Lave/ S. Chaiklin (eds.), Understanding practice: perspectives on activity and context: 3-32). Cambridge: Cambridge University Press.

Lave, J. (1996): The savagery of the domestic mind. In L. Nader (ed.): Naked science: anthropological Inquiry into boundaries, power, and knowledge: 87-100). New York/ London: Routledge.

Lave, J./Murtaugh. M./de la Rocha, O. (1984): The dialectic of arithmetic in grocery shopping. In Rogoff, B. and Lave, J. (eds.) Everyday cognition: its development in social context: 67-94). Cambridge, Mass.: Harvard University Press.

Lindblom, C. E. (1959): The science of 'muddling through'. Public Administration Review, XIX, 79-88.

Lölke, U. (2002): Zur Lokalität von Wissen: Die Kritik der local knowledge-Debatte in Anthropologie und internationaler Zusammenarbeit. Hamburg: Institut für Afrika-Kinde (Focus Afrika, IAK.Diskussionsbeiträge, 21).

Lovell, N. (1998): Introduction. In: Lovell, N. (ed.), Locality and Belonging (pp.1-24). London/ New York: Routledge (European Association of Social Anthropologists).

Lyotard, J. F. (1986): Das postmoderne Wissen (The postmodern Knowledge). Graz: Böhlau Verlag.

Maasen, S. (2007): Wissenssoziologie. Bielefeld: Transcript (Themen der Soziologie).

McCarthy, D. (1996): Knowledge as culture: the new sociology of knowledge. London/New York: Routledge.

Malinowski, B. (1948): Magic, science and religion and other essays. Garden City, N.Y.: Doubleday Anchor.

Marsden, D. (1994): Indigenous management and the management of indigenous knowledge. In S. Wright (ed.), Anthropology of Organizations: 41-55). London, New York: Routledge.

Menkhoff, Th,/Evers, H-D./Wah, C Y. (eds.) (2010): Governing and managing knowledge in Asia. Singapore etc. World Scientific (Series on Innovation and Knowledge Management, 9.

Mersmann, C. (1993): Umweltwissen und Landnutzung in einem afrikanischen Dorf: zur Frage des bäuerlichen Engagements in der Gestaltung der Kulturlandschaft der Usambara-Berge Tansanias. Hamburg: Deutsches Übersee-Institut.

Metzger, D. G./Williams, G .E. (1966): Some procedures and results in the study of native categories: Tzeltal 'firewood'. American Anthropologist, 68, 389-407.

Miehlau, S./Wickl, F. (2007): Lokales Wissen und Entwicklung. Bad Honneff: Horlemann Verlag.

Murdoch, J./Clark, J. (1994): Sustainable knowledge. Geoforum, 25, 115-132.

Nas, P. J. M. (ed.) (1995): Issues in urban development: case studies from Indonesia. Leiden: Research School CNWS.

Nader L. (ed.) (1996): Naked science. Anthropological inquiry into boundaries, power, and knowledge. New York/ London: Routledge.

Nasar, J. L. (1998). The Evaluative Image of the City. Thousand Oaks etc.: Sage Publications.

Nazarea, V. D. (1999): Introduction: a view from a point: ethnoecology as situated knowledge. In V. D. Nazarea (ed.), Ethnoecology. Situated knowledge / Located lives: 3-20). Tuscon: University of Arizona Press.

Nygren, A. (1999): Local knowledge in the environment-development discourse: from dichotomies to situated knowledges. Critique of Anthropology 19, 267-288.

Pennington, D. C. (2000): Social cognition. London: Routledge/ Philadelphia: Taylor/ Francis (Routledge Modular Psychology).

Preston, V. A./ Taylor, S. M. (1981): Personal construct theory and residential choice. Annals of the Association of American Geographers, 21, 437-461.

Pasquale, S./Schröder:/Schulze, U. (eds.) (1998): Lokales Wissen für nachhaltige Entwicklung: ein Praxisführer. Saarbrücken: Verlag für Entwicklungspolitik.

Posey, D. A./Dutfield, G. (1996): Beyond intellectual property: toward traditional resource rights for indigenous peoples and local communities. Ottawa etc.: International Development Research Centre.

Pottier, J. (1993): Harvesting words? Thoughts on agricultural extension and knowledge ownership, with reference to Rwanda. Entwicklungsethnologie, 2, 28-38.

Pottier, J./Bicker, A./Sillitoe, P. (eds.) (2003): Negotiating local knowledge: Power and identity in development. London: Pluto Press (Anthropology, Culture, and Society)

Prattis, J. I. (1973): Strategizing Man. Man, 8, 45-58.

Quinn, N. (ed.) (2005): Finding Culture in Talk. A Collection of Methods. New York/ Houndmills: Palgrave Macmillan (Culture, Mind, and Society, The Book Series of the Society for Psychological Anthropology).

Quinn, N./ Holland, D. (1987): Culture and cognition. In D. Holland/ N. Quinn (eds.), Cultural models in language and thought: 3-40). Cambridge: Cambridge University Press.

Raethel, A. (1993): Auswertungsmethoden für Repertory Grids. In: Scheer, J. W. and A. Catina (eds.), Einführung in die Repertory Grid-Technik. Bd. 1: Grundlagen und Methoden: 41-67). Bern etc.: Verlag Hans Huber.

Richards, P. (1980): Community environmental knowledge in African rural development. In D. Brokhensha, D. M. Warren/ O. Werner (eds.) Indigenous knowledge systems and development: 181-194). Washington, D.C.: University Press of America, Inc. (The International Library of Development and Indigenous Knowledge).

Rogoff, B./ Lave, J. (eds.) (1984). Everyday cognition: its development in social context. Cambridge, Mass.: Harvard University Press.

Saegert, S./ G. H. Winkel (1990): Environmental Psychology. Annual Review of Psychology, 41, 441-477.

Salmond, A. (1982): Theoretical Landscapes: On cross-cultural conceptions of knowledge. In D. Parkin (Ed.), Semantic Anthropology: 65-87). London etc.: Academic Press (ASA Monographs, 22).

Sankoff, G. (1971): Quantitative analysis of sharing and variability in a cognitive model. Ethnology, 10, 389-408.

Schank, R. C./Abelson, R. P. (1977): Scripts, plans, goals, and understanding: an inquiry into human knowledge structures. Hillsdale: Erlbaum Publishers.

Schareika, N. (2004): Lokales Wissen: ethnologische Perspektiven. In N. Schareika/ Th. Bierschenk (eds.), Lokales Wissen – Sozialwissenschaftliche Perspektiven: 9-39). Münster: Lit Verlag (Mainzer Beiträge zur Afrika-Forschung, 11).

Scheer, J. W. (1993): Planung und Durchführung von Repertory Grid-Untersuchungen. In Scheer, J. W./ A. Catina (eds.), Einführung in die Repertory Grid-Technik. Band 1: Grundlagen und Methoden: 24-40). Bern etc.: Verlag Hans Huber.

Scheer, J. W./ Catina, A. (eds.) (1993): Einführung in die Repertory Grid-Technik. Band 1: Grundlagen und Methoden. Bern etc.: Verlag Hans Huber.

Schönhuth, M./Kievelitz, U. (1995): Participatory learning approaches: Rapid Rural Appraisal / Participatory Appraisal: an introductory guide. Roßdorf: GTZ.

Scott, J. P. (1998): Seeing like a state: how certain schemes to improve the human condition have failed. New Haven/ London: Yale University Press; The Institution for Social and Policy Studies at Yale University (Yale Agricultural Studies, The Yale ISPS Series).

Seur, H. (1992): The engagement of researchers and local actors in the construction of case studies and research themes: exploring methods of restudy. In N. Long/ A. Long (eds.), Battlefields of knowledge: the interlocking of theory and practice in social research and development: 115-143). London/ New York: Routledge.

Sillitoe, P. (1998a): The development of indigenous knowledge: a new applied anthropology. Current Anthropology, 39, 232-252.

Sillitoe, P. (1998b): What know natives? Local knowledge in development. Social Anthropology, 6, 203-220.

Sillitoe, P. (1998c): Knowing the land: soil and land resource evaluation and indigenous knowledge. Soil Use and Management , 14, 188-193.

Sillitoe, P. (ed.) (2009): Local science vs. global science: Approaches to indigenous knowledge in international development. London: Berghahn (Studies in Environmental Anthropology and Ethnobiology).

Sillitoe, P., Dixon, P.-J./Barr, J. (2005): Indigenous Knowledge Inquiries. A Methodologies Manual for Development Programs and Projects. London: Intermediate Technology Publications.

Siverts, H. (1991): Technology and knowledge among the Jivaro of Peru. In Gronhaug, R./Haaland, G./Henriksen, G. (eds.), The ecology of choice and symbol: essays in honour of Fredrik Barth: 297-311). Bergen: Alma Mater Forlag AS.

Sperber, D. (1982): Le savoir des anthropologues. Paris: Hermann (Collection Savoir).

Spradley, J. P. (1980): The ethnographic interview. New York etc.: Holt, Rinehart/ Winston.

Steht, N. (2001): Moderne Wissensgesellschaften. Aus Politik und Zeitgeschichte B 36: 7-13.

Stokols, D./Altman, I. (eds.) (1987): Handbook of environmental psychology, Vol. 1 und 2. New York: Wiley.

Strathern, M./da Cunha, M.C./Descola A. C. A./Harvey: (1998): Exploitable knowledge belongs to the creators of it: a debate. Social Anthropology, 6, 109-126.

Strauss, A. L. (1987): Qualitative analysis for social scientists. Cambridge etc.: Cambridge University Press.

Strauss, C./Quinn, N. (1997): A cognitive theory of cultural meaning. Cambridge etc.: Cambridge University Press (Publications of the Society for Psychological Anthropology, 9).

Tambiah, S. J. (1990): Magic, science, religion, the scope of rationality. Cambridge: Cambridge University Press.

Tanner, C./Foppa, K. (1996): Umweltwahrnehmung, Umweltbewußtsein und Umweltverhalten. In Diekmann,A./Jaeger, C. C. (eds.) Umweltsoziologie: 245-271). Opladen: Westdeutscher Verlag (Kölner Zeitschrift für Soziologie und Sozialpsychologie, special issue).

Thrift, N. (1996): Flies and germs: a Geography of Knowledge. In: Thrift, N. (ed.): Spatial Formations: 96-124. London etc., Sage (Theory, Culture and Society).

Tognoli, J. (1987): Residential environments. In: Stokols, D./Altman, I. (eds.) Handbook of environmental psychology, Vol. 1 und 2: 655-690). New York: Wiley.

Van der Ploeg, J. (1989): Knowledge systems, metaphor and interface: the case of potatoes in the Peruvian highlands. In: N. Long/ A. Long (eds.), Battlefields of knowledge: the interlocking of theory and practice in social research and development: 177-193). London/ New York: Routledge.

Van Ufford, Q. (1993): Knowledge and ignorance in the practices of development policy. In: M. Hobart (ed.): An anthropological critique of development. The growth of ignorance: 135-160). London, New York: Routledge.

Von Cranach, M. (1995): Über das Wissen sozialer Systeme. In: Flick, U. (Ed.), Psychologie des Sozialen: Repräsentationen in Wissen und Sprache: 22-53). Reinbek bei Hamburg: Rowohlt Taschenbuch Verlag.

Vayda, A. P. (1983): Progressive contextualization. Methods for research in human ecology. Human Ecology, 11, 265-281.

Warren, D. M./Slikkerveer, L. J./Brokhensha, D. (eds.) (1995): The cultural dimension of development: indigenous knowledge systems. London: Intermediate Technology Publications (IT Studies in Indigenous Knowledge and Development).

Weller, S. C./Romney, A. K. (1988): Systematic data collection. Newbury Park etc.: Sage Publications (Qualitative Research Methods, 10).

Werner, O./Fenton, J. (1970): Method and theory in ethnoscience and ethnoepistemology. In R. Naroll/ R. Cohen (eds.) Handbook of Method in Cultural Anthropology: 537-578). New York: The Natural History Press.

Werner, O./ Schoepfle, M. (1987): Systematic fieldwork (2 vols.). Newbury Park: Sage Publications.

Zeleny, M. (2010): Knowledge of Enterprise: Knowledge management or knowledge technology? In Th. Menkhoff et al. (eds.), Governing and managing knowledge in Asia: 23-57). Singapore etc. World Scientific (Series on Innovation and Knowledge Management), 9.

Conflicting Frames of Reference

Environmental Changes in Coastal Indonesia

CHRISTIAN REICHEL, SOFIE ELENA MARTENS AND ARNE HARMS

INTRODUCTION

Marine ecosystems worldwide are degrading at a rapid scale as a result of an-thropogenic factors, such as overfishing, increasing pollution, and the impacts of global climate change. In many locations, these factors have caused radical de-clines in targeted fish stocks and shifts in fish size and species composition, sometimes leading to the collapse of coastal and oceanic fisheries (Hughes et al. 2005).

Coral reefs are among the most valuable and diverse, yet also the most frag-ile, marine ecosystems. They provide crucial environmental and economic ser-vices including coastal protection, seafood, and medicines (Cassels et al. 2005: 336). The fish associated with coral reefs constitute the most diverse vertebrate fauna in the world, and these reefs still comprise a reservoir of so far unknown marine biodiversity (Montgomery 1990: 329). Although global warming is one of the major threats to these coral reefs, the human population explosion in Southeast Asia has put additional pressure on marine resources (Pockley 2000; Burke et al. 2002: 26). Furthermore, the overfishing of reef fish results in a sim-plification of food webs and a significant loss in biodiversity. As a consequence, the vulnerability of reef ecosystems to environmental changes is further in-creased (cf. Berkes et al. 2006). However, new approaches have emerged in re-cent years, which do not exclude human actors in order to protect the natural system, but rather emphasize the interdependencies between the social and natu-ral realms. Furthermore, it is now widely recognized that culturally mediated perceptions, forms of knowledge-specific and quotidian interactions, and cogni-tions are highly important for the way human actors understand and cope with the dynamic processes related to environmental changes (Casimir 2008: 36; cf. Antweiler, this volume).

Indonesia, consisting of more than 17,000 islands, is the world's largest archipelago and its flora and fauna display a high degree of endemism (Cassels et al. 2005: 337). In total, the country is home to up to 86,000 km² of coral reefs, thus representing more than 50 per cent of the reefs in Southeast Asia, and approximately 14-18 per cent of all reefs on earth. However, official numbers suggest that over 85 per cent of Indonesian reefs are threatened by human activities, with half of them at high risk (Burke et al. 2002: 38). On the other hand, the increase of coastal populations, coupled with a concomitant depletion of resources and an intensification of marine exploitation, will further increase the pressure on environmental resources, which implies, among other things, even greater difficulties in effectively managing coastal zones and seascapes.

On a national level, attempts to protect these unique marine ecosystems and to maintain biodiversity by and through the establishment of *Marine Protected Areas (MPAs)*, have been checked by the poor management of these protected areas and an overall intensification of marine resources exploitation. Here, the repeatedly reiterated official commitment to protecting the environment stands in an uneasy relation with the recently announced Indonesian Blue Revolution, which will entail yet again the intensified exploitation of marine resources to boost the national economy. But the controversies and conflicts regarding the nexus of environmental changes, social-ecological well-being, and economic practices is not limited to the national sphere, but is better understood as being both influential for, as well as generated by, localized encounters (Tsing 2005). While national and international initiatives to conserve and exploit marine resources have already received considerable critical attention, we feel that localized engagements with ideas about environmental change as well as culturally mediated experiences of a changing environment still deserve further investigation.

In this chapter we will illustrate our argument with information from two different localities in coastal Indonesia, namely the Taka Bonerate atoll and the Spermonde Archipelago in South Celebes (the Indonesian province Sulawesi Selatan). Both case studies are based on anthropological, in-depth fieldwork undertaken by the authors. Christian Reichel conducted research for six months, from 2005 to 2006, on several islands in Taka Bonerate, while Sofie Martens investigated the local knowledge base and environmental perceptions of fishermen in the Spermonde area over a period of five months from 2007 to 2008. Although the studies differed slightly in their approaches and thematic foci, both employed a variety of methods to collect and validate the data presented here.

The main methods applied included participant observation, semi-standardized interviews, group interviews, free listings, and elicitation tasks, as well as the analysis of cognitive ecological networks (cf. Antweiler, this volume, for a discussion of cognitive anthropological methods).

Map 1: The Indonesian Archipelago and the location of the research sites

Source: Mapsof.net 2011.

After a brief overview of relevant theoretical developments, we focus on the ways environmental changes are debated and practically related to in these two Indonesian contexts.

Both of these settings are understood and engaged with in remarkably differing ways, despite being affected by similar environmental changes. To be more precise, while dramatic environmental changes in the first case study figure prominently in violent conflicts about increasingly scarce resources, this very scarcity is, in the second case, related to in a strikingly different way. As a window onto these fluctuating relations, we concentrate on local environmental knowledge (LEK) and its many layers. That is to say, while we acknowledge the importance of LEK for environmental interactions, we emphasise that LEK itself is generated, reworked, and reiterated not only in respect to the material conditions of existence, but also within wider frames of reference. This LEK, therefore, cannot be reduced to a solely ecological activity, but has to be understood as bordering on and overlapping with, for instance, religious formations, which will be demonstrated by an examination of local understandings of the seascape.

LOCAL ENVIRONMENTAL KNOWLEDGE AND SEASCAPES: THEORETICAL PERSPECTIVES

While necessarily localized knowledge about the environment has played a rather minimal role for the largest part of the history of anthropology, forms of knowledge subsumed thereunder have received a growing interest in recent decades (cf. Bicker et al. 2004; Nazarea 2006; Sillitoe 1998). Needless to say, the practice of anthropology was and is marked by an engagement with forms and varieties of knowledge and related practices that are, to a substantial degree, developed in and tied to local natural environments. The documentation and analysis of what today would have to be called 'local environmental knowledge' remained therefore for the most part at the core of the discipline (Descola/Palsson 1996: 1-4), albeit frequently only as a means to reach and uncover hidden, universal functions or patterns (see, for instance, Malinowski 1922; Levi-Strauss 1966). Beyond such rather abstracting approaches to indigenous cultures, localized knowledge about the environment became of overarching interest in the context of a revived interest in the environment itself. In the wake of dramatic environmental changes brought about by a reflexive modernization (Beck 2008), sustainability, adaptation, and resilience (cf. Deswandi et al., this volume) emerged as key concepts for ecological theory and politics (cf. Adger et al. 2005). Hence, knowledge about the environment became of interest as a means of achieving more robust, if not sustainable, ecological relations, as well as a means to articulate or legitimize political claims (cf. Hornidge, this volume). However, in the ever-messy interplay of place-based identities, asymmetrical power relations, and harsh environmental and economic changes, specific local knowledge may (increasingly) play a role also in inter- or inner-ethnic social conflicts. In other words, specific local knowledge may, both as a signifier and in its signified contents, increasingly emerge as an important factor.

Arguing in this manner, we do not wish to contribute or add another twist to the basically mono-causal assumption according to which scarcity or environmental changes lead to conflicts. Instead, we take our departure from the truism that environmental changes force societies to react or coevolve, and that societal consequences unfold in necessarily historical patterns and across varying schemes and scales. Nevertheless, as the rich body of literature on social-ecological systems and the politics of nature indicates, the path taken and the situation evolved depend largely on the specifics of local knowledge, as well as on the politics of its articulation and implementation (Nazarea 2006; Dressler et al. 2010). In short, local knowledge has to be understood as generated, articulated, and contested, both within often quotidian environmental engagements (In-

gold 1993) and what has come to be called the cultural politics of natural resources (Baviskar 2008). Taken together, material engagement and political embeddedness serve as the reiteration or very often modification of handed-down
local knowledge. Nonetheless, while LEK often may be written about as overly
flexible, if not waning and easily being defeated by the onslaught of modernity,
we wish to reiterate once again (see Hoeppe 2008; Antweiler, this volume) the
persistence of such localized knowledge. Differing from influential environmental narratives, engendered by romanticizing perceptions of Naturvölker and influential environmental organizations, we localize the persistence (or non-
persistence) of such local knowledge formations, less in naiveté or as an insight
into wholly sustainable lifestyles, but more in the persistence of underlying
frames of reference. Again, frames of reference do not imply an underlying,
causal, or cognitive structure in the (e.g. Marxist) sense of structure and super-
structure; rather, they serve as a cultural backdrop or the conditioning of actions
and legibility that easily transcend the cultural domains with which modern science is concerned.

While they are historically and ecologically constituted, and while they may
frame distinct experiences and actions, their validity is constantly negotiated. In
concrete encounters with the materiality of daily life, as in the more abstract,
epistemic difficulties of changing natures or in ontological musings entailed in
some ritual practices, frames of references are therefore experienced, reiterated,
or modified in necessarily messy encounters (Ingold 2000; Tsing 2005;
Frömming 2006). While this constant modeling and remodeling is clearly, as
stated earlier, also a condition of local environmental knowledge, the difference
between the two pertains to the mode of abstraction and to structural flexibilities.
Local knowledge is therefore closely tied to practice; indeed, it may be treated,
as some observers do, as hardly distinguishable from practice (see Ingold 1993;
Palsson 1994). Frames of reference, on the other hand, have always to be translated into practice. They serve as the backdrop, underlying motivation, or semantic condition for actions, as well as more practice-related forms of knowledge,
for instance, LEK. Therefore, as some practices and forms of knowledge fundamentally change or wither, underlying frames of reference may even persist unchanged. While this has been quite well-elaborated in recent historical studies,
we want to add that these underlying frames of reference, perhaps even more
than environmental changes or local environmental knowledge, structure conflicts around increasingly scarce resources such as forests, reefs, or fish.

Mirroring culturally mediated assumptions about the centrality of land-based
relations, as well as the consequential structuring of scientific inquiry, local environmental knowledge about forests, bushes, farms, and parks is today much

better understood than for seascapes. With the overarching importance of sedentary lifestyles rooted firmly on the ground, relations to, on, and in the sea still remain widely unaccounted for. It might even be argued that the presumably delocalized relations and subjectivities of post-modern transnationalities receive higher attention than the multifarious relations the huge coastal populations have to, on and in the seascape. While an uncanny sea might still haunt western thought and scientific practice (Corbin 1994), and while its material qualities might seriously impinge certain types of investigation (Helmreich 2009; Orlove/ Caton 2009), the sea nevertheless plays a tremendously important role for coastal populations worldwide, not only as the space for economic activities, leisure, or transport, but also as an animated seascape (Carrier 2003; Jackson 1995). We therefore, for the sake of this paper, emphasise two related, only analytically separable, aspects of the intimate entanglements of seascapes and their adjoining coasts: the seascape as a dialectical field of and for cultural constructions and as managed commons. On the one hand, we understand seascapes as an interface of material reality and cultural practice, which holds true for the social construction of the seascape – albeit in a weaker sense than with respect to landscapes in general. Reefs may be degraded but simultaneously nourished and revived by human influences,[1] or, more generally, anthropogenic climate change may trigger profound changes in seascapes that will undoubtedly produce new ecosystems. Beyond that – and from a narrower social scientific perspective – perceptions, experiences, and narrations of marine areas are also generated in a dialectical encounter of respective materiality (riffs, rough sea, storms, current) with particular forms of knowledge. In a sense then, both the material reality as necessarily perceived and the forms of local environmental knowledge are embedded in wider frames of reference. Likewise, the seascape is often thought of as being animated by biotic and divine entities, as well as by a plethora of hybrid forms (see below).

While the divine and hybrid entities which populate the seascape may give important insights into the workings and imaginations of respective cultural formations and into moral orders and underlying cosmologies, they may also be analyzed as important patterns or articulations of the local management of the commons. Certainly, the seascape as commons may, precisely because of its vastness, rich resources, and fundamental openness to a multitude of actors, be extremely challenging for sustainable management strategies. This – as the relevance of differing frames of reference and local environmental knowledge for

---

1   The rompong (see below) has to be understood as but one instance of the social structuring of the seascape.

actual social and environmental interactions – we hope to substantiate by and through our first case study in South Sulawesi.

CASE STUDY 1: TAKA BONERATE – SOUTH SULAWESI

Taka Bonerate, with an area of 2,220km², is the largest atoll in Indonesia and the third largest atoll in the world. The area is located in the Flores Sea between the south-western tip of Sulawesi and the island of Flores. Due to its high biodiversity and the high degree of endemic animal and plant species that exist underwater, the atoll was declared a Marine National Park in 1992. The inhabitants of Taka Bonerate consist mainly of two ethnic groups: the Bajau and the Bugis. Since the Bajau used to almost exclusively live at sea in their approximately 12 meter-long boats (also known as *soopes*) without permanently settling on any land, they are sometimes mistakenly identified as sea nomads.

Nowadays, this term is only used to a limited extent, as the Bajau in Southeast Asia and Taka Bonerate have largely abandoned their nomadic lifestyles and live in permanent settlements on the mainland or the islands. Life on the boats is mostly limited to Sakai fishing tours, which last up to several months. Despite these changes, the Bajau's culture and use of resources is still firmly linked to the sea. The Bajau are nominally committed to Islam, but their religious world view is shaped by the analogue idea of gods (*dewa*), sea spirits (*hantu laut*), and demons (*jinn*) living in the sea. In order to avoid upsetting these supernatural creatures of the sea, whose powers are delivered to everyone regardless of whether they are located on the coast or at sea, there are different rules of behavior and taboos that protect the moral principles and include practical orientation rules in the Bajau community (Frömming/Reichel 2011).

Figure 1: Bajau woman preparing fish

Source: Christian Reichel, Taka Bonerate.

A minority of rich Buginese business people in Taka Bonerate have a monopoly over all major political and economic positions in the villages. They have so much power and influence that, despite the reluctance of the Bajau living in Taka Bonerate, they can enforce their own interests. While there is no open conflict between the two ethnic groups, in most cases their contact is limited to a purely economic level. As many Bajau do not sell their catch directly to the markets but rather to Buginese middlemen in the fish trade, they are in a dependent relationship with them, which is underpinned by a profound, all-encompassing patron-client system in which an interdependent, mutually beneficial relationship exists between a punggawa (a patron, which in most cases is a Bugis) and his sawi client (usually a Bajau) (for further discussion on the patronage system see Deswandi et al., this volume).

Until the 1990s, the atoll islands in Taka Bonerate and the adjacent reef ecosystems were relatively untapped by influences from outside the region. Far-reaching changes have only taken place in the last couple of decades, affecting local ecological, economic, and social realms alike. These developments are mainly explained by the constant growth of the internal migration of fishermen from other provinces, who are attracted by the region's wealth of marine resources, as well as the increasing access to and growing inclusion in the international trade of high-priced marine products.

This has resulted in noticeable social tensions and provoked countermeasures from inside the communities. Recently, the disparate economic and political interests of various stakeholders in resource exploitation, as well as the modification of knowledge systems and underlying frames of reference, have led to the emergence of a large number of partially open or latent conflicts. In addition, population growth and the ongoing destruction of coral reefs are adding further pressure to the situation.

"If you own a garden, you build a fence to prevent wild boars from intruding and eating what's being grown. The fishermen from outside are like wild boars that eat our crops and destroy our garden. In doing so, they not only destroy our livelihood, but they also destroy *semangat* - the cosmic order that is hidden beneath the diversity of life and which ties everything together. In ten to twenty years, the people on this island will suffer from hunger because all of the coral reefs and *semangat* will be destroyed. [...] We are already unable to fish with bait because we don't catch anything anymore. The fishermen from outside show up with modern equipment and steal our fish. Whether large or small, they take hundreds of tons of all kinds of fish each year. I was never in agreement with the Taka Bonerate being declared a national park. Since then, a large number of fishermen have been coming from the outside because the fishing authority issues so many fishing permits. When the local fishermen use destructive fishing techniques, they go to jail. The fishermen from outside have enough money to buy themselves out of problems. There is war at sea and the inhabitants of Taka Bonerate should fight for their garden." (Bajau fisherman and Imam from Rajuni Kecil, February 25, 2006)

The resulting frustration of many local fishermen includes the large potential for conflicts,[2] which are not just initiated between local fishermen and those from outlying areas, but also solely amongst local fishermen. The society is therefore divided and there is a tense relationship between the use of traditional strategies and the maximization of personal profit.

While many Buginese tend to make the most gains with respect to the supply of new markets, and take up lucrative middleman positions as punggawa, many Bajau can be seen as laggards. Due to the greater competition for marine resources within the atoll, they are forced to give up their traditional fishing methods and thereby apply more effective yet destructive tactics in order to make a somewhat more lucrative catch.

---

2   In both research areas, fishing is considered an almost purely male occupation. Thus, women have generally no direct experiences of fishing at sea. Nevertheless, they are highly involved in the processing and distribution of the catch, as well as the regular collection of sea shells on the reef flats. As an often mentioned exception, Bajau women are locally known for joining their husbands on fishing trips and working with them side by side.

Figure 2: Traditional Tuna fishing

Source: Christian Reichel, Taka Bonerate.

"When I fish with bombs, I can catch 100 kg of fish in a day. When I fish with a net or bait, I only catch an average of five to ten kilograms." (Bajau fisherman from Rajuni Besar, December 11, 2005)

The equipment the fishermen have to use in order to apply these new methods is associated with significantly higher purchase and maintenance costs, which they usually cannot finance. In turn, the majority of fishermen take out a loan from a *punggawa* or work as a *sawi* for him. Although the *punggwa* can provide the sawi with social security, the sawi quickly develops a one-sided dependency on the *punggwa* due to the debts that are owed.

Due to the dual objectives of using natural resources as intensively as possible and generating maximum profit as quickly as possible, an increasing number of fishermen are no longer relating their trade to the idea of there being gods (*dewa*), sea spirits (*hantu laut*), and demons (*jinn*) in the sea. They are also abstaining from observing religious restrictions that limit the use of natural resources. This development has brought about the disintegration of various religious beliefs and simultaneously divided the members of coastal communities into two groups: one consisting of fishermen who continue to use behavioral rules and taboos in dealing with natural resources, while the other consists of fishermen who fail to do so in order to make a maximum profit.

On November 15, 2005, this very emotional constellation of tensions between the atoll's natural resources and its cultural significance escalated to violence on the island of Tambolongan, which neighbors Taka Bonerate. The event is outlined by the following excerpt from the field diary of the author Christian Reichel.

"For about the last ten years, fringing reefs around the island of Tambolongan have been visited by bomb fishermen from the island of Polassi. Due to increasingly smaller catches, a group of fishermen who wanted to put up a fight against destructive fishing methods formed on the island. On the grounds that the police were corrupt and would do nothing against the destructive fishing, they built their own protection zone and attempted to drive the bomb fishermen a way. According to several informants, the police of the Selayar kabupaten (district) were involved in a complex branched network of bomb fishermen that had mafia-like structures. The police were allegedly bribed by an influential island punggwa for whom several fishermen worked. Accordingly, despite great efforts by the protectors of the reef, no legal action was taken against the fishermen who were using destructive fishing techniques. To avoid having the lucrative revenue stream dry up, the police used every means possible to hinder the reef protectors' protests. They also tried to disable the group's leader, Bapak Mudai, a *punggwa* on the island of Tambolongan who declared the fight against all fishermen using destructive techniques. The conflict escalated when Bapak Mudaiand his group used six boats to try and ram a boat of these fishermen. It resulted in a battle at sea in which two people died and many more were injured. To this day, four people are missing. Just days after this incident, several police officers stormed the island of Tambolongan to arrest Bapak Mudai. Although there were white flags hoisted in the village, the police were very brutal and arrested 39 people. Since Bapak Mudaire fused to come out of his house, it was shot at repeatedly until his death was certain. For many people in the region, Bapak Mudai was a martyr. Due to the strong suggestions of corruption, the highest-ranking police chief in Selayar was suspended from duty. However, he did not have to go to jail." (Christan Reichel, translated and written into field notes, February 18, 2006)

Using this regional example, it is clear that the atoll's various inhabitants interpret their environment differently and construe a specific form of the seascape. Apart from purely economic motives for profit maximization, it is primarily religious notions about the spirituality of the natural areas that affect the local frames of reference and forms of resource use.

Figure 3: Group Interview with Bajau fishermen

Source: Christian Reichel, Taka Bonerate.

The basis for the way in which this seascape is interpreted by various resource users is therefore not universally constant, but rather subject to local character. It was Gadamer (1975) who pointed out that during every attempt to understand something, the individual finds himself in a hermeneutic situation, i.e. there is a preconception of understanding that influences the interpretive result.

Although the local fishermen were involved in regional trade networks for hundreds of years, the extremely high demand for fishery products is a recent phenomenon that has only existed since the 1980s. This has resulted in many of the fishing activities changing from subsistence usage to a highly profitable export-oriented utilization of resources.

The consequences of this development are disastrous, not only for the natural resources of the two areas, but also they affect conflicting usage interests and patterns of interpretation of the seascape which cannot be equally satisfied. This in turn promotes a variety of more or less open conflicts, extending over several administrative levels. The increase in population and the ongoing destruction of the resource base stir further competition and add more pressure to the situation.

"Even in Taka Bonerate, the tense relationship between destructive and non-destructive fishermen always has the potential to reach a tipping point and end in violent conflict. The police and the military have supported the bombing fishermen from Polassi and supplied them with bombs. Since their pay is so low, they are dependent on the destructive fishermen's bribes. Several years ago, fishermen from Passitalu Tengah and Jinato tried to cultivate Agar-Agar. However, the fields were destroyed by the army because they were afraid that this alternative source of income would drastically reduce the amount of bomb fishing that went on and thereby the amount of brides they would receive." (Anthropologist from the Hassannudin University in Makassar, March 2006)

The government is attempting to intervene in the conflict in a regulatory manner. However, these efforts do not yet seem to be producing the desired effect. Financial assistance from national and international development funds cannot contribute to the reduction of conflicts because a large part of the state structure is involved in fighting corruption, and inadequate participation in the local perception of the seascape is tolerated. The result is therefore a one-sided, top-down form of management which is not attuned with either the cultural or economic conditions and looks past the original goal of sustainable management.

CASE STUDY 2: SPERMONDE ARCHIPELAGO – SOUTH SULAWESI

The Spermonde Archipelago is a coral reef platform covering 40,000 ha of coastal waters along the west off-shore of Makassar City, South Sulawesi. It consists of approximately 121 coral islands, 54 of which are densely populated (Jompa et al. 2007: 268; Glaser et al. 2010). It is not surprising that the already mentioned nationwide degradation of coastal ecosystems is also noticeable in the Spermonde area. The province of South Sulawesi is among the most densely populated areas in Indonesia and the South Sulawesians are well-known throughout the country for their historical role in maritime trade. The port of Makassar especially is of high importance for the fishing industry in the region and has been connected to international markets for several centuries. Similar to the conditions in Taka Bonerate, the coastal ecosystem has been affected by destructive fishing practices, particularly cyanide and blast fishing[3], resulting in serious degradation of coral habitats. The archipelago is closely connected to the trade in live reef and ornamental fish species, with key markets in Hong Kong and Singapore. This development has led to a severe decline in live coral cover

---

3 Blast or dynamite fishing is the practice of using dynamite or other kinds of explosives to kill or stun schools of fish. Blast fishing is quite a common practice and has been used in the Spermonde area since the 1940s (Pet-Soede et al. 2001: 49). Cyanide fishing has been practiced since the 1980s to catch high-valued target species for the trade with live food and ornamental fish (Briggs 2003: 41). The export of fish for the live food trade reached its peak some years ago. Nevertheless, it is still an important factor because the rarity of a species increases its price, making it lucrative for the fishermen to engage in this kind of endeavor.

and fish stocks from outer to inner reefs. An estimated 60 to 80 per cent of coral reefs throughout the archipelago were already classified as severely damaged in 2003 (Briggs 2003: 61). Other anthropogenic factors, e.g. sewerage and ship traffic, related to the increase in population, are adding to the pressure.

Coastal communities in the Spermonde area rely heavily on the exploitation of their marine resources, including the revenues generated by the fishing of live reef food fish and its trade. Indeed, trade has always been the focal point of economic activities in the archipelago. The island communities represent a variety of ethnic identities. The dominant ethnic group is Makassarese, and Bahasa Makassar is the main language used in daily activities. Social life on the islands, especially in the socioeconomic sphere, is dominated by a dynamic patronage system based on a complex network of debt relations (cf. Deswandi et al., this volume). In the case of the Spermonde, Yanurita and Neil (2007) even argue that the whole archipelago is connected and united through a social network evolving from these relations. They are, although voluntary in theory, first of all unequal relations, where the follower is dependent, usually financially, on the patron.

In the Spermonde area, the exploitation of marine resources is framed by a distinct understanding of the local seascape as *bebas* (free) or 'open to all', i.e. open access to the resources. Local traditions in marine tenure and the sustainable management of fishing grounds are absent. Theoretically, the villagers all have equally free access to the reefs and flats for resource exploitation, which includes the application of destructive fishing gear, while an increasing number of small-scale fishermen exploit the same areas.

Figure 4: The beaches are crowded with small fishing boats

Source: Sofie Martens, Spermonde.

Whereas in other parts of Indonesia complex management systems have been developed, as for instance the *sasi* practices in the Maluku province (cf. Zerner 1994), there are no similar practices described for the Spermonde area. Furthermore, fishing efforts in the archipelago are connected directly to international markets and, consequently, it is extremely difficult to implement policies to constrict resource exploitation on the local level (Matsui 2007). As part of the national initiative for the protection of the marine environment, a number of marine protected areas (MPAs) have been declared in the Spermonde region. However, management of these MPAs has been rather ineffective and with only a very limited impact on marine conservation goals. The exact locations of MPAs are often not even known or not relevant to the fishermen:

"Indeed there were protected areas here, once. Established by the Fisheries Department, right? But the people did not care. At Bone Batang they also built once a house there. [...] A house of the navy. To do duty there so that there are no bombers. But the officer had not even arrived, the house was already destroyed. [...] Yes, indeed, one cannot go bombing, if there is an officer, if there is none, surely the area is bombed. [...] For the other fishermen, it is free here! " (Fisherman, 50 yrs, January 25, 2008)

Within this wider framework of an open seascape, distinct domains of ecological knowledge are present, which relates to differences in the practical engagement with the sea and results in a differentiation between the underwater realm of the divers, mainly working with spear guns or cyanide, and the realm of the hand-line fishers experiencing the seascape from the surface. Especially the deeper parts of the reef area are almost invisible for handline fishermen and are often described as the knowledge domain of the divers (*penyelam*) only. This relates to fish behavior as well as the general characteristics of the habitat, as exemplified in the following quotations:

"I do not know. The divers, they know because they can observe these things. We cannot see under water. The divers know. They say to us, there is fish spawn. If they are divers. We cannot see these things." (Fisherman, 45 yrs, March 31, 2008)

"Yes, we do not know about the coral species. It is the divers right, they see everything down there. They see the coral patches, what kind it is, big or small. The hand-line fishermen also know these things but only partially.Whether there is a huge or a small place. Like this." (Fisherman, 42 yrs, December 17, 2007)

In general, the study revealed an intimate and extensive knowledge of the seascape, the habitat and feeding behaviors of target species, profitable fishing locations, sea currents, fishing gear, and bait. This knowledge is widely shared and agreed upon among the fishermen. Other aspects of fish biology connected to the life history of exploited fish species, especially spawning behavior, seasonality, and sexual dimorphism, are only poorly understood and conceptualized. Furthermore, this knowledge was referred to as irrelevant for artisanal fisheries. However, to draw a clear and mutually exclusive distinction between the users of destructive and more selective and environmentally friendly hand-lining techniques would be arbitrary. Practices such as the use of cyanide and blast fishing are generally believed to hold many advantages in comparison to other fishing techniques. They are effective, quick, relatively easy to apply, and they hold the promise of good revenue for a small financial input. Additionally, the extraction of corals for aquaria or as construction material is widespread. Local fishermen switch between different practices according to seasonal conditions. However, age and a strong financial dependency are crucial factors in limiting the options.

Environmental change, especially the decline in live coral cover and fish stocks, is attributed mainly to the deployment of cyanide, explosives and, additionally, trawling. However, it was evident during the interviews that the decline in fish abundance was not necessarily perceived as a negative development.

Fish, although characterized as social beings, are mainly regarded as a commodity. Therefore, any local evaluation is, with very few exceptions, based on the economic value of species. They are divided into high-value fish that yield a good price per kilo (*ikan timbangan*) and low-value fish which would not provide the fishermen with a sufficient income and are therefore often described as 'useless'. In fact, the majority of fishermen interviewed considered the current situation as being more desirable than in the times when fish were still abundant:

"In the past, life on the island has been very difficult because there were no species being exported. Life is much better now. When they started to export, the people were making progress. Before, we caught so many fish that they had to throw them away at the auction. They caught more than the people could buy." (Fisherman, 48 yrs, February 23, 2008)

"The neighborhood was really different in the past. You had to search for big houses, in the 70s the houses were different. Today you could say that the houses are decent, so there has been improvement. [...] The situation of the fishermen has improved, because the prices changed so much. [...] In the past we were poor, I remember the 70s, I sometimes did not eat for two or three days.[...] Indeed, it was different in the past. Indeed, there were many fish, but less fishers. Now there are many fishers and the prices further increase. Grouper is being stored, Spanish Mackerel is also stored and sold abroad. Only that. They were not exported in the past, but sold at the local fish market only." (Fisherman, 44 yrs, March 15, 2008)

Similar statements were given by many fishermen who believe that nowadays they have more options to earn their living. Indeed, even community members with a low income can afford more goods from Makassar than before. Since the fish have become less numerous and catch rates have decreased, the prices have increased accordingly, making the resources more valuable for them. In local reasoning, fewer fish resources are dissipated today, whereas the income of the fishermen stays more or less the same or even increases.

Figure 5: Houses on the island of Barrang Lompo

Source: Sofie Martens, Spermonde.

Despite this overall acceptance of the advantages of destructive practices by the fishermen and their communities, a growing number of community members support the idea of conservation, demanding a more selective and therefore sustainable exploitation of the environment. This development is highly influenced by the global knowledge of sustainable resource use, introduced to the local context by scientists, government officials, and foreign traders alike. No matter how high the prices for fish, the increasing scarcity of resources and the growing number of fishermen engaging in fishing activities still stir the competition for fish and challenge the notion of open access to the Spermonde area for everyone. Indeed, local fishermen often commented negatively on the sea as being overly "crowded" nowadays, impeding their fishing activities. Although the common norm still applies in most cases, it is nevertheless subject to certain constraints and changes.

One of these constraints relates to the spiritual world. Fishermen who are rooted in local traditions cannot rove the area as they please, but have to act according to certain beliefs in order to secure fishing success. In Indonesia, many places in the landscape are believed to be inhabited by spiritual beings, and this also holds true for the seascape. In the Spermonde, the belief in the so-called *penjaga taka* (guardian of the reef), i.e. non-human spirits inhabiting the reefs,[4] is important in structuring the daily engagement with the sea.

These spirits can only be found on patches of corals and not in areas with sandy bottoms. The *penjaga taka* are highly localized and closely associated with a certain reef area, which is referred to as their home.[5] Knowledge about these spirits and certain behavioral rules are seen as crucial when entering their realm, as they are considered to be of an ambiguous nature. Most often these non-human sprits are described as dangerous beings, testing and tempting the fishermen at sea or even hurting or killing them when they are displeased with their conduct.[6] These spirits are also related to catch rates. On the one hand, it may help the fishermen to catch many fish on the reef, but on the other hand, it is also possible that the fishermen do not catch any fish at the location, if the spirit is displeased. Thus, the goodwill of these spirits is believed to be crucial, not only for the physical well-being of the fishermen, but also for their economic performance. However, as the reefs in the Spermonde region are increasingly destroyed, the seascape changes its face and at the same time the belief in these spirits is fading.

One example for the rules-in-use regulating fishing activities relates to the *rompong*, a rope with palm leaves attached that is anchored to the sea bottom. The leaves attract a broad range of small fish species that gather between them. As a rompong is built, and therefore individually owned, the owner has priority if he wants to catch at that spot and can order other fishermen to leave. Hand-line fishermen are allowed to fish close to the rompong every time because they do not destroy the habitat using hand-lines. However, if a group of fishermen

---

4 Indeed, the terms penjaga taka (guardians of the reef), penjaga laut (guardians of the sea), hantu laut (sea ghosts), penghuni taka (inhabitants of the reef), and setan je'ne (water demons) were often used interchangeably.

5 The origin of these penjaga taka seems to be unclear. They are nonetheless distinguished from the revengeful ghosts of humans killed by an accident at sea, who may pose a threat to the fishermen as well.

6 Since spirits are perceived as dangerous for the fishermen, it is important for them to know how they can protect themselves. This protection may comprise the recitation of formulae or prayers from the Qu'ran or the deployment of objects which are believed to possess the ability to fend off the spirits.

wants to use blast fishing near a rompong, they are supposed to ask for permission first. Usually, this issue is solved by splitting the catch, satisfying all parties. In this example, the personal investment of time and money provides the individual fisherman with temporary ownership rights over a confined marine territory. In order to regulate the joint exploitation of the same finite area, other locally enforced rules have been established as well (cf. Deswandi et al., this volume). One example is the sharing of fish between hand-line fishermen and bombers, as described by one informant:

"We are all fishermen here, so we cannot be angry at the bombers. When we see a boat that is using bombs, we join them diving. If I collect 30 fish, I keep 20 and give 10 to the bombers. So when I am on a fishing trip and I hear bombs, I go there and dive." (Fisherman, 62 yrs, February 14, 2008)

These obligations to share, if observed, often prevent an increase of tensions between varying groups of resource users.

Regarding these rules-in-use, Glaser and colleagues speak of an emerging local territoriality and new institutional arrangements. The authors further identify a number of other newly emergent rules, of which the self-defined "island exclusion zones" are among the most effective (Glaser et al. 2010: 1222; cf. Deswandi et al., this volume). Indeed, it is not only the individual investment of fishermen that grants them ownership rights, but also their place of residence. On several islands, the communities claim exclusive exploitation rights to the reefs and associated resources surrounding their islands. Consequently, if outsiders want to fish near such an inhabited island, they have to consult with community leaders first or face the sometimes violent response when caught. Since these rules have evolved on the basis of local conditions, the extension of the zones and specific rules of access may vary extensively among the islands. However, these locally constructed regulations especially apply to fishermen using bombs or cyanide in these zones, although this is rarely the case, since the waters around the islands are consistently overfished and polluted by sewerage. It was stated in the interviews that one of the main reasons for the restriction of destructive gear can be seen in the function of the reefs as a natural barrier against the sometimes stormy sea. Most islands are elevated only slightly above sea level, with the surrounding intact coral reefs standing as their sole protection. Bombing in the close vicinity of inhabited islands therefore threatens the livelihood of islanders and is often banned by the communities through the definition of exclusion zones. One of the crucial aspects of these zones is that they have emerged to exclude anyone who is defined as an outsider. The rules were not established to protect the fragile marine resources, but rather to ensure that the community or certain individuals benefit from their exploitation.

The norm that the sea is 'open to all' evokes a view of the seascape as an open and unregulated playground. The examples given above illustrate the existing constraints to this widespread norm. Therefore, notions of territoriality and ownership were and are indeed present in the local context. Whether some of these rules are truly emergent, or rather constantly adjusted to changing environmental and societal conditions, is an issue that needs further elaboration. However, in consideration of the fact that the competition among fishermen is increasing while the resource base is dwindling, certain societal regulations governing access to restricted territories may gain in importance (cf. Glaser et al 2010), whereas constraints related to the religious realm may fade. In future, the perception of the seascape as an open space may be contested and negotiated anew, challenged by an adjustment of rules-in-use in response to increasing multiple pressures.

CONCLUSION

This chapter argues for the importance of underlying frames of reference for the emergence and development of the potential for conflict in the context of changing environments. It is these frames which fundamentally structure the way environmental change is experienced, understood, and also acted upon. Nevertheless, they are constantly contested and modified in concrete encounters with the local surroundings.

In two short case studies, we have illustrated the complex relationships and dependencies of various interest groups, local environmental knowledge, and underlying frames of reference in the Spermonde Archipelago and Taka Bonerate Atoll. Both ecosystems are of central importance for local fishermen and we have therefore tried to establish how cultural constructions and environmental realities mutually change or co-evolve in uneasy relationships.

Although different socioecological dynamics and conflicting interests have already led to various conflicts surrounding the precarious resource situation in some areas of Indonesia, our case studies from South Sulawesi nevertheless indicate that similar environmental changes in the same region may lead to quite different social, economic and cultural changes. When the natural environment changes through overfishing or the extinction of certain species, or when the social environment changes through integration into national markets or as a result of increasing competition, forms of local environmental knowledge change as well. While this may imply changes in adaptive capacities or have consequences for other forms of knowledge, it by no means occurs in a unitary manner (Linkenbach 2004).

While many fishermen in the Spermonde Archipelago perceive the changes occurring in a positive light, since they profit financially as a result of increased fish prices, the same process in the Taka Bonerate Atoll leads to conflicting interests that cannot be satisfied equitably. The respective frames of reference of the actors play a significant role in these different developments. In Spermonde, the former understanding of the seascape as open to all is undergoing certain adjustments under the pressure of growing competition. Notions of territoriality and ownership seem to gain in importance in the context of resource exploitation, especially excluding resource users from outside of the relational proximity of the island communities. These locally constructed rules-in-use and obligations to share structure local interactions and may prevent a rise in tensions in the domain of marine exploitation.

For some fishermen in Taka Bonerate, marine resources are just 'consumer goods', which should be exploited in order to gain maximum profit; for others the interaction with and use of the seascape is essential for cultural and religious self-images. The concept of *semangat*, for instance, plays a pivotal role in this respect, as s illustrated by the above statement of the Imam from the island of Rajuni Kecil. *Semangat* is closely related to the notion of seascape and constitutes important local values, norms, and beliefs, as well as the cultural identity of fishing communities.

This dualism in turn promotes a variety of more or less open conflicts that are currently taking place and are exacerbated by intensifying population pressure and increasingly scarce resources – all while anticipated global climate changes continue to loom. The perception of and (religious) reactions to environmental changes are culturally specific and therefore require detailed, on-site research in order to be understood. Hence, the main assumption is that the effects of environmental changes can only be understood by their impact at local levels. A fundamental understanding of the cultural meaning, as well as the handling and processing of environmental changes and related disasters, is also required in order to develop alternative, more sustainable, approaches.

ACKNOWLEDGEMENTS

We would like to thank the institutions involved in the Indonesian-German research program SPICE II, but especially the Leibniz Centre for Tropical Marine Ecology (ZMT), Bremen, and the Center for Coral Reefs Research (PPTK) at Hasanuddin University, Makassar, for all their support and assistance for our master projects. Our special thanks also go to the communities in the Spermonde and Taka Bonerate. We are grateful to them for sharing their lives and knowledge with us.

REFERENCES

Baviskar, A. (2008): Introduction. In: Baviskar, A. (ed.), Contested Grounds: Essays on Nature, Culture, and Power, New Delhi: Oxford University Press, 1-12.

Beck, U. (2008): World Risk Society, Cambridge: Polity Press.

Berkes, F./Hughes, T.P./Steneck, R.S./Wilson, J.A./Bellwood, D.R./Crona, B/Folke, C./Gunderson, L.H./Leslie, H.M./Norberg, J./Nystöm, M./Olsson, P./Österblom, H./Scheffer, M./Worm, B. (2006): Globalization, Roving Bandits, and Marine Resources. Science 311/5767, pp. 1557-1558.

Bicker, A./ Sillitoe, P./ Pottier, J. (eds.) (2004): Development and Local Knowledge: New Approaches to Issues in Natural Resource Management, Conservation and Agriculture, London: Routledge.

Briggs, M. (2003): Destructive Fishing Practices in South Sulawesi Island – East Indonesia and the Role of Aquaculture as a Potential Alternative Livelihood, Bangkok: APEC Grouper Research and Development Network.

Burke, L./Selig, E./Spalding, M. (eds.) (2002): Reefs at Risk in Southeast Asia, Washington, DC: World Resource Institute.

Carrier, J. G (2003): Biography, Ecology, Political Economy: Seascape and Conflict in Jamaica. In: Stewart, P. J. / Strathern, A. (eds.), Landscape, Memory and History, London: Pluto Press, 210-228.

Casimir, M. J. (2008): The Mutual Dynamics of Cultural and Environmental Change: An Introductory Essay. In: Casimir, M. J. (ed.), Culture and the Changing Environment – Uncertainty, cognition and risk management in cross-cultural perspectives, New York, Oxford: Berghahn Books, 1-58.

Cassels, S./Curran, S. R./Kramer, R. (2005): Do Migrants Degrade Coastal Environments? Migration, Natural Resource Extraction and Poverty in North Sulawesi, Indonesia. Human Ecology 33/3, 329-363.

Corbin, A. (1994): The Lure of the Sea: The Discovery of the Seaside in the Western World, 1750-1840, Cambridge: Polity Press.

Descola, P./Palsson, G. (1996): Introduction. In: Descola, P. / Palsson, G. (eds.), Nature and Society: Anthropological Perspectives, London: Routledge, 1-21.

Dressler, W./Büscher, B./Schoon, M./Brockington, D./Hayes, T./Kull, C./McCarthy, J./Streshtha, K. (2010): From Hope to Crisis and Back? A

Critical History of the Global CBNRM Narrative. Environmental Conservation 37/1, 1-11.

Frömming, U. U. (2006): Naturkatastrophen: Kulturelle Deutung und Verarbeitung, Frankfurt am Main: Campus.

Frömming, U.U./Reichel, C. (2011): Vulnerable Coastal Regions: Indigenous People under Climate Change in Indonesia. Regional examples. In: Bergmann, S./Gerten, D. (eds.), Religion in Environmental and Climate Change, New York, London: Continuum, 215-235.

Gadamer, H.-G. (1975): Wahrheit und Methode. Grundzüge einer philosophischen Hermeneutik, Tübingen.

Glaser, M./Baitoningsih, W./Ferse, S. C. A./Neil, M./Deswandi, R. (2010): Whose sustainability? Top–down participation and emergent rules in marine protected area management in Indonesia. Marine Policy 34/6, pp. 1215-1225.

Helmreich, S. (2009): Alien Ocean: Anthropological Voyages in Microbial Seas, Berkeley: University of California Press.

Hoeppe, G. (2008): Knowing the Sea in the 'Time of Progress': Environmental Change, Parallel Knowledges and the Uses of Metaphor in Kerala (South India). In: Casimir, M.J. (ed.), Culture and the Changing Environment: Uncertainty, Cognition and Risk Management, Oxford: Berghahn, 301-324.

Hughes, T. P./Bellwood, D. R./Folke, C./Steneck, R. S./Wilson, J. (2005): New paradigms for supporting the resilience of marine ecosystems. Trends in Ecology and Evolution 20/7, 380-386.

Ingold, T. (1993): The Temporality of the Landscape. World Archeology 25/2, 152-174.

Ingold, T. (2000): The Perception of the Environment: Essays on Livelihood, Dwelling and Skill, London: Routledge.

Jackson, S. E. (1995): The Water is not Empty: Cross-Cultural Issues in Conceptualising Sea Space. Australian Geographer 26/1, 87-96.

Jompa, J./Moka, W./Yanurita, D. (2007): Condition of Spermonde Ecosystem: Its Relationship with the Utilization of Maritime Resources of the Spermonde Archipelago. In: Koji Tanaka (ed.), Natural Resource Management and Socioeconomic Transformation under the Decentralization in Indonesia: Toward Sulawesi Area Studies, Research Report, Kyoto: Center of Intergrated Area Studies Kyoto University, 265-279.

Levi-Straus, C. (1966): The Savage Mind, Chicago: University of Chicago Press.

Linkenbach, A. (2004): Lokales Wissen im Entwicklungsdiskurs: Abwertung, Aneignung oder Anerkennung des Anderen? In: Schareika, N. / Bierschenk, Th. (eds.): Lokales Wissen –sozialwissenschaftliche Perspektiven, (= Mainzer Beiträge zur Afrika-Forschung, 11), Münster: Lit-Verlag, 233-257.

Malinowski, B. (1922): Argonauts of the Western Pacific: An Account of Native Enterprise and Adventure in the Archipelagoes of Melanesian New Guinea, London: Routledge & Kegan Paul.

Matsui, K. (2007): Impact of Decentralization on Maritime Resource Management: A Case of the Spermonde Archipelago Area, South Sulawesi, Indonesia. In: Tanaka, K. (ed.), Natural Resource Management and Socioeconomic Transformation under the Decentralization in Indonesia: Toward Sulawesi Area Studies, Research Report, Kyoto: Center of Intergrated Area Studies Kyoto University, 79-89.

Montgomery, W. L. (1990): Zoogeography, Behavior and Ecology of Coral-Reef Fishes. In: Dubinsky, Z. (ed.) Coral Reefs, Amsterdam: Elsevier, 329-364.

Nazarea, V. (2006): Local Knowledge and Memory in Biodiversity Conservation. Annual Review of Anthropology 35, 317-335.

Orlove, B./Caton, S. C. (2009): Water as an Object of Anthropological Inquiry. In: Hastrup, K. (ed.), The Question of Resilience: Social Responses to Climate Change, Copenhagen: The Royal Danish Academy of Sciences and Letters, 31-47.

Palsson, G. (1994): Enskilment at Sea. Man 29/4, 901-927.

Pelras, Ch. (2000): Patron-client ties among the Bugis and Makassarese of South Sulawesi. In: Tol, R./van Dijk, K./Acciaioli, G. (eds.), Authority and Enterprise among the Peoples of South Sulawesi, Leiden: KITLV Press, 15-54.

Pet-Soede, C./Van Densen, W. L. T./Pet, J. S./Machiels, M. A. M. (2001): Impact of Indonesian coral reef fisheries on fish community structure and the resultant catch composition. Fisheries Research 51/1, 35-51.

Pockley, P. (2000): Global warming identified as main threat to coral reefs. In: Nature 407/6807, 932.

Sillitoe, P. (1998): The Development of Indigenous Knowledge: A New Applied Anthropology. Cultural Anthropology 39/2, 223-252.

Tsing, A. L. (2005): Friction: An Ethnography of Global Connection, Princeton: Princeton University Press.

Yanurita, D./Neil, M. (2007): Utilization of Marine Resources in the Spermonde Archipelago.In: Tanaka, K. (ed.), Natural Resource Management and Socioeconomic Transformation under the Decentralization in Indonesia: Toward Sulawesi Area Studies, Research Report, Kyoto: Center of Intergrated Area Studies Kyoto University, 281-295.

Zerner, Ch. (1994): Through a Green Lens: The Construction of Customary Environmental Law and Community in Indonesia's Maluku Islands. Law and Society Review 28/5, pp. 1079-1122.

FIGURES

Map 1: The Indonesian Archipelago. Location of the research sites is indicated. Source: Mapsof.net 2011: http://mapsof.net/map/sulawesi-in-indonesia#.TmkB R3OXMzU, 05.09.2011

"We Observe the Weather because we are Farmers"
Weather Knowledge and Meteorology
in the Mekong Delta, Vietnam

JUDITH EHLERT

> The ancestors could predict the flood just by looking at the water. If, for example, they looked at the water in front of their house and it was red in lunar May, the flood would be big in that year. The ancestors had already done research by looking and observing.
>
> OLD FARMER/INTERVIEW (SEPTEMBER 25, 2008)

INTRODUCTION

The Mekong Delta in Vietnam is commonly known as the 'rice-bowl' of the nation. Bypassing the other five upstream riparian countries China, Myanmar, Laos, Thailand, and Cambodia, the Mekong River brings massive seasonal freshwater sources to the delta's basin, located in Vietnam.

Map 1: Mekong River Riparian Countries

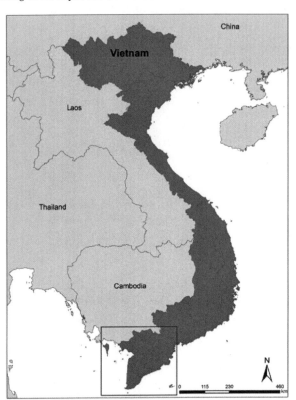

Source: Cartography: V. Graw & P. Nienkemper; Data: Department of Environment and Natural Resources of Can Tho City, 2009.

The annual abundance of river water that is passed downstream via a complex river and channel network system creates wide floodplains and contributes to the rich wetlands and ecosystems in the delta. The catchment area of the Mekong River Basin in Vietnam's South is populated by about 18 million people, which makes up 22 per cent of Vietnam's total population (Le et al. 2007). The rural population has adapted its livelihood strategies to the water and flood regime in the area. Intensive agriculture and aquaculture production proliferate because of the rich water resource base being regulated for irrigation and flood control pur- poses by the massive construction of dams, dykes, and sluices (Pham 2012; Biggs et al. 2009; cf. Brocheux 1995).

Figures 1 and 2: Local Livelihoods – Rice Cultivation and Fishery

Source: Judith Ehlert, 2008.

Being a traditional rice cultivating, area and therefore highly dependent on seasonal water resources, traditional local flood and weather knowledge form the
touchstone for agricultural production in the Mekong Delta. 'Traditional
knowledge' on weather and flood forecast practices denotes longstanding
knowledge that has been generated through the close observation of the local
environment and the interpretation of such to infer short, medium, and long-term
weather and flood patterns. In the following chapter this kind of local knowledge
will also be called 'weather lore'. Without access to any other weather information in the past, a farmer's delicate ability to foretell the weather was based
on specific environmental indicators. Traditional ecological knowledge on
weather and flood prediction developed out of the necessity to organize efficiently agricultural decision-making and production in the context of seasonal
climatic conditions and river water sources in the delta.

However, those environmental conditions are changing. According to the
emic perspective, increasingly more unreliable flood and weather patterns constitute a qualitative change to the natural environment. Instead of distinct weather periods distinguishing the wet from the dry season (Biggs 2004: 81), local
farmers and fishermen observe increasingly irregular precipitation periods (see
also Adger et al. 2001). They are further aware of a growing frequency and
magnitude of storms hitting the delta. A farmer's statement, 'We cannot count
on nature anymore' (01.09.08), provokes the question as to how reliable locally
grown weather knowledge is in this context of environmental change and the
increasing anthropogenic control of the water environment. Hence, besides
changing rain patterns, human interference into ecology is held responsible for
changing local flood characteristics.

The following discussion reflects on the integration of traditional weather
lore and scientific weather forecasting as a local strategy to adapt to the respective changes of the natural environment. It focuses on the traditional and modern
weather forecast practices upon which agricultural lifestyles and decision-
making in the Mekong Delta depend. In regard to changing flood and weather
conditions, farmers and fishermen draw on their exquisite ability to observe and
interpret immediate weather events on the basis of locally developed weather
lore. Besides this, they make use of science-based meteorological forecasts,
which have become widely accessible in rural areas. Local weather 'knowing'
underlines the process through which actors are capable of drawing on plural
modes of environmental knowledge, with reference to flood and weather variability, in order to back up agricultural decision-making. This process of local
knowledge hybridization serves as an adaptive strategy to encounter environmental change and will therefore be examined closely. Against the background

of the growing accuracy of modern meteorological prediction and the development of new information technology that disseminates weather information on a broad scale to rural areas, the reliability that farmers ascribe to their own traditional weather lore will be investigated. The discovered pragmatic rather than cosmological human-water relationship, as well as the deep cultural appreciation of science and technology in Vietnam, makes the re-evaluation of relevant knowledge for local weather management an interesting case. Huu and Cohen (1997: 13) claim that "the shifting patterns of the constellations, the rhythms of the universe and the changes of the night sky throughout the seasons, so exquisitely understood by farmers, have become irrelevant" in the modern delta society. This claim will be put to the test in this chapter.

In doing so, the following discussion is based on empirical data that was collected during a one-year field research (04/2008-04/2009) in the rural flood-prone districts of Can Tho City, one of the 13 Mekong Delta provinces. The rigorously formalized research culture in Vietnam demanded high flexibility in doing ethnographic research at the commune level. Living in farming families during the flood season however enabled an in-depth insight into everyday agricultural lifestyles and into the weather-related organization of daily farming routines. Besides approaching local weather lore through observation, local weather knowledge, which is very often captured in environment-related proverbs, was discussed in 11 group discussions with farmers and fishermen and followed up in 25 semi-structured interviews. All interviews were conducted with the help of a female English-Vietnamese translator and later on coded for analytical purposes.

The chapter begins with the presentation of different local weather lore indicators by discussing their highly contextualized nature. Traditional weather knowledge is then contrasted with the modern weather information that is spread widely through Vietnam's vast media network to the delta region. How both knowledge reference systems are integrated into people's everyday farming routines and seasonal agricultural decision-making is depicted in the next step, strengthening the argument of a certain cultural-ecological pragmatism inherent in people's relationship with their natural environment. Finally, the conclusion takes up a more structural (policy) perspective on the question of how to adapt to and manage environmental change efficiently by means other than 'just' traditional and modern weather knowledge.

TRADITIONAL WEATHER KNOWLEDGE AND MODERN METEOROLOGY

The introductory quote to this chapter, 'doing research by looking and observing', captures the very essence of what is meant here by traditional weather lore and represents a substantial feature of local knowledge, which is methodologically rooted in natural experimentation and therefore strongly bound in local empiricism (Agrawal 1995; Antweiler 1998); it is the fine-tuned ability of farmers and fishermen to observe closely the surrounding environment, and to do research by inferring interpretations from contextualized and dense weather observations. Due to the lack of modern and scientific weather forecast information in rural areas, farmers in the past have had to rely on observations of their very close environment and to base their decision-making regarding rice crop cycles on such observations. Farmers used to 'read' natural signs of botanic, atmospheric and astronomic variability as well as insect behavior to infer upcoming weather fronts.

The interpretation of animal, insect, and plant behavior and of astronomic and atmospheric indicators partly characterizes farmers' agricultural lifestyles up to today. Their weather lore refers to the behavior of insects, especially of dragonflies and ants, of frogs and toads, of birds, and of livestock, which they cognitively connect to upcoming weather events. Very commonly, people for example relate the flying behavior of dragonflies to short-term weather changes. According to local observations, these insects fly high in when there is a sunny sky, fly low in case of rain and at an average altitude when it is cloudy. In contrast to such a short-term weather indicator, the behavior of ants is related to flood levels expected for the following season, as they move their nests up to higher ground at the onset of a high flood. As for most weather lore, this experience is also captured in a local saying: "In the 7th month of the lunar year[1], ants move. Just afraid there is flood again."

---

1   The 7th lunar month refers to August on the Gregorian calendar.

Table 1: Selection of weather-related Proverbs

Proverbs	
Vietnamese	**English**
Mùa lũ, đồng trắng, nước trong; Thả câu câu cá Ăn no đi nằm.	In flood seasons, white fields, transparent water; dropping the fishing line to catch fish Eating until full, and going to sleep.
Dầy sao thì nắng, vắng sao thì mưa.	Many stars mean sunshine, few stars mean rain.
Sao mờ thì cạn, sao sáng thì mưa.	Dull stars mean dryness, bright stars mean rain.
Ếch kêu uôm uôm Ao chuôm đầy nước.	Frogs cry 'uôm uôm' Small ponds are full with water.
Trăng quầng thì hạn; Trăng tán thì mưa.	Moon with round halo means droughts; moon with broken halo means rain.
Trời vàng thì gió, trời đỏ thì mưa.	Yellow sky means wind, red sky means rain.
Hoẵng tác trên đồi thì mưa Hoẵng tác dưới bưa thì nắng.	Munjtacs cry on the hills means rain; munjtacs cry on deltas means sunshine.
Lam nham tháng sáu hơn làu bàu tháng bảy.	Little rain in lunar 6th months is better than a lot of rain in lunar 7th months.
Ráng vàng thì nắng, ráng đỏ thì mưa.	Yellow clouds mean sunshine, red clouds mean rain.
Quạ tắm thì ráo, sáo tắm thì mưa.	Crows bath means dryness, mynahs bath means rain.
Tháng tám heo may Chuồn chuồn bay thì bão. Cơn đằng Đông vừa trông vừa chạy Cơn đằng Nam vừa làm vừa chơi Cơn đằng Bắc thì rắc vài hạt.	Lunar 8th months, monsoons; dragonflies fly means storms. Rain in the East, both looking and running; rain in the South, both working and playing; rain in the North, just some drops (for drying rice).
Én bay thấp mưa ngập bờ ao; Én bay cao mưa rào thì tạnh.	Swallows fly low, rain fill ponds; swallows fly high, heavy showers will stop.

Chớp Đông nhay nháy,	Lightning flashes in the East,
Gà gáy thì mưa.	roosters crow means rain.

Experiences	
Chiều hôm trước gà đi ngủ sớm thì hôm sau sẽ có mưa.	Chickens sleep early in the evening means rain for the next day.
Khi trời đang mưa mà mối hoặc kiến ra khỏi tổ nhiều thì trời nắng.	When it is raining and woodworms or ants move out of their nests in great numbers, it will be sunny.
Khi cóc nghiến răng hoặc khi gà trèo lên cây cao, thì trời đang nắng sẽ chuyển mưa.	When toads grind their teeth or when chickens fly to high trees, the sunny weather will turn to rainy.
Gà lên cây rỉa lông thì trời sắp mưa.	Chickens come to high branches to preen themselves means it is going to rain soon.

Source: Author's compilation.

As one can infer from Table 1, local farmers have a substantive repertoire to describe the signs of weather variations by the nuanced references they make to the material world in which they live.

Further examples are the sky and the appearance of clouds as atmospheric indicators by which to predict short-term weather changes in terms of precipitation and wind. According to other proverbs, the exact description of the shapes and colors of clouds make a difference to foretelling the weather:

"Chicken-fatted clouds mean wind, dog-fatted clouds mean rain; clouds with the shape of a gourd flower [pumpkin] means inundation, clouds with rose-mallow shape [hibiscus] means rains."

Figure 3: Clouds and Sky as Weather Indicators

Source: Judith Ehlert, 2008.

In addition, farmers interpret the growing behavior of plants in order to predict the seasonal availability of water resources. A classic observational experience was that the closer the banana bunches hang to the ground, the higher the flood level the following year (see Picture 5).

Another botanic indicator was a special grass called *Co Tay* that grows along the edges of the canals and channels. If the top of the grass very suddenly grows high, again a high water level is anticipated for the upcoming flood season. In traditional weather lore both botanic phenomena were decisive factors for seasonal forecasts.

In agricultural societies such as Vietnam, weather change forecasts are deeply related to star constellations and the Moon (Huu/Cohen 1997: 12): "Vietnam is a nation of cultivators bonded to the land and water, intimate with the power of the Sun and the Moon, and the life-giving potential and destructiveness of rain."

Most ancient calendars were observational lunar calendars, meaning that time changes were marked either by the first glimpse of the crescent or the full Moon (Aslaksen 2010: 14). This close human-astronomic relationship is still expressed in the original meaning of the Chinese New Year – called *Tet* in Vietnamese, which stands for the communion of human beings with nature. The name originates from 'tiet', meaning the knotty internodes between two sections of a bamboo stem, symbolizing the transition between two seasons, each characterized by different weather patterns (Huu/Cohen 1997: 6). According to the rule of thumb, *Tet* falls on the day of the second new Moon after the December solstice on approximately December 22, which is between January 21st and February 20th of the western calendar (Aslaksen 2010: 11/ 21ff.). Commune elderly told about the traditional practice of predicting the flood for the upcoming season during *Tet* by 'weighing the bottle'. A number of hours before the New Year they fill a plastic bottle with river water and weigh it. At the same time on New Year's Day they use the same bottle, fill it again with water from the same river spot and weigh the bottle another time. If the bottle in the New Year turns out to be heavier, the next flood will be higher than the previous one (September 11, 2008).

In ancient societies in general, the Moon played an important role as an astronomic 'time keeper'. According to Giddens (1990: 17), the separation of 'time' and 'space' constitutes a typical feature of modernity:

"[...] the time reckoning which formed the basis of day-to-day life, certainly for the majority of the population, always linked time with place [...]. No one could tell the time of day without reference to other socio-spatial markers: "when" was almost universally either connected with "where" or identified by regular natural occurrences. The invention of the mechanical clock and its diffusion to virtually all members of the population (a phenomenon which dates at its earliest from the late eighteenth century) were of key significance in the separation of time from space."

In contemporary rural Vietnam, references to the Moon as a 'time keeper' are still prevalent but complemented by the Gregorian calendar, applied especially in formal communication within the bureaucratic apparatus. For instance, making appointments with local officials or for farmers' meetings are organized on the basis of the globally bound reference system of time. Nonetheless, this 'formal meeting culture' is complemented by a distinct calculation and perception of time prevailing in the spiritual-religious sphere and in agricultural life following the Chinese calendar, which is often called the 'lunar calendar'[2] locally and which is typically to be found in each household (Huu/Cohen 1997: 8f.). Farmers relate seasonal water availability and respective agricultural activities to

---

2   Contrary to local declarations, however, the Chinese calendar is not a pure lunar calendar that totally ignores the Sun and the tropical year. In fact, the Chinese calendar is an integrated lunisolar calendar, meaning it is a solar calendar that happens to use the lunar month as the basic unit rather than the solar day as marking the beginning of a new month. Therefore, the year in the lunisolar calendar is an approximation of the seasonal year (Aslaksen 2010: 9ff.)

specified lunar months. Cropping patterns and the agricultural rhythm, for example, are captured in the following local saying:

"Lunar 1st months are the months to grow sweet potatoes; Lunar 2nd months are to grow beans; Lunar 3rd months are to grow potatoes, lunar 3rd month, plough to break the field; Lunar 4th, sow rice seeds; Lunar 5th, rains fill the fields; People, wives together with husbands; Husbands plough wives transplant, you feel happy inside."

Notwithstanding the romanticized image transmitted in those local sayings, it reflects the deeply contextualized nature of the agricultural lifestyle. The descriptions of astronomic, atmospheric, botanic, and animal or insect phenomena are all made on the basis of very local everyday surroundings inherent in the typical rural lifeworld. The distinction between dog fat and chicken fat colors to describe the appearances of clouds well expresses the strongly context-bound nature of such knowledge and the fine-tuning of local observation as the ultimate method in traditional weather forecast. The immediate local world constitutes the reference point and common standard along which communication, interaction, and shared interpretation meaningfully take place. People use their local environment to designate the world in which they live (Strecker 2004: 66; Berger/Luckmann 1966), and traditional weather knowledge is characterized by concepts of space and time deeply rooted in localities and seasonal cycles and localized in social activities.

In contrast to such contextualized indicators, modern meteorology is strongly characterized by its delocalized nature and numerical and abstract representation of natural phenomena (Huber/Pedersen 1997: 583):

"The weather forecast as we know it today is the outcome of [the] transformation of time and space, of quantification, measurement and representation. Traditional forecasts never went beyond weather rules (such as a 'red sky in the morning is the sailor's warning'). The predictive power of modern meteorology is based on the knowledge of physical laws of causation and probability, and on the quantification and modeling of nature."

In the Mekong Delta, this modern knowledge is spread to rural areas via the dense television and radio network in Vietnam. The decentralized hydrometeorological forecast system of the country comes under the auspices of the *Ministry of Natural Resources and the Environment (MoNRE)*, which is in charge of gathering and processing meteorological and hydrological data. Furthermore, its mandate is to disseminate flood and storm warnings for the main rivers in a timely manner (Nguyen/Nyuyen 2008: 18f.). The *Southern Regional Hydrome-*

teorological Center is in charge of weather data collection for the Mekong Delta. It integrates the macro data it receives from the *Mekong River Commission* and *MoNRE* with data from the various station networks in the region. After processing this data, it transmits weather information to the provincial weather stations, agriculture departments, and, if necessary, to the provincial Committees of Flood and Storm Control. These information transmissions, as well as daily forecasting news, are broadcasted via local radio and TV stations as well as newspapers (interview with staff of a weather station, Can Tho City, August 01, 2008; Bui/Le 2006: 72f.; Nguyen/Nguyen 2008: 20). Meteorological knowledge is disseminated through the vastly developed mass media network in Vietnam. The state-owned Vietnam Television estimates that about 13 million of the 16 million homes in Vietnam have a TV and thus access to broadcasted news[3]. In addition, Voice of Vietnam's radio stations broadcast the news twice a day through fixed and mobile public loudspeakers or radio (Pehu et al. 2003: 3).

Figure 4: Public Broadcasting

Source: Simon Benedikter, 2011.

---

3   This estimation is provided by Vietnam Television itself.

WEATHER KNOWLEDGE HYBRIDIZATION AND ADAPTATION TO FLOOD AND WEATHER CHANGES

As mentioned above, the rural population has growing access to alternative weather knowledge. What is thus of interest in the following is the relative relia-bility that farmers and fishermen ascribe to their own environmental knowledge in this context. In line with Nygren (ibid: 282) it is argued that it is the relative status of traditional and modern weather knowledge that constitutes the critical question for the analysis of such knowledge encounters. First, however, local patterns of knowledge transmission, which already indicate a certain human-nature relation in the delta and are argued to have an effect on the respective management of local weather knowledge, are examined.

Local Weather Knowing and Cultural-ecological Pragmatism

Weather knowledge is transmitted from generation to generation in the form of proverbs, local sayings, and songs. 'We observe the weather because we are farmers' expresses the common ability of farmers to adapt to weather variations through environmental observation. In the Mekong Delta, the skills of close ob-servation of the environment and its correct interpretation are broadly assigned to the 'ordinary' farmer as such. This contrasts with cases of weather knowledge as encountered in the Philippines (Galcgac/Balisacam 2009), India (Anandaraja et al. 2008), and Tibet (Huber/Pedersen 1997), for example, in which 'weather makers' and 'forecasters' constitute a highly recognized and institutionalized profession. Especially in the latter case of Tibet, Huber and Pedersen assess a strong cosmological relationship between the weather and the 'moral climate'. According to local Tibetan understanding, sinful human action negatively im-pacts on weather events. In order to avoid negative weather, local agricultural communities used to pay service fees to the weather maker's rituals as an insur-ance against damage to crops (Huber/Pedersen 1997: 587). In contrast to this strong institutionalization, farmers in the Mekong Delta very vaguely explain that their weather knowledge had been passed on to them by their 'ancestors'. Most commonly, weather lore is acquired through the personal accumulation of experiences and informal experiments (cf. Antweiler 1998). Only age was men-tioned as a decisive factor in the ability to foretell the weather – community el-ders were assigned more in-depth skills for weather and flood forecasting than the younger generations, who were even said to prefer to listen to the weather forecast on radio and TV.

It is argued that this missing specialization and formalization of weather knowledge in the Mekong Delta is related to the relatively weak cosmological relationship between humans and nature in contemporary Mekong Delta society. Traditionally, the Vietnamese believed in being descendants of the royal water dragon 'Lac Long Quan' and the mountain fairy 'Au Co'. The dragon symbolizes a supernatural power over the weather and therefore over crop production. This belief system is still found in folkloristic dragon dances expressing sacrifices to the gods of agriculture and the plea for timely rain (Huu/Cohen 1997: 68f.). Nevertheless, such traditions are no longer relevant for the conduct of people's everyday life, in which they follow a rational way of going about their daily business (ibid: 8): "Scientific thinking has transformed Vietnam. Mystical beliefs and practices are vanishing, while religious origins of customs have given way to secular social customs [...]." Local people's connection to water is rather qualified by rational pragmatism than spiritual attachment. Water (and weather) is considered a taken-for-granted resource in the delta (Taylor 2006: 47f.), and religious water festivals marking the beginning and the end of the rainy period are not celebrated much by local kinh[5] farmers but only by the ethnic Khmer in the Mekong Delta. For the local Vietnamese in the research site, these festivals play a less important social role. Consequently, secularization and pragmatism characterize the contemporary water-society relationship in the delta.

The utilitarian handling of the environment is rooted in the dominant modernist, technocratic, and materialist views on nature in Vietnamese society (Ehlert 2012). People trust in science and technology and value it as a driving force that brought them out of food insecurity in the late 1970s, after nationwide irrigation campaigns pushed rice production enormously following the Vietnam War (Biggs 2004). The rural population ascribes the region's success in rice export to the technocratic approach pursued in order to control the water environment. In line with this, Taylor (2006: 49) argues that the rapid uptake of new crops and technology happened because of cultural disposure to the new developments of people living along communicative water corridors in the Mekong Delta. The cognitive rationality and exposure to modernity along the waterways has increasingly replaced cosmological traditions, which used to connect humankind to nature, with a certain kind of environmental pragmatism. This emic concept of the ecology opposes the assumption of a strong cosmological innateness characterizing the human-water interface in the Mekong Delta and the eco-romantic position of certain scholars in the field of local, respectively indigenous, knowledge (Berkes 1999; cf. Neubert/Macamo 2004). Such pragmatism also finds its expression in the management approach of local weather knowledge. Local forecast knowledge that no longer corresponds to actual weather events is overthrown, since it no longer serves its purpose. Local knowledge on weather is passed from generation to generation, but only as long as it provides correct weather and flood prediction. It was found that while short-term weather forecast practices are still very important for everyday agricultural and fishery activities, seasonal traditional foretelling methods, managing flood prediction, are no longer perceived as relevant for local flood season management. Flood forecasts based on botanic indicators such as the 'banana bunch' or 'weighing the bottle' (see above) were mentioned by commune elders but were totally unknown to the younger generation. The older generation itself considers those methods nowadays as unreliable for assessing seasonal flood phenomena correctly, and since they are considered obsolete they are no longer passed on to the next generation.

Farmers gave the following reasons as to why those long-term prediction methods would no longer work in the given environmental context by referring to the growing human interference in river ecology as reasons why locally-grown flood predictions do not correspond to actual flood events. The way that humans have appropriated the environment for development purposes by flood control measures has altered the ecology in such a way that traditional practices of seasonal prediction no longer 'work' in an ever more complex and extra-local system of flood management.[4] The rural population perceives outside conditions such as flood control measures for upstream riparian countries (see Map 1) and the complex Vietnamese dyke system itself as strongly influencing local flooding. Extra-local conditions increasingly determine local seasonal water environments, and the contemporary flood infrastructure calls into question the reliability of their local flood prediction practices more and more. The human-regulated control system in place affects the seasons, and in this man-made environment, which is characterized by the construction of dams and dikes for flood control, intensive irrigation and hydropower, traditional methods fail to predict floods. Local flooding nowadays is seen as less determined by nature than by the controlled water release and withdrawal from upstream river stretches, rendering the traditional ways of 'foreseeing' the flood unreliable and the passing down of these ancient skills obsolete:

---

4   This result accords with the findings of Thim Ly (2010: 82ff.), who describes the case of riverbank villagers in Cambodia. Since the construction of the Yali-Falls dam, their traditional flood prediction methods that are based on rain indicators no longer prove reliable in the context of uncontrollable water release from the hydropower dam.

"Today, the condition in the area nearer to the origin of the flood[5] is different and the man-made dyke system makes flooding more and more unpredictable. It is hard to say how long a cycle between big floods is. Floods do not come naturally anymore." (Interview, vice president of a district people's committee, Thot Not, 05.06.08)

The impact of human interference in the ecology of the delta and the natural water regime was also mentioned in a discussion between one female farmer in her mid-70s and a husband and wife, both in their 50s and engaged in farming as a primary occupation. The method of natural experimentation and methodological empiricism became apparent in the interview statement of the elderly woman, who had realized that in some years the banana bunch in front of her house and close to the channel had bent down heavily but that the big flood the following season failed to appear. The husband and wife commented on the old female's observation that even if the river flood coming down from Cambodia into the delta was high, they could not see it in their commune, since the flood would have been irrigated towards the sea via major irrigation channels before actually reaching their commune located further downstream (interview, Vinh Thanh, September 01, 2008).

---

5   The 'origin of the flood' is an expression used by the local population when referring to the water volumes that seasonally stream down from neighboring Cambodia, entering the Mekong Delta in Vietnam through the north-western border provinces of the delta.

Figure 5: Banana bunch as a Weather Indicator

Source: Judith Ehlert, 2008.

Besides such direct anthropogenic factors, local farmers further referred to more abstract phenomena such as 'climate change' that would annul their calendaric time rules, which used to distinguish perfectly the wet from the dry season in the past:

"The proverbs about flood cannot be used anymore because the weather has changed. It is not like in the past. In the past we calculated by lunar calendar and the Chinese calendar. They calculated very well but now the calendar has gone wrong. The weather – we cannot rely on the 'time' to predict the weather. In the past, the weather was more moderate. From March to October there was the rainy season. From November to December it was all sunny and there was not one drop of rain. But nowadays rain and sun come very sudden, not like in a circle anymore. When we harvest the rice, sometimes there is rain and we cannot dry the rice. Now there are rains and whirlwinds completely different from the past. Also in the world there are many disasters happening. The earth has gone wrong in some way. This earth is old and ruined. [...] The climate has changed [...]." (Interview, two very old farmers, Vinh Thanh, September 05, 2008)

Due to the growing imponderability of seasonal weather events, farming communities make use of scientific weather information in order to better cope with flooding. The rural population has high confidence in the accuracy of the modern ways of flood forecasting, as expressed in the following statement taken from a discussion with two elderly traditional fishermen who had changed to the aquaculture business:

"The majority of people just listens to the weather forecast because now science already made a big progress and the traditional experiences are sometimes not so correct. Because everything we have depends on science. It is thanks to science that we make the second rice crop. Only some of the traditional experience is still used. Nowadays we just rely on the government and the science." (Interview, Thot Not, October 06, 2008)

The environmental pragmatism mentioned earlier is again well-reflected in the consistent handling of local weather knowledge that has turned obsolete or less reliable (see above). Nevertheless, in contrast to such long-term weather lore, traditional weather indicators are continuously used for organizing daily agricultural work routines, especially for post-harvesting activities. The movements of clouds and the flying patterns of dragonflies, for example, remain the most important and trusted signs announcing short-term weather fronts:

"Proverbs are never wrong. Clouds like chicken fat means that it will be windy, clouds like dog fat means it will rain. Those experiences and proverbs can never be wrong. If you guess the weather by looking at the sky, your prediction is completely correct." (Interview, two very old farmers, Vinh Thanh, September 05, 2008)

On the one hand, one can thus observe the neglect of traditional methods for seasonal (long-term) forecasts and on the other hand the concurrent upholding of short-term weather lore methods. While short-term weather lore methods are still widely applied by the young and the older generation of farmers and fishermen on a daily basis, the more far-reaching decision-making processes for the agricultural cycle are increasingly backed by modern meteorology and science. The obsolescence of some parts of local weather lore then goes hand in hand with the growing availability and access to modern weather knowledge that is spread through the mass media and agricultural extension services.

The contestation of traditional long-term weather lore, which fails the test of informal experiments and is therefore cast aside, ably brings environmental and epistemological pragmatism to the point. The study proves the stock of local knowledge to be highly capable of revising itself in accordance with problem-orientations in people's everyday life (cf. Linkenbach 2004). Modern meteorology substitutes for this failure of local flood prediction and gains in accuracy due to better technological equipment and satellite observation. Access to scientific weather and flood information broadens the local knowledge base. The intermingling of local environmental knowledge and external weather information – entering locality via radio or TV – in local social spaces endows actors with diverse frames of reference at hand for local problem solving – in this case for efficient and risk-minimizing agricultural decision-making. Following the social constructivist stance towards knowledge, according to Berger and Luckmann (1966: 26), "T[t]he sociology of knowledge must concern itself with everything that passes for 'knowledge' in society." This actor's orientation helps to deconstruct static knowledge categories such as traditional versus modern knowledge. By avoiding a focus on respective end-state (knowledge) typologies, Berger and Luckmann underline the agency function that enables actors to draw on diverse knowledge-embedded practices and cosmologies in order to manage, construct, and reproduce everyday farming realities. As such, actors are understood as competent agents, who are capable of processing social experience and of reflexivity in their intercourse with the social and natural environment in which they act (Weber 1972).

What one can observe at the moment is the symmetrical coexistence and hybridization of the diverse ways by which actors practice 'weather knowing'. The integration of the cropping and water calendars represents an interesting example of the hybrid forms of weather knowledge by mixing the Chinese and the Gregorian calendars: In the past, meaning before the introduction of massive flood-control infrastructure and irrigation systems from the 1980s onwards, the weather in general and the availability of water resources specifically constituted the main determinants for agricultural activities (see above). The Chinese calendar presented a perfect means for the adaptation of agricultural and aquacultural production because it informed about the seasonal flood and daily tidal variations – the tide itself dating from characteristics of the Moon[6]. Farmers in the past had cultivated 'floating rice' that used to grow in tune with rising water-levels in the field. In order to raise crop productivity however, high-yield but less water-resistant rice species were introduced in the 1980s. With the advanced and complex system of irrigation and flood control in place nowadays, agricultural productivity became less dependent on the weather and more on the prevention of crop pests and diseases. In the context of agricultural intensification and high-yield cropping, new pests and diseases have developed and made rice production more vulnerable. Agricultural extension staff therefore calculate a

---

6 Since the Chinese calendar takes account of the Moon and is based on an approximation of the seasonal year at the same time, the calendar was an approved device for local flood season management – especially in Can Tho City, which is highly affected by tidal variation in the delta – and to minimize the risk of crop damage caused by excess water.

farming calendar that takes into consideration the development and movement of bugs and the seasonal water availability, by drawing on scientific (weather) information. The farming calendar guides agricultural activities in regard to water management on field-level, sowing, and cropping activities in order to coordinate agricultural work in a timely manner within the different field sections; otherwise, later harvesting plots risk high exposure to pest diseases (Le Meur et al. 2005: 24). The interdependency and complexity in decision-making is growing relative to the intensification of agriculture. Such changing conditions require the Chinese calendar, which beforehand operated as main agricultural guide, to be complemented by the farming calendar. The farming calendar is based on scientific knowledge in order to minimize the risk of agricultural loss, and it computes dates for post-flood water management activities according to the Gregorian calendar. Before passing on the dates and information to the farming communities, however, the Gregorian dates are commuted into dates on the Chinese calendar. By leaving the 'formal sphere of extension experts' (see above) the information is 'translated' back into dates on the Chinese calendar, and then adapted to local farming routines. This procedure represents a micro-example for the hybrid character of the local knowledge system and constitutes a case for the embeddedness of scientific knowledge in everyday agricultural practice. This hybridization of the local knowledge stock is highlighted by the following statement:

"Nowadays the weather and climate show unusual changes. Therefore scientific research is needed in order to support farmers in their production. If we combine science and technology with the local experience appropriately, the effectiveness will be great."[7]

CONCLUSION: KNOWLEDGE AND ENVIRONMENTAL ADAPTATION

The Mekong Delta, with its thriving ecological and technological transformations, represents an interesting case for studying the epistemological dynamic between humans and nature. Ambitious economic development visions for the Mekong Delta have fostered large-scale technical interventions in the form of dams and dykes and pushed the creation of a 'modern hydraulic society' (Wittfogel 1957; Evers/Benedikter 2009). Vietnam vigorously pursues its effort towards becoming an industrialized country by 2020 with the special promotion of

---

7   Originating from a focus group discussion with district-level agricultural extension officers discussing the pros and cons of technology and local experience in agricultural production (Vinh Thanh, February 09, 2009).

a prospering Mekong Delta (VCP 2001). These anthropogenic transformations were shown to stimulate the generation, revision, and innovation of locally available environmental knowledge by putting it in a constant state of flux (Descola/Palsson 1996). Starting the analysis from such local knowledge encounters, in which 'traditional' weather lore and 'modern' meteorological information were intimately intertwined in socio-geographical space and local practice (Nygren 1999), emphasized the dynamic character of local knowledge stocks and people's hybrid ways of knowing the weather as a strategy to cope with irregular weather patterns. In the long run, traditional weather lore will gradually become marginalized, since the transformation from an agricultural to an industrialized society renders weather lore irrelevant for growing urban lifestyles and off-farm job opportunities in the delta. Nonetheless, as long as agriculture constitutes people's main source of living, they will continue to define what is 'traditional', 'innovative', and 'modern' in terms of local weather knowledge. As soon as the traditional indicators fail to live up to actual weather events, they are thrown out and replaced by more reliable modern sources of information. The application of hybrid forms of knowing the weather serves as the best possible adaptation to encounter and to act upon weather and flood changes. As such, the study aimed first at depicting the parallelism and overlapping of multiple knowledge reference systems with which people operate in the conduct of modernizing everyday life. The Vietnamese official policy framework of "Living with Flood" denotes a strategic program that seeks to maximize the benefits from flooding while at the same time minimizing agricultural loss and human casualties (for a critical account, see Ehlert 2012). The growing supply and investment in local weather information infrastructure is part of this official policy framework, in which flood and weather forecasting constitutes one of the most pro-active measures (Lebel/Sinh 2007: 44). According to Contreras (2007: 231f.) and access to weather forecast information via the Internet or radio contributes to the ability of local communities to take appropriate action and preparedness measures on time. In the light of growing frequencies and magnitudes of storms in the delta, warning systems will thus play an increasingly important role in the future. Cyclone *Nargis*, which devastated Myanmar's Irrawaddy Delta in 2008, aroused a public discussion in Vietnam on respective future scenarios for the Mekong Delta, since both deltas feature a flat topography and are characterized by the construction in rural areas of houses that are built traditionally with very light materials (Ehlert 2012); the people in the Mekong Delta would not be accustomed to fighting storms (statement by Major General Nguyen Son Ha, a member of the National Council for Search and Rescue, Saigon Times Weekly, May 24, 2008: 42).

This perspective shows that local knowledge and the provision of external weather information are but one way of coping with environmental change. In order to put into practice an adaptive strategy towards environmental change, it would further need the promotion of safe house construction methods and coherent and participative flood management strategies for better integrating land and water use changes following urbanization and industrialization (Lebel et al. 2009). Second, the study concludes that knowing the weather serves rather as a coping mechanism within the overall context of environmental change (see also Hornidge in this volume). The adaptive challenge to environmental change, however, lies in more sensitive approaches towards the ecology for development planning and the drastic pursuit of modernization in the region. This nevertheless remains a question of political will and of negotiating development alternatives with the dominant water control paradigm in the delta.

REFERENCES

Adger, W. N./Kelly, P. M./Nguyen Huu Ninh (2001): Environment, Society and Precipitous Change. In: W. N. Adger/P.M. Kelly/Nguyen Huu Ninh (eds.): Living with Environmental Change. Social Vulnerability, Adaptation and Resilience in Vietnam, London and New York: Routledge Research Global Environmental Change, 3-18.

Agrawal, A. (1995): Dismantling the Divide between Indigenous and Scientific Knowledge. Development and Change 26/3, 413-439.

Anandaraja, N./Rathakrishnan, T./Ramasubramanian, M./Saravanan, P./Suganthi, N.S. (2008): Indigenous Weather and Forecast Practices of Coimbatore District Farmers of Tamil Nadu. Indian Journal of Traditional Knowledge, 7/4, 630-633.

Antweiler, C. (1998): Local Knowledge and Local Knowing. Anthropos 93, 469-494.

Aslaksen, H. (2010): The Mathematics of the Chinese Calendar. Singapore: National University of Singapore. Draft version. (http://www.math.nus.edu.sg/aslaksen/calendar/cal.pdf) [accessed 01/2011].

Berger, P./Luckmann, Th. (1966): The Social Construction of Reality. A Treatise in the Sociology of Knowledge, New York: Penguin Books.

Berkes, F. (1999): Sacred Ecology. Traditional Ecological Knowledge and Resource Management, Philadelphia and London: Taylor & Francis.

Biggs, D. (2004): Between the Rivers and the Tides: A Hydraulic History of the Mekong Delta 1820-1975, PhD. Washington: University of Washington.

Biggs, D./Miller, F./Chu Thai Hoanh/Molle F. (2009): The Delta Machine: Water Management in the Vietnamese Mekong Delta in Historical and Contemporary Perspectives. In: F. Molle/T. Foran/M. Käkönen, (eds.), Contested Waterscapes in the Mekong Region. Hydropower, Livelihoods and Governance. London and Sterling, VA: Earthscan, 203-225.

Brocheux, P. (1995): The Mekong Delta: Ecology, Economy, and Revolution, 1860-1960, University of Wisconsin-Madison and Center for Southeast Asian Studies: Monograph Number 12.

Bui, Duc Long/Le Thi Hue (2006): Vietnam Country Report: 2005 Rainfall, Floods and Disaster Forecasting Preparedness. Paper presented at the 4th Annual Mekong Flood Forum, Siem Reap, Cambodia, 18-19 May 2006.

Contreras, A. P. (2007): Synthesis: Discourse, Power and Knowledge. In: Lebe,l L. /Dore, J./ Daniel, R./Saing Koma, Y. (eds.): Democratizing Water Governance in the Mekong. Chiang Mai: Mekong Press, 227-236.

Descola, P./Palsson, G. (1996): Nature and Society: Anthropological Perspectives, London: Routledge.

Ehlert, J. (2012): Beautiful Floods. Environmental Knowledge and Agrarian Change in the Mekong Delta, Vietnam, Berlin, Münster: Lit Verlag.

Evers, H.-D./Benedikter, S. (2009): Hydraulic Bureaucracy in a Modern Hydraulic Society – Strategic Group Formation in the Mekong Delta, Vietnam. Water Alternatives 2, 416-439.

Galacgac, E. S./Balisacan C. M. (2009): Traditional Weather Forecasting for Sustainable Agroforestry Practices in Ilocos Norte Province, Philippines. Forest Ecology and Management 257, 2044-2053.

Giddens, A. (1990): The Consequences of Modernity, UK: Polity Press.

Huber, T./Pedersen, P. (1997): Meteorological Knowledge and Environmental Ideas in Traditional and Modern Societies: The Case of Tibet. The Journal of the Royal Anthropological Institute 3/3, 577-597.

Huu, Ngoc and Barbara Cohen (1997): Tet. The Vietnamese Lunar New Year, Hanoi: The Gioi Publishers.

Le, Anh Tuan/Chu Thai Hoanh/Miller, F. /Bach Tan Sinh (2007): Flood and Salinity Management in the Mekong Delta, Vietnam. In: Tran Thanh Be/Bach Tan Sinh/Miller, F. (eds.), Challenges to Sustainable Development in the Mekong Delta: Regional and National Policy Issues and Research Needs, Thailand: The Sustainable Mekong Research Network (Sumernet), 15-68.

Le Meur, P.-Y./Hauswirth D./Leurent, T./Lienhard, P. (2005): The Local Politics of Land and Water. Case Studies from the Mekong Delta, Études et Travaux en ligne, 4: Les Éditions du GRET.

Lebel, L./Bach Tan Sinh (2007): Politics of Floods and Disasters. In: Lebel, L./Dore, J./Daniel, R./Y. Saing Koma (eds.), Democratizing Water Governance in the Mekong, Chiang Mai: Mekong Press, 37-54.

Lebel, L./Bach Tan Sinh/Garden, P./Suong Seng/Le Anh Tuan/ Duong Van Truc (2009): The Promise of Flood Protection: Dikes and Dams, Drains and Diversions. In: Molle, F./Foran, T./Käkönen, M. (eds.), Contested Waterscapes in the Mekong Region. Hydropower, Livelihoods and Governance, London/ Sterling, VA: Earthscan, 283-306.

Linkenbach, A. (2004): Lokales Wissen im Entwicklungsdiskurs: Abwertung, Aneignung oder Anerkennung des Anderen? In: Schareika N./Bierschenk, Th. (eds.), Lokales Wissen – Sozialwissenschaftliche Perspektiven. Münster: Lit, 233-257.

Neubert, D./Macamo, E. (2004): Wer weiß hier was? 'Authentisches' lokales Wissen und der Globalitätsanspruch der Wissenschaft. In: Schareika N./Bierschenk, Th. (eds.), Lokales Wissen – Sozialwissenschaftliche Perspektiven. Münster: Lit, 93-122.

Nguyen, Van Sanh/Nguyen Duy Can (2008): Study on Local Community Institutions to Cope with the Flood Situation of the Mekong Region, Scientific Report (Draft). Sumernet: The Sustainable Mekong Research Network.

Nygren, A. (1999): Local Knowledge in the Environment-Development Discourse: From Dichotomies to Situated Knowledges. In: Critique of Anthropology 19/3, 267–288.

Pehu, E./Janakiram, S./Winder, D./ O'Farrell, C/Young, J. (2003): Visit to Vietnam 16th-25th October 2003. Report of Project Preparation Phase, DFID/FAO/ODI: Collaborative Program for Knowledge Systems in Support of Rural Livelihoods.(http://www.fao.org/rdd/doc/Vietnam Assessment.pdf) [accessed 01/2011].

Pham, Cong Huu (2012): Floods and Farmers. Politics, Economics and Environmental Impacts of Dyke Construction in the Mekong Delta/ Vietnam, Berlin, Münster: Lit Verlag.

Saigon Times Weekly (2008): Real and Present Danger. 24 May 2008, no. 22.

Strecker, I. (2004): Was sagen die Sterne? Zur Rhetorik lokalen Wissens in Hamar (Südäthiopien). In: Schareika N./Bierschenk, Th. (eds.), Lokales Wissen – Sozialwissenschaftliche Perspektiven. Münster: LIT, 59-91.

Taylor, P. (2006): Rivers into Roads: The Terrestrialization of a South-east Asian River Delta. In: Leybourne, M./Gaynor, A. (eds.), Water. Histories, Cultures, Ecologies, Crawley: University of Western Australia Press, 38-52.

Weber, M. (1972): Wirtschaft und Gesellschaft. Grundriss der verstehenden Soziologie, J. Winckelmann, ed., 5th rev. edn. Tübingen: Mohr.

Wittfogel, K. A. (1957): Oriental Despotism – A Comparative Study of Total Power, Yale University Press.

VCP – Communist Party of Vietnam, Central Committee (2001): Strategy for Socio Economic Development 2001 – 2010. Presented by the Central Committee, 8th Tenure, to the 9th National Congress April 2001.

"Why did the Fish Cross the Road?"

Environmental Uncertainty and Local Knowledge in Bangladesh

PAUL SILLITOE AND MAHBUB ALAM

LIVING WITH THE DELTA INSTEAD OF DOMINATING IT

In Bangladesh, the koi mach fish (*Anabas testudineus*) can 'walk' out of water and may on occasion be seen crossing the road, going from one water body to another.[1] But you are less likely to see these fish moving across the land today than two decades ago. Its disappearance is one of many changes that have occurred following the construction of massive flood defenses under the *World Bank* funded *Flood Action Plan (FAP)*, which featured multi-billion dollar engineering measures comprising embankments and sluices intended to control the annual monsoon flood and protect the Bangladeshi floodplain from extensive inundation.

If current climate change predictions prove correct, Bangladesh is likely to suffer catastrophic flooding, as it is situated on one of the world's largest low-lying deltas (Yu et al. 2010). Instead of seeing two-thirds of the country inundated for some three months of the year, we are likely to see a large area permanently under water all year round. For example, if sea levels rise one meter in the Bay of Bengal, it will permanently inundate 18 per cent of Bangladesh's land area, displacing 11 per cent of its population, an estimated 15 million or so people (Karim/Rahman1995). The current FAP defenses will prove inadequate, and may even arguably make matters worse by impeding the natural flow of water.

---

1 The climbing perch or gourami 'walks' on land by pushing itself along with fins and tail, using gill plates for support.

In this event, powerful voices will probably lobby development agencies for further, even more massive engineering interventions to protect the floodplain. We think that those advocating such solutions to possible climate induced environmental change need to learn from the FAP experience, which has revealed the hubris of high-tech approaches that assume they can contain and manage such natural forces (Brammer 2004). The flood defenses have made life more difficult, not better for the poor – the avowed target group of development agencies. For instance, disruption to the flow of monsoon waters greatly disadvantages poor fishermen. It is therefore time for us to learn from such people and understand how to live with the delta, not dominate it.

Figure 1: Embankment and sluice gate at Khalilpur, Pabna

Source: Sarder Shafiqul Alam, Bangladesh Center for Advanced Studies 2005.

The Bengal region is one of the most disaster-prone on the planet and regularly hits the news headlines, notably because of its floods. Some cite the increased intensity and frequency of extreme weather events as evidence that climate change is already affecting Bangladesh and neighboring countries. These events not only involve floods but also hailstorms, cold spells, droughts, and dense fog, and in coastal regions cyclones, too (Huq/Rahman 1994). Many people in North Bengal rank floods as the region's second most pressing problem, putting drought as the first, which they say has been increasing in severity since 1977, with many summer house fires attributed to extremely dry weather (RDRS 2009).[2] In its Fourth Assessment report, the *Intergovernmental Panel on Climate Change (IPCC* 2007) gives the following changes in climate trends, variability and extreme events:

- In Bangladesh, the average temperature has registered an increasing trend of about 1°C in May and 0.5°C in November during the 14 year period from 1985 to 1998;
- The annual mean rainfall exhibits increasing trends in Bangladesh. Decadal rain anomalies are above long-term averages since 1960s;
- Serious and recurring floods have taken place during 2002, 2003, and 2004. Cyclones originating from the Bay of Bengal have been noted to decrease since 1970 but the intensity has increased;
- Frequency of monsoon depressions and cyclones formation in Bay of Bengal has increased;
- Water shortages have been attributed to rapid urbanization and industrialization, population growth and inefficient water use, which are aggravated by changing climate and its adverse impacts on demand, supply and water quality;
- Saltwater from the Bay of Bengal is reported to have penetrated 100km or more inland along tributary channels during the dry season;
- The precipitation decline and droughts has resulted in the drying up of wetlands and severe degradation of ecosystems.

This chapter reviews local farmer and fishers' assessments of, and adaptations to, environmental changes resulting across the Bangladeshi floodplain with the construction of the FAP flood defenses and their impact on subsistence activities. It examines how local people assess these environmental changes, both their short- and long-term impacts, and how they cope with them. Using data from the Tangail region, it draws attention to issues that should be considered in the event of any similar climate change-instigated engineering measures or, as politicians are fond of saying, 'learn the lessons' of experience. In addition to standard anthropological methods such as participant observation, informal conversation, in-depth interviews, etc., we employ techniques advanced in indigenous knowledge

---

2   Severe droughts have occurred in the years of 1977, 2002, 2005, 2006 and 2008.

and participatory development work during this research (see Sillitoe et al. 2005).

ENGINEERING THE ENVIRONMENT

The annual hydrological cycle of Bengal is a challenging one of extremes, with floods at one time of the year and droughts at another (Chowdhury 1996; Hofer & Messerli 2006). Recent engineering interventions to meet these challenges have had mixed results, making life even more difficult for many. They have compromised the accommodation reached by generations of Bengalis in securing their livelihoods, increasing the risks and uncertainties faced by many, notably the poorer.

In the wake of the catastrophic floods of 1987 and 1988, the government of Bangladesh adopted the *Flood Action Plan* drawn up by the *United Nations Development Program* and funded by the *World Bank*, with a view to easing the country's flood problems (World Bank 1990; Boyce 1990). Before this, in the early 1960s, many polders had been constructed on riverbanks in coastal areas and judged a success at mitigating the effects of floods. The *Bangladesh Water Development Board* employed many foreign experts together with local engineers to implement the plan, spending large sums on technological interventions. The FAP involved the construction of large embankments on both sides of all major rivers, such as those of the Jamuna-Brahmaputra and Padma-Ganges river systems, to prevent them bursting their banks. A major part of the plan featured compartmentalization, an "innovative scheme" of flood regulation.[3] Its objective was to allow the regulation of flood levels within areas enclosed by embankments (flood control compartments) through a system sluices (drainage regulators). It was intended that farmers could control flood water levels within compartments to suit their cropping requirements, notably the cultivation of rice, largely introduced high yielding varieties (Rashid/Mallik 1995). Notice that the pan largely overlooks fisheries that contribute significantly to households' livelihood regimes.

---

3   The nearby large Tangail FAP compartmentalization project has impacted significantly on the environment of the Charan beel (lake) villages.

Figure 2: From a sluice gate looking into a compartment at Khalilpur, Pabna

Source: Sarder Shafiqul Alam, Bangladesh Center for Advanced Studies, 2005.

The FAP sought to enhance road communications, too. National and local governments and NGOs also contributed to the road building program, sometimes employing poor people in 'food for work' schemes, while some NGOs such as *CARE* only took on destitute women to do this work. The construction of roads further complicated things, as many ran from east to west across the delta, when the river systems drained into the Bay of Bengal to the south. The building of roads contrary to the direction of rivers and without adequate water culverts under them further interrupted the drainage system, resulting in extensive water logging for extended periods, particularly in the southern part of the country.

While some parties strongly opposed the FAP 'structural solution' to the flood problem, the plan went ahead with strong international support (Boyce 1990; Paul 1995). The interests of certain stakeholders clearly prevailed above others, such as those of consultants; for instance, as Muhammad (2004: 3447) points out: "Consultants, local and imported, have been the major beneficiaries [...] consultant fees have been a significant share of project costs." It had a dramatic impact on water resources across the country, as predicted. Although the construction of the embankment defenses reduced the risk of flood over large areas, it also had some, often unforeseen, negative impacts (Brammer 2004; Cook 2010). Many people have seen their livelihoods affected and point to the detrimental effects on the local ecology. The considerable physical changes to watercourses that have resulted across the floodplain many consider environmental disasters. For instance, Schmuck-Widmann (2001: 117) observes that "the Jamuna was dyked and its course narrowed [...]. Usually, erosion is quite predictable, but this technical manipulation makes the river totally unpredictable."

In coastal areas, such as Khulna, the construction of polders was intended to reduce salinity by keeping salty water away from agricultural land (see Reichel et al., this volume, for comparative discussion of marine degradation in South Celebes), but it resulted in long-term water logging, the coasts experiencing unusual floods due to the inland interruption of the natural drainage system. In the Beel Dakatia area, thousands of acres of farmland were under water for over two decades (Rahman 1995; Naseem et al. 2001). Not only did farming cease, but aquatic resources were also badly affected, including fish stocks. The farming and fishing communities in the locality resorted to hunting migratory birds to earn a living, further impacting negatively on biodiversity.

Another problem is the Farakka Barrage, the world's longest, situated in India, which since 1975 has been diverting the Ganges into the Hooghly river basin. The long-running international political disputes between the neighboring states of Bangladesh and India over water resources, of which the Barrage is an instance, further complicate the complex hydrological circumstances of the Bengal Delta (Islam 1987; Crow 1995; Subedi 2005).[4] While the Barrage scarcely impacts on the annual floods – not really diminishing the volume of water arriving in the monsoon season – it has a dramatic effect in the dry season, greatly reducing water flow and impacting negatively on the hydrology and ecology of the delta downstream (Swain 1996). It has increased water contamination, disrupting domestic water supply and threatening public health, reduced fishing returns and hindered navigation, and raised soil salinity, contributing to a fall in agricultural production. The Barrage's river diversion has displaced populations within Bangladesh, creating environmental refugees, some of whom have migrated to India, exacerbating political tensions. According to many rural people, India also poisons the flood water with industrial waste. They attribute the wound disease epidemic that accompanied the 1988 flood to these toxins, which resulted in some fish species declining dramatically and even becoming locally extinct, including *boro baim* (*Mastacembalus armatus*), *shail* (*Channa striatus*), *salam puti* (*Puntius sophore*), *kora puti* (*Anodontostomata chacuda*) and *tengra* (*Batasio batasio*). The Hindu fishermen Bancha Ram Das recounted how "after

---

4   Deforestation in the hilly Indian states of Meghalaya, Assam and Tripura is another contentious cross-border environmental issue, in this case increasing the danger of flash floods that extensively damage farmland in the north-eastern region Bangladesh, where the large hoar lake and grassland ecosystem occurs.

the flood of 1988 a wound disease attacked many fish. Some fish such as *gazar* and *alang* have completely disappeared. Other fish attacked by the wound sickness such as the *boro baim* eel, *shail* snake head, and *salam puti* and *kora puti small carps* have fallen greatly in numbers. As far as we know, the flood waters came across many parts of India. People think this water brought in some bad things that caused the fish diseases." According to Nilkamal Das, "the fish we call *salam puti* disappeared from Charan [became locally extinct] after that flood [...] at that time we saw lots of dead fish floating in the water caught by wound diseases ... Brother, you can't imagine what happened after the flood of 1988. We can't tell you how many dead fish we found on the bank of the beel. We were unable to go there because of the bad smell."

Figure 3: The inter-relationships of floodplain resources and livelihoods

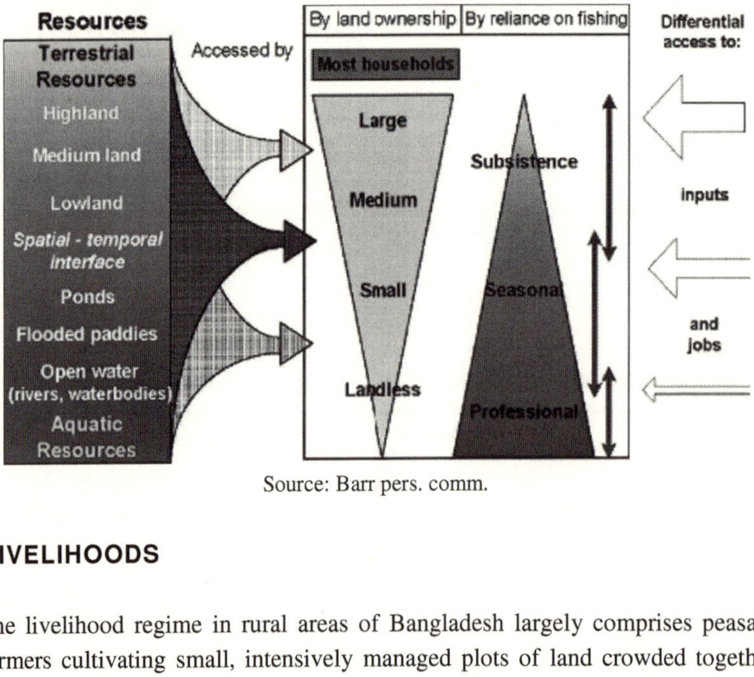

Source: Barr pers. comm.

LIVELIHOODS

The livelihood regime in rural areas of Bangladesh largely comprises peasant farmers cultivating small, intensively managed plots of land crowded together across the floodplain. They feature a mix of landowners, sharecroppers, and landless laborers who differ considerably in wealth. There are also some full-time fishermen and a few following other occupations such as weaving and making pottery (Clement et al. 2000). The pattern of livelihoods found on the floodplain broadly ranges from land-holding households that largely engage in farming to landless ones that depend heavily on fishing (Figure 1). Muslim families dominate rural society, with Hindus in the minority and usually the poorer of the two groups. According to the 2004 census, 89.5 per cent of the population of Bangladesh is Muslim, 9.6 per cent Hindu, and the remainder recorded as 'other'; the percentage of Hindus in the Charan region is marginally higher at 14 per cent and the Muslims lower at 86 per cent of the region's population.

Farmers cultivate rice as a staple, together with other crops such as mustard, onions, beans, and jute, for subsistence and sale at local markets. Households also keep some ducks, chickens and a few sheep, with cows and a few water buffalo supplying milk and serving as draught animals. The number of crops that they are able to cultivate in a year varies from one to three, depending on the extent and duration of the inundation of their plots, which may disappear under water for a few weeks to several months during the monsoon, depending on their elevation. While lower lying land may be inundated for considerable periods, it is cultivated using traditional chamara deepwater rice varieties that grow quickly and keep pace with rising water levels, surviving submersion by elongating hollow internode structures that allow gas exchange with the atmosphere. The annual deposition of sediment also maintains natural soil fertility. When the flood waters recede in the month of Kartic (October to November), the exposed soil is rich in ras, 'sap' or fertile moisture, and at full water capacity supports a range of crops. While higher unflooded land is more readily farmed all year round, it is naturally less fertile and its cultivation requires costly irrigation, particularly in the boro dry season.

The arrival of high yielding varieties (HYV) of paddy and associated technology packages in the last three decades or so[5] have led to considerable changes in farming practices (Hossain 1989; Conway and Barbier 1990; Alauddin and Tisdell 1991), and the introduction of genetically modified crops is likely to lead to further changes. The HYV 'green revolution' is the agricultural equivalent of engineering's embankment construction, regarding the changes that have resulted and new uncertainties that stretch the capacity of local coping mechanisms. The new seeds demand inputs of inorganic fertilizers to maintain fertility and spraying with biocides to control pests and diseases. They also require regular supplies of water, which are largely pumped up from deep tube wells, as surface water sources such as beel lakes cannot meet the considerable irrigation demands of HYV varieties. The following comments of Fazlul Haque, a sharecropper, indicate the extent of the changes farmers face:

---

5   According to Fazlul Haque, a local share-cropper, the government introduced high yielding varieties into the Charan area in 1978.

"All of us depend on IRRI varieties (locally all HYV varieties are called IRRI, after the International Rice Research Institute in the Philippines, the source of HVV rice). I cultivate the IRRI varieties 29, 14, Gazi, BR 3 and Hybrid in the months of Poush and Magh. These have replaced the local varieties such as Kaliboro and Kunailboro. They have increased the cost of rice cultivation. But the yield has increased dramatically. The cost of labor, fertilizer and tilling is rising so high that rice cultivation is no longer profitable. When I first bought seeds, the price was Tk. 8.00 per kg. Now the price is very high. They cost me Tk. 40.00 per kg. from a local NGO. I bought five kg of Hybrid seed. I tried to preserve some seed but failed. It did not produce any seedling. The need for fertilizer is 7.5 mounds for an acre. The government says that farmers will get fertilizer on time. This is untrue. There is no fertilizer in the market or anywhere. The real price of fertilizer is Tk. 750.00 but I won't get it even for Tk. 1000.00.[6] The fields need fertilizer as soon as the flood water recedes. Fertilizer that is required within 20 days is applied 40 days late. It affects the yield. The late application of fertilizer decreases what we expect by one half. This is a common occurrence. The fertilizer used to be available in the market earlier. Now I go to the dealers' shop and queue up for three or four days to get small amounts of fertilizer that do not meet my needs. The demand for fertilizer [to maintain yields] has been increasing alarmingly. And fertilizer and pesticide are degrading the quality of soil. Irrigation is a big constraint nowadays. We face big difficulties because of price hikes. Often we farmers have to give one quarter of our crop to the irrigation provider. Electricity failure is a regular experience too."

---

6   The value of the taka (Tk), the currency of Bangladesh, was Tk105 to €1 at the beginning of 2012.

Figure 4: The seasonally changing extent of Charan beel lake

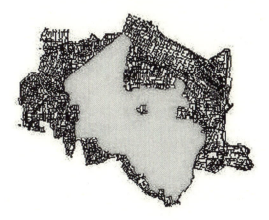

Dry season

Monsoon flood

Source: Data from colleagues on our DfID projects; maps produced at Newcastle University's Centre for Land Use and Water Resources Research.

During the rainy season and monsoon floods, many people turn to fishing to supply some of their food, when fish are in abundant supply (Tsai & Ali 1997). A few people, largely Hindus of the low *jele* caste, fish full-time for much of the year. They sell the bulk of their catch to the local community and beyond. In the dry months when fish numbers plummet, the fishermen turn to other occupations to eke out a living such as day laborers or rickshaw pullers. But they face increasing problems and their numbers have been decreasing. They are the poorer members of the community (Table 1).

Table 1: Fishing and other occupations (%) (respondents =70)[7]

	Land holding categories		
	1	2	3
Full-time fishing	37	28.8	10
Part-time fishing	63	71.2	90
Proportion (%) of income from fishing	69.6	66.9	24.9
Other occupations			
Farming	32	57.14	90
Day labour	20	5.7	
Rickshaw puller	8	5.7	
Fish trade	8	5.7	
Animal rearing	4	5.7	
Govt. service	-	-	10

Land holding categories: 1 = <0.05 acre [n=25]; 2 = 0.05-0.2 acre [n=35]; 3 = >0.2 acre [n=10][8]

Source: Authors' compilation.

The 'professional' fishermen organise themselves in cooperatives in order to lease access to water bodies from the government (Table 1), but powerful Muslim families deprive them of any control. Furthermore, Muslims who cannot find other work have encroached, often violently, on their traditional fishing rights. For instance, the Agcharan Fishermen's Cooperative (comprising Hindu fishermen) used to control all Charan beel but has seen the powerful Khan families of Pachcahran gradually take it over, initially annexing one-eighth of the water body and then a quarter and now a half; the fishermen describe the Khans as 'invaders' (Alam 2001b). When full-time fishing was seen as an unclean occupa-

---

7 We thank our colleagues Mizanur Rahman and Somen Dewan for help with the survey that supplied data, conducted in Agcharan and Pascharan villages of the Charan region.

8 While stratification according landholding is questionable, for using a single criterion (Scoones 1995), landholding in Bangladesh correlates well with wealth ranking (Adams et al. 1997).

tion inherited by low caste persons, it protected fish stocks, as other members of society avoided it because it was 'polluting' (Alam 2001a). The Hindu fishermen employ techniques that ensure the conservation of fish numbers [e.g. use nets of a gauge that allow fry to escape – Table 2]. With no such customary practices, the Muslim newcomers have reduced fish stocks by using tackle such as small mesh nets and closing sluices to trap fish in limited areas. They reportedly bribe the Fisheries Department staff, who are supposed to enforce bans on illegal fishing methods to conserve fish fry. Consequently, fish populations are declining through overexploitation. The extensive disruptions to the hydrological cycle, notably through the construction of flood protection devices, have exacerbated the problem, and fisher families consequently displaced have joined the human flood of dispossessed persons who eke out an existence by day laboring, pulling rickshaws, petty trading, and so on in towns and rural areas.

Local people say that the FAP has damaged livelihoods in two ways as a result of embankment and sluice gates interrupting the monsoon flood. Firstly, it has devastated fisheries, and secondly, together with the HYV revolution, it has made farming more vulnerable to shocks.

HYDROLOGICAL UNCERTAINTIES

Every year, in the month of *Ashar* (June and July), the monsoon rains bring large volumes of water to the Bengal delta, although the extent of flooding can vary from one year to another (Chowdhury 1996; Hofer & Messerli 2006). While there is some predictability at the regional level, there is considerable uncertainty at the local one. The land floods to different depths depending on elevation, with the highest settled land standing clear, unless the flood is exceptional. People in Charan village talk of flood waters reaching five hands (pach hat) deep on cultivable land, which about is about 2.25m, but some years they are half this depth. The water fills all the water bodies – the canals, lakes, ponds and ditches – and the rivers swell, regularly bursting their banks and braiding to produce new channels and islands. The large rivers become virtual inland seas, the opposite bank not visible.

While the embankment system aims to contain watercourses and prevent flood waters spreading out over wide areas as previously, this concentration of water flow can have devastating consequences if the engineering fails (Brammer 2004). The confinement of river courses between embankments results in increased silt deposition on the confined river bed, which, as people observe, may build up to dangerous extents, the river becoming higher than the surrounding land. When the embankments that control such rivers burst, the resulting flash floods can devastate considerable areas of crops. Such unpredictable and un-manageable flash floods have increased considerably in occurrence, and river bank erosion has increased alarmingly with such events, wreaking increased and devastating damage locally.

Not all erosion events are totally destructive, though. The swirling action of rivers can produce doho 'whirlpool pits' that can subsequently provide shelter for fish. There are several such whirlpool refuges in the Shapai and Langulia rivers of the Charan region. One that resulted in the destruction of a banana stand and is called *kalakupar doho* (the banana garden whirlpool pit), and another is called *bhangabarir doho* (whirlpool pit at eroded house), after the bank erosion that destroyed some houses near Balla village. Erosion and sedimentation are particular concerns for char island dwellers, as they destroy and create the land on which they depend (Schmuck-Widmann 2001).

Water levels start to fall from the month of Ashin and rivers return to their courses. Many rivers previously had currents of saf pani 'clean water' flowing constantly along their 'roots', even in the driest drought month of *Chaitraya*, and contained some fish throughout the year. But many now dry up in some years, together with canals and lakes. It is common today to see carts and rickshaws using dry riverbeds as thoroughfares. The associated droughts and increasing irregularities in the seasons are possible evidence of the impacts of climate change, which may be compounding the problems resulting from flood control engineering.

Figure 5: Sluice gate above river at Banla Khola, Pabna

Source: Sarder Shafiqul Alam, Bangladesh Center for Advanced Studies, 2005.

The total drying up of waterways and water bodies has predictably impacted on the ecosystem, with has declined in plant and animal life. And when the monsoon rains replenish the dry riverbeds, the water is *ghola, turbid*, unsuitable for plants and creatures that depend on clear water, but some introduced plants are thriving in these conditions, notably the water hyacinth (*Eichhornia crassipes*), which grows vigorously and clogs up waterways. When it rots it further reduces water quality to the detriment of local aquatic life. The reduction of river beds to pools of water is also impacting on human health, resulting in skin diseases contracted from bathing, and also linked to increases in illnesses such as diarrhoea and hepatitis.

FISHING UNCERTAINTIES

Large quantities of fish fry used to come with the Ashaira pani, 'the Ashar month's flood water', to join those hatched from eggs spawned in local water bodies. Older people recall how large numbers of fish used to arrive in local water bodies and comment on the marked decline. Fishermen used to catch more fish than they could sell and sometimes threw many back into the water. There is widespread agreement in the Charan region that the crash in fish populations is one of the most significant changes they have witnessed in the last 30 years or so. People named a total of 23 fish species as either extinct locally or greatly reduced in numbers, including the fish that 'walks' out of water.[9] All respondents in a random questionnaire survey of 70 men, including both full- and part-time fishermen, thought that catches have declined significantly, for which they offered the following four reasons: a decrease in fisheries' area, fish disease, overfishing, and related to this the use of fine mesh current *jal* 'nets'.

The most frequently cited reason is that the construction of embankments, sluice gates, roads, and associated barriers has disrupted natural water movement. In the Tangail area, fisheries have been badly affected by such attempts to control water flow, with the disruption of water supply to canals and beel lakes seriously hitting poor Hindu fishermen's livelihood activities (Alam 2001a). Embankments along rivers such as the *jamuna* obstruct the entrance of fish fry into many local water bodies such as lakes and canals. The sluice gate between the river and the beel 'lake' at Bhuapur in the Charan region remains closed, for instance, at the beginning of the monsoon, disrupting the flow of the naya pani 'new water' and impeding fish movement and the arrival of the *nayali mach*, 'new fish' (FAP 20 1994). Furthermore, the silting up of local rivers and linking

9 On the richness of fish resources in the region previously, see Doha 1973; also Alam 2001.

canals because of reduced water flow has diminished routes for fish movement and effectively decreased the areas into which they migrate in large numbers.

The contemporary fall in water levels, even the drying up of rivers and other water bodies in the dry season, attributed in part to these infrastructure developments, amplifies these effects (Minkin/Boyce 1994), and many of the 'mother fish' that remain locally die before they spawn. Some government agencies and NGOs have started projects to build on the local practice of *katha* 'sanctuary pit' construction (Table 4), which mimics the natural doho 'whirlpool pit' and provides deepwater locations in lakes where fish can take refuge, often with tree branches in them to give further shelter. However, there are problems protecting the fish in these places from poaching, and sometimes they dry up completely.

It is not only interventions in the delta's river system but also the growing human population's demand for food that is relentlessly increasing the pressure on fish populations through overfishing and unrestricted hatch collection (Lewis, Wood and Gregory 1996:56). Increasing numbers of newcomer Muslim fishermen are using fine meshed nets that catch not only *renu pona* 'fry' but also fish eggs (Table 2). The fewer fish arriving are caught at an early stage in their development and fewer are entering extensive water bodies, where they are less easily caught and they have a chance to grow large and spawn.

Table 2: Fishing equipment (respondents=70).[10]

	Land holding categories		
	1	**2**	**3**
Types of gear used (%)			
Seine net (Ber jal)	48	85.7	80
Current net (Current jal)	-	5.7	30
Seine net (Dhora jal)	12	2.9	-
lift net (Khora jal)	8	5.7	-
Push net (Thela jal)	68	62.9	70
Cast net (Jhaki jal)	68	51.4	80
Trap (Polo)	-	5.7	20
% possessed boat	52	62.9	40
% borrowed money to purchase gear	84	82.9	50
% borrowed money from:			
NGO	85.8	86.2	40
Private lender	14.3	17.2	10
Av. rate of interest (%) per month	4.4	3.7	4.5

Land holding categories: 1 = <0.05 acre [n=25]; 2 = 0.05-0.2 acre [n=35]; 3 = >0.2 acre [n=10]

* Note all respondents bought gear, none made their own.

Source: Authors' compilation.

With disruption to the natural reproduction cycle and falls in fish numbers, development agencies have turned to promoting aquaculture as a way of increasing fish supply (Lewis et al. 1996). Large artificial ponds today are a common sight in villages and are stocked with exotic fish such as *Tilapia (Oreochromis mosambica)*, *Karfew (Cyprinus carpio)*, silver carp (*Hypophthalmichthys molitrix*), and grass carp (*Ctenopharyngodon idellus*), which escape regularly from such ponds when overfilled during the monsoon flood and compete with local species, further stressing these populations, damaging fisheries, and increasing the uncertainties that fishermen face. (In addition, people complain that these introduced fish have 'no taste at all'). The promotion of these fish has impacted negatively on aquatic resources and the local ecology, placing some local species at a competitive disadvantage.

---

10 For details of fishing equipment, see Ahmed 1970.

OTHER AQUATIC RESOURCE UNCERTAINTIES

The decrease in aquatic plants (Karim 1993), attributed to changes in the annual flood pattern, has also impacted on fish, reducing places of shelter, such as leaves to hide under, and food for fish. This disruption to the ecology has also impacted on poorer families that depend on certain plants that have decreased in occurrence as food, particularly in crisis times. These include the stems of the padma lotus (*Nymphaea caerulea*), which used to grow prolifically in lakes, and the roots of the *shaluk* lily (*Nymphaea nouchali*) and *ghetu* (*Aponogeton natans*) plants. The poorest families, notably of day laborers who have an uncertain income, may fall back on these wild food sources in difficult times, women and children gathering them from water bodies (Sadeque 1990). The decreased availability of these plants increases the uncertainty of already precarious livelihoods and may threaten the survival of the poorest in the rural community. In discussing these matters, Situ Mia mentioned the local saying "surviving on taro leaf and ghetu" ("*kochu ghechu kheye beche thaka*"), which captures the hardship people face when they have recourse to such food sources. He spoke of the privation they experience in having to "eat this pig food" (the nomadic pig herders of Bengal feed their animals on these plants) and pointed out that "nowadays, low-lying land is not getting sufficient flood water [for these plants to flourish] and more powerful farming families are grabbing the land to farm [and so reducing the areas where these plants grow]. It is hard for poor people who depend on these resources, who cannot really survive here anymore."

Some fish also feed on aquatic animals, including various insects and water snails, and people say they are declining in numbers, too, together with frogs. Aquatic creatures also serve as food for ducks, which many women keep together with chickens, which means that they cannot afford to keep their flocks. Residents in the Charan region also say that there were large numbers of kasim turtles (*Chelydra serpentine*) previously, and specialist turtle hunters used to come from Modhupur district to catch them. The turtles have not been seen for some years. Similarly, the villagers no longer see the shushuk river dolphin (*Platanista gangetica*) that used to be a regular visitor to the Langulia and Shapai rivers.

Some bird populations, notably those that feed on fish, have also declined, such as the bok Asian Openbill stork (*Anastomus oscitans*), which people recall was once so common that large areas of lakes appeared white. Changes to natural vegetation around villages have also impacted on bird life, the increased occurrence of droughts affecting plant communities, with a decline in the bushes that provide shelter for animals, notably birds. As some char dwellers[11] living on the nearby Jamuna River commented to Schmuck-Widmann (2001: 113), "before the river became 'crazy' [...] the region was covered with trees and bushes; many song birds and animals lived in the forest." The cumulative effect of these changes is clearly considerable and has not only reduced local biodiversity worryingly (Shiva 1992; Mokhlesur 1995), but also increased livelihood uncertainties for those least able to handle them.

FARMING UNCERTAINTIES

The decline in chamara 'deepwater rice' cultivation has also affected fish populations. The long stems of these rapidly growing rice varieties, which keep up with rising floodwaters (to depths of 5 meters), not only provide shelter for fish but also snag food. There is a folk rhyme that intimates the paddy's merits (see Ehlert, this volume, for Vietnamese proverbs):

Istir maijhe mamara jadi thake nani,
Uncle is the best of all relatives if grandmother is still alive,
Dhaner maijhe chamara jadi thake pani
Chamara is the best of all paddies if the water level is high.

Deepwater rice is one of the two main aman monsoon season rice crops (the other consists of transplanted varieties grown on unflooded or shallowly flooded land). Broadcast sown in February-March, chamara paddy is harvested in October-November. In the other months, farmers cultivate a *rabi* ('winter crop') such as mustard, onions, potatoes or pulses that draws on soil moisture left after the deepwater rice harvest.

There are two other rice crops. The aus, sown January-February and harvested May-June as flood waters start to rise, is a short-duration, rapidly growing, and low-yielding crop, but it traditionally tides people through the lean period before the next aman harvest. The winter boro crop, which, although high yielding, was previously limited in area because it requires irrigation, is sown in October, grows through the dry winter, and is harvested before the monsoon rains. The introduction of tube wells from the mid-1980s to tap into aquifers led to this crop's rapid expansion. The control of water levels via sluice gates within the FAP polder compartments has further contributed to considerable changes in the floodplain farming regime. These technical interventions allow farmers to culti-

---

11 These are people who live on char, which are unstable islands that form in braided river courses.

vate both transplanted aman and winter boro paddy crops in a year (Hossain 1991; Ullah 1996; Alauddin/Hossain 2001). Furthermore, these rice varieties have been the target of 'green revolution' HYV plant breeding programs (Alauddin/Tisdell 1991; Dasgupta 1998; Muhammad 2004).

The tube well and compartmentalization schemes combined with HYVs have squeezed out other local rain-fed cropping regimes that cannot compete economically and thus produce lower returns (Rashid/Mallik 1995) but at some cost to many households, increasing the uncertainties they face. The tube well pumps usually belong to wealthier farmers, who may restrict others' access to irrigation water. And there are the environmental costs of exploiting groundwater supplies, which at current rates are unsustainable, together with the dangers of increasing soil salinity using water that has not been chemically monitored for salts (Barr/Gowing 1998). The consequences of such overexploitation are immediate, too, as poignantly illustrated in those regions of Bangladesh where the lowering of aquifer water tables has resulted in the oxidative release of arsenic from rock strata, poisoning many people. Some also use pumps to take water for irrigation from beel 'lakes' during the dry season, further reducing water levels and to the detriment of aquatic resources.

The change in flooding patterns and depths, resulting from FAP attempts to control watercourses, threatens the long-term fertility of the land. Farmers report a worrying gradual decline in soil quality. Before the construction of embankments, flood water spread across the land, depositing silt widely (Huq/Kamal 1993; Brammer 1996). Together with rotting crop residues, dead fish and other aquatic debris left behind by receding flood waters, this ensured that the soil maintained high kuwat 'organic matter' content. The flood defenses have interrupted this natural process (FAP 16 1993) and soils are now becoming harder, 'like rock or brick' people say, and karkosh 'harsh', their structure degraded with falling kuwat 'organic matter' content and less ras 'sap' fertile moisture: "In former times the river transported more fertile sediment [...] but 'today only sand'" (Schmuck-Widmann 2001: 113). The occurrence of flash floods makes matters worse, as these deposit quantities of coarse, sandy riverbed material that is low in natural fertilizers.

One response to declining soil fertility is to use inorganic fertilizers. The cultivation of HYVs requires the application of such fertilizers to maximise yield, together with applications of biocides, as noted, to control crop pests and diseases and the supply of adequate water through irrigation. Some think that the use of chemical fertilizer, which in solution finds its way into water courses, has contributed to the decline in fish populations. Biocides too, made up of strong insecticides, poison fish eggs and fry (Islam 1993) but the expansion of boro crop cultivation, doing away with the previous winter's break in rice cultivation across much of the floodplain, and the consequent year-round rice mono crop, inevitably results in increases in pest and disease outbreaks that require control.

ECONOMIC UNCERTAINTIES

There is a large body of literature on the outcome of the "Green Revolution's transformation of agricultural practices" (Griffin 1979; Conway/Barbier 1990; Joshi 1999; Scoones/Thompson 2011). The changes have not all been as positive as proponents argued; in particular, they have increased the vulnerability of poorer people. While the grain yields of HYV paddy are higher than traditional varieties with the correct application of inputs, and they have arguably warded off starvation (in the short-term anyway), reduced Bangladesh's food import deficit, and can earn farmers good financial returns when sold on the market, this focus on economic production and returns overlooks environmental and wider socioeconomic issues.

Regarding uncertainties, people now face not only increased natural uncertainties but also human induced ones in the shape of the capitalist market. The introduction of HYVs has undermined farmers' independence by making them dependent on the market for necessary inputs (Hossain 1989; Alauddin and Tisdell 1991). Furthermore, they have no control over these uncertainties and can become prey to market fluctuations, particularly the smaller and poorer farmers who lack the financial resources to buffer themselves against such fluctuations (Dasgupta 1998). Consequently, they commonly have to borrow money to purchase necessary inputs essential to ensuring that the new varieties give good yields, and if the price of the resulting crop is down for any reason they may be unable to repay loans and end up going deeper into debt, until they are forced to sell land to repay what they owe. They may eventually become landless. The winners under these highly imperfect market conditions are the wealthier landowners – often the moneylenders – whose land holdings increase in size.

The farmers also have less control over their supply of seed, with crop breeding centers constantly introducing new varieties as they battle to keep ahead of threats to yields such as newly evolving disease strains and pests. Farmers are likely to lose control completely if genetically modified (GM) crops become widespread – such as the Sub1a gene that 'waterproofs' rice plants, increasing their resilience to both floods and droughts (Adriano 2011) – which feature so-called 'terminator genes' that ensure the production of sterile seeds. As such, they are at the mercy of the multinational seed production companies (Shiva 2000).

The consequences of the disappearance of local varieties from the farming system, under pressure from HYVs, are the subject of much debate. The threats posed by such loss of biodiversity are considerable (Shiva 1992, 1993), and it could even undermine the breeding programs that are responsible for the losses, by ultimately reducing the genetic bank on which they draw – as evident in experiments on transferring 'snorkel' genes isolated from deepwater rice varieties to increase yields of submerged paddy (Hattori et al. 2009). Many local rice varieties have superior features to HYVs, as some are more drought tolerant, such as the *kunail boro* and *kali boro* local varieties of winter season paddy. Others yield in a shorter period, such as traditional aus season varieties, and many local paddies, notably the chamara deepwater varieties, are flood tolerant. They are also often more flavourful and preferred at mealtimes. Fazlul Haque recounted how "in the aman season I used to cultivate such varieties as *parja, kaika* and *junukra* that used to yield in a good timely way, and the *chamara* paddy that grew with the flood. The *chamara* only had a few varieties. The aus paddy had many varieties called *haita, ashakumra, bhaturi,* and *chapila* that grew in good time before the monsoon rains arrived and were full of flavour." Transgenic crops in particular – such as beta-carotene, producing so-called 'golden rice' (Ye et al. 2000; Potrykus 2001) – may also pose a threat to the environment because if their genetically engineered traits escape into the wild, they could cause unknown changes in ecosystems.

The decline in local varieties relates both to current market economic arrangements and changes in the landscape wrought by FAP engineering interventions, with introduced HYV paddies favored by these water level controlling interventions, which have proved irresistible forces, even for the most conservative farmers unable to establish profitable specialist niches for local rice varieties (Hossain 1991; Ullah 1996; Alauddin/Hossain 2001). Moreover, the economic outlook is not so rosy if we factor in the cost to farmers of long-term environmental impacts – currently treated by companies and agencies as so-called externalities (i.e. costs left off the balance sheet) – such as diminishing natural soil fertility, declining water quality and threats to supply, and the increasing occurrence of potent crop pests and virulent diseases, which are an increasing economic burden on farmers who have to purchase necessary fertilizers, water, and biocides in a race to stay ahead of these morphing environmental problems. It is possible that surface water-using, rain-fed local varieties are more cost-effective if we compare all such expenses against returns.

POLITICAL UNCERTAINTIES

The foregoing economic review omits consideration of the costs incurred by the landless members of rural society, such as *jele* caste fisherfolk. Some argue that the new cropping regimes have increased the demand for labor, particularly at bottleneck points in the farming year such as transplanting and harvest. They consequently benefit the poor, too, through increased employment opportunities, but this is questionable, particularly in view of the exploitative nature of local labor markets. While Bangladesh enjoys higher crop yields and seeks food self-sufficiency, this has not reduced poverty; rather, it has changed its character, with new forms of social exclusion and inequality. The discrediting of existing knowledge and techniques (invariably subsistence-oriented, and often environmentally well-adjusted and sustainable), with the intrusion of foreign technology, further advances outside hegemony and bolsters the power of wealthy élites that occupy positions interfacing with the national and international bodies in charge.

Figure 6: Flooded homestead at Gopal Ganj

Source: Sarder Shafiqul Alam, Bangladesh Center for Advanced Studies, 2008.

The poor are overlooked and lose further control over their own lives, paradoxically when agencies believe they may be ameliorating their grinding poverty (Dasgupta 1998). Agricultural growth driven by capitalistic market forces favors the dominant classes, extending their control over resources. Analysis of constraints perceived by different livelihood groups, according to the Sustainable Livelihoods Framework (Carney 1998), shows that it is not only lack of natural resources that is a problem for landless and marginal farmers and fishermen but also social arrangements and local institutions that limit their access to resources (Table 3 – see also Deswandi et al., this volume).[12]

---

12 We thank our colleagues Julian Barr and Graham Haylor for these data, collected during a problem census to identify floodplain production constraints, conducted along standard participatory lines during our DfID project work (Crouch 1991).

Table 3: Constraints according to transformed problem census data

Livelihood Group	Vulnerability context			Assets (deficiency of)					Structures			Processes		Ó
	Tre nds	Sho cks	Seaso-nality	Natu-ral	Soci al	Phy-sical	Hu man	Finan cial	Publ ic	Pri-vate*	Intra-HH	Local institut.	Formal govern.	Points
Landless	2		23	15	6	5	3	4	8	5		32		100
Sharecroppers	10	1	8	11			10	12	15	23		10		100
Medium/large land owners	9	2	4	6		26	7	8	13	15		6	4	100
Seasonal fishermen	41		6					20				13	20	100
Professional fishermen	44				7			16			1	33		100
Poor women	1	8	19	33		2	1	14	1	8		10	5	100
Wealthy women		8	6	13	5	3	14	9	14	2	6	22		100

Source: Authors' compilation.

The policy of flood protection and its associated conversion of low-lying depressed areas to year-round farmable land through the construction of embanked polders have had, for example, not only negative environmental consequences, disrupting fish reproduction and reducing fish stocks, but also political repercussions, interfering with poor people's traditional access to common resources (Table 4). Such resources, providing uncertain or poor returns and being uneconomically labor-intensive, were not previously attractive propositions. The poor often rely on such common land and water bodies (Mokhlesur 1995) to eke out their meagre livelihoods (Sadeque 1990) and interventions may increase the value of such resources, attracting the wealthy and powerful who seek to control them. If they evict the poor, following an intervention that increases productive capacity, the consequences can be dire. While landowner farmers profit from the combination of an extended growing season and HYV crops, the Hindu fishers lose out (Jansen 1990). The polders have displaced the Hindu *jele* caste fisherfolk from a large part of their traditional fishery grounds, where customary access rights pertained, thus further destabilizing their livelihoods and increasing the uncertainties they face (Rahman 1986; Ahmed 1997). Before the FAP interventions, fishermen effectively enjoyed open access rights over low-lying fields when flooded. After the interventions, they were excluded because of the attenuated flooding of arable land, which is now farmed more or less the year round, with water levels managed by sluice gates. Some landowners have even established private aquaculture ponds within these areas, where previously monsoon flooding would have dispersed stocks. The FAP has also made it more feasible to control water bodies that nominally remain open fisheries. These become highly productive resources when combined with development-funded fish stocking programs and poor people find access restricted (even where projects try to work through local cooperatives). The wealthy, overlooking these environmental implications, justify such processes as the inevitable cost of increasing efficiency, but for the poor they amount to increasing the affluence of the rich – and at their expense.

Table 4: Access to water bodies (respondents=70)

	Land holding categories		
	1	2	3
% fish in:			
Lake	96	100	90
River	68	45.7	20
Pond	44	57.0	30
Canal	52	42.9	50
Lease water body fishing rights directly from Dept. Fisheries:			
% as individual	16	42	30
% as member of co-operative	60	58	30
% sub-lease fishing rights in water body [from local lessee]	64	97	60
Av. cost of lease (Tk./season per person)	1200	1800	1800
% respondents fish in katha	48	62.8	60
Av. no. of katha used per person	1.58	2.1	1.7
% respondents directly lease katha	44	0	30
% sub-lease katha access [from local lessee]	8.3	62.8	40

Land holding categories: 1 = <0.05 acre [n=25]; 2 = 0.05-0.2 acre [n=35]; 3 = >0.2 acre [n=10]
* Lease periods = 6 months. Katha 'pits' used from November to April

Source: Authors' compilation.

We witnessed such politicking firsthand on a partner DfID natural resources project in Rajshahi District, where rich landowners advocated the draining of the beel 'lake' by excavating a canal to give them access to more land for rice cultivation. They claimed to have title deeds to the land under water, which is not as improbable as it sounds in a country where the drying up of water bodies occurs naturally across the floodplain. The landowners saw the project as an opportunity to speed up this slow natural process to their advantage. The poor, particularly those who relied heavily on fishing, were encouraged to speak out at segregated stakeholder sessions and predictably opposed the suggestion to deprive them of a common resource. The wealthy minority were angry, expecting their poor and landless clients to go along with whatever they mooted, as was usual (Islam 1974). Furthermore, an environmental assessment (Barr 2000: 33-34) indicated a range of negative consequences for fish breeding, biodiversity, the water table, and so on. One village leader, addressing a meeting, warned everyone against collaborating with the project and talked of protecting the beel lake, as it was part of a British plot to retake colonial control of Bengal. More worryingly, the landowners forbade people to fish over their land under the lake. In another display of power, following elections, landowners refused to enter into sharecropping arrangements with poor members of their villages, or employ them as day laborers, effectively depriving them locally of an important source of income by entering into arrangements with people from elsewhere. The issue was finally resolved by setting up a committee with members from all sections of the community to disburse funds for attending training courses, supporting duck rearing, purchasing tree seedlings, and so on. It was not exactly business as usual, but the wealthy regained indirect control of the incoming resources to their advantage. Some colleagues justified the episode as a mutual learning experience for all, empowering the poor by including them as stakeholders in the discussions. The experience was not the naive exception, to judge from the burgeoning literature on conflict management in development contexts (Warner/Jones 1998; Matiru 2000; Castro/Nielsen 2001; Warner 2001).

The polder system has reshaped the landscape and relations between various stakeholders and the land, permanently altering fishing and farming opportunities. Conflicts of interest are not only between fishers and farmers but also different groups of farmers. These focus on operational constraints and problems within flood control compartments and largely concern the regulation of water volumes. Disagreements center on the timing of the operation of sluice gates, particularly during the monsoon. Landowners on higher land want to postpone the release of water, while those on lower land, where inundation is deeper, want to discharge it accordingly (Lewins 2004). The outcomes of these tussles depend for the large part on power relations within communities, the larger and wealthier landowners seeking to use the influence they have to prevail over others. They may, for instance, pressurize those in debt to them and may use access to winter water, as tube well owners and operators, as a lever, too. Farmers whose plots are more deeply immersed have more influence over decisions on timing where low-lying land predominates within a polder, as at Charan, with their larger numbers. The result of these discussions is always uncertain regarding water release, and it impacts unpredictably on farmers' cultivation decisions.

CLIMATE CHANGE UNCERTAINTIES

The adverse effects of climate change could negate recent increases in agricultural production. In its fourth assessment, the *UN Intergovernmental Panel on Climate Change* reported that, by 2050, rice and wheat production in Bangladesh might fall by 8 per cent and 32 per cent, respectively, and that approximately 1,000 square kilometers of cultivated land, including areas culturing sea products, are likely to become salt marsh (Ministry of Food and Relief Division 2010). The Bay of Bengal, as noted, is a region likely to experience substantial climate change impacts as a result of two processes: Firstly, increases in sea levels, with the permanent inundation of low-lying regions, and secondly, the melting of Himalayan glaciers, increasing the danger of large-scale flash floods (Hofer/ Messerli 2006). The pattern of the seasons is changing, too. For example, north-westerly winds bringing *kal baishaki* thunderstorms arrived in April previously and people could prepare for them, but now they occur unpredictably and without warning, very often damaging crops. Small farmers are particularly vulnerable, having limited capacity to cope with such events, thus exacerbating livelihood uncertainties. Some perceive an increase in the occurrence of natural disasters in the last twenty years as evidence of climate change. In coastal regions, recent tidal surges have broken all records. Cyclone Aila (2009) not only killed hundreds of people but also devastated mangroves and polders; residents of Satkhira, a badly affected district, say that if the embankments are repaired they will need to be raised some two meters to offer any form of surge protection (Khan 2009).

Local people are aware of changes in weather patterns, as they have to contend with the often devastating consequences (see Ehlert, this volume). They have picked up on the global climate change debate to varying extents and combine what they hear with their own cultural insights and cosmology to understand events and manage their responses accordingly. Local solutions include, for instance, changing subsistence strategies, adopting new farming methods, modifying fishing technologies, and migrating elsewhere. It is necessary for those who plan measures to cope with the consequences of climate change, such as policymakers and their scientific advisors, to appreciate these views and related responses, which represent profound knowledge of local ecology and livelihood strategies built up through generations of experience, albeit these may be expressed in idioms that appear strange (Sillitoe 2000). It is difficult, for example, for outsiders to comprehend how beliefs in demon fish lurking in lakes, and the practice of Hindu puja rituals to the Durga and Gonga deities, can have any relevance to environmental issues, although they intimately inform the understanding and practices of Bangladeshi fishermen. Similarly, the Bawa festival in the Charan region, which attracts people from far and wide and occurs in the month of *Poush* (December to January), when people parade to the *beel* 'lake' with fishing gear, dancing to the accompaniment of singing and blowing buffalo horns to celebrate the fish catch, tells us something about local views of aquatic resources.

Figure 7: Flooded railway line at Brahman Baria

Source: Chaman Sikandar Julkernine, 2004.

LOCAL KNOWLEDGE AND CLIMATE CHANGE

The main natural uncertainties that people face include the extent of flooding each year, the possibility of sudden flash floods (especially if flood defenses fail), and in the dry season the occurrence of droughts and the disappearance of watercourses. Climate change threatens to exacerbate these weather-related uncertainties considerably. Uncertainties over fish populations concern flood control interruptions to water flow bringing new fry, the impacts of overfishing (often using inappropriate gear), and ecosystem issues, which include exotic fish escaping from overfilled aquaculture ponds. Hydrological interventions have also impacted on wild plants, increasing livelihood uncertainties for the poor in particular, who rely on some of these for food in hard times; they have also impacted on wildlife populations, further exacerbating insecurities. The uncertainties faced by farmers include concerns over continued soil fertility in line with changes to the flooding regime combined with the heavy use of fertilizers, which together with biocides are polluting water sources in uncertain ways; for instance, in the dry season the supply of irrigation water is uncertain for many Economic uncertainties concern the working of the market. Farmers, dependent on erratic market arrangements for the supply of inputs necessary to maximize HYV yields, including sound seed, face uncertain market fluctuations. Further uncertainties concern crop breeding generally, with the loss of many traditional varieties to genetic counterparts. Political uncertainties revolve locally around changes in patron-client relations and conflicts over access to common resources and the operation of flood control facilities such as sluice gates. And on top of these uncertainties are those of population growth, which is increasing pressure on all resources.

Local perceptions and practices need to be accommodated in the formulation of any effective climate change mitigation and adaptation strategies, in line with arguments put forward with respect to local knowledge, which have been in development for some decades now (Sillitoe 1998; Sillitoe Bicker/Pottier 2002; Sillitoe, Dixon/Barr 2005 – see also Hornidge, this volume). The challenges faced in relating such knowledge to these problems are great, a socio-cultural and epistemological gulf opening up between the contrasting philosophies of living with nature versus dominating nature. The assumption is that while the different paradigms cannot be reconciled, nonetheless it should be possible to devise a way of exchanging knowledge across the gap. We should beware interpreting and testing local experience and knowledge according to our canons alone, reproducing our dominant worldview, which may be misleading, even inimical, to the interests of the poor. There is a danger of distorting their knowledge, allowing scientific and development discourse to define them instead.

Failure to accommodate local perceptions and practices in formulating climate change mitigation and adaptation strategies may lead people to reject these measures as not matching their understanding of problems and needs – as has happened previously in development contexts – or result in top-down impositions that communities will resist. The rise of "ecological nationalism" across Bangladesh and India (Cederlof/Sivaramakrishnanan 2006), which challenges changes to farming systems relating to their environmental impacts, is a possible response to ignoring local ways and knowledge. One experience we had with a senior DfID natural resources advisor, who took us to an FAP-constructed embankment with a large trench dug through it and asked "Why are these peasants doing this, don't they understand that the embankment is there to protect them and their land?" graphically illustrates the point. Enquiries in the local community soon revealed that the embankment had prevented floodwaters draining away and desperate farmers had breached it so that they could proceed with cultivating their otherwise inundated plots in good time.

This is not to argue that there is no place for outside technical or other assistance, only that this needs to be sensitive to the local context. Rapid and extensive change may render local knowledge less effective, even inadequate, with the new environmental uncertainties leading to knowledge uncertainties as a result. The assault on the water environment, for instance, resulting from extensive flood prevention engineering schemes, threatens to do violence to people's understanding of fish and other aquatic resources. We should not romanticise local knowledge and practices (see Antweiler, this volume), as these may be unable to cope with some of the new challenges posed by climate change, putting poor and vulnerable communities with few other resources and low resilience particularly at risk. A related issue with respect to such transformations increasing uncertainties is the evident loss of local knowledge under the pressure of economic and environmental changes, which are eroding the knowledge base that people may draw on in response to climate change impacts and for survival. This is evident, for instance, in the loss of local crop varieties, as noted earlier. As these disappear, so does associated farmers' knowledge. Such local knowledge is often not formally recorded and learned but passed on in the doing – so, if the activities to which it relates cease, the knowledge may disappear within a generation, which has recently led to calls in biodiversity conservation contexts for the protection of bio-cultural diversity (Posey 1999; Stepp, Wyndham/Zarger 2002; Laird 2002).

Furthermore, the assistance may be two-way. While climate change uncertainties may challenge local knowledge and practices, communities are not helpless and will respond in some measure; indeed, they will have to, to survive. Policymakers, scientists, and technocrats may have something to learn from people's ability to innovate and modify existing practices and to develop locally embedded adaptation strategies to reduce their vulnerability. One example concerns the floating gardens pioneered in parts of Bangladesh that allow households to grow vegetables such as cucurbits and okra on flooded land. They comprise rafts made from water hyacinths, some eight meters by one, with a layer of compost on top; the previous year's rotten beds often serving as compost. Such cross-cultural lessons may go in many directions; for example, the Bangladeshi floating garden experiments might draw on the famous floating islands of Lake Titicaca and the Aztec chinampas cultivation system in the Valley of Mexico (Orlove 2002; Ayres 2004).

AVOIDING PREVIOUS MISTAKES

So, 'Why did the fish cross the road?' 'To join another school', namely the one that considers local knowledge. The consequences of FAP engineering interventions, combined with the introduction of HYVs and associated technology, illustrate the dangers of imposing solutions on people without a full understanding of their situation and knowledge. The lessons are pertinent because we face the challenges of climate change, where FAP embankment-like mistakes could prove disastrous for communities. We may even need to cultivate a different mindset, learning from local views evolved over generations, to confront these challenges. The inhabitants of the Bay of Bengal are arguably well equipped to handle the uncertainties of climate change, living in a region where such ambiguity is commonplace, and where floods, droughts, and cyclones have been features of everyday life for millennia.

The delta environment of Bengal is naturally a dynamic one where the landscape can change dramatically in short periods of time, with new char 'sediment islands' appearing and old ones being swept away and the braided rivers suddenly changing their courses and leaving behind new ox-bow lakes while old beel 'lakes' gradually fill with sediment and disappear. The inhabitants of the region have adapted to this uncertain environment, not seeking to control it as in western engineering but living with it by, for example, quickly colonizing new char (Elahi/ Rogge 1990; Schmuck-Widmann 1996; Mamun 1996): "The *char*-people appreciate the *bonna* [flood], because it irrigates and fertilizes the fields, kills pests and enables the fish to move and spawn" (Schmuck-Widmann 2001: 74). Their view is epitomized in the borrowed Arabic phrase 'Insha'Allah', 'it is God's will'; a more fatalistic and arguably realistic attitude faced by these natural forces than the confident, controlling western view. Agencies need to realise that cultural diversity and local people's knowledge and practices should contribute significantly to our understanding and protection of natural environments.

ACKNOWLEDGMENTS

We thank the UK Department for International Development (Natural Resources Systems Programme projects R6744 and R6756) and UNESCO (Local and Indigenous Knowledge Systems – LINKS – Programme) for funding the research reported on here. The fieldwork was conducted in Agcharan and Pascharan villages of Charan mauza under Kalihati thana, in the district of Tangail, central Bangladesh. The views expressed are those of the authors and not necessarily of DFID or UNESCO.

REFERENCES

Adams, A.M./ Evans, G./Mohammed, R./ Farnsworth, J. (1997): Socioeconomic stratification by wealth ranking: is it valid? World Development 25 (7), 1165-1172.

Adriano, J.D. (2011): 'Waterproofing' gene may also protect rice from droughts (http://www.scidev.net/en/news/-waterproofing-gene-may-also-protect-rice-from-droughts.html).

Ahmed, M. (1997): Socioeconomic and policy issues in the floodplain fisheries of Bangladesh. In: Tsai, Ch. F A/Ali, Mohammad, Y. (eds.): Openwater fisheries of Bangladesh, Dhaka: University Press Limited, 89-98.

Ahmed, N. (1970): Fishing gear of East Pakistan. Dhaka: East Pakistan Government Press.

Alam, M. (2001a): Slaves of water: indigenous knowledge of fisheries on the floodplain of Bangladesh, Unpub. PhD thesis: University of Durham.

Alam, M. (2001b): Access to fishing waters: experience of the Hindu fishers of Charan. Grassroots Voice 4(3): 29-69.

Alauddin, M./Hossain, M. (2001): Environment and agriculture in a developing economy: problems and prospects for Bangladesh, Cheltenham: Edward Elgar.

Alauddin, M./Tisdell, C. (1991): The "green revolution" and economic development: the process and its impact in Bangladesh, Basingstoke: Macmillan.

Ayres, A. (2004): Xochimilco's Sunken Treasure. New Scientist 192 (2442): 50-51.

Barr, J.F./ Gowing, J.G. (1998): Rice production in floodplains: Issues for water management in Bangladesh. In: Pereira, L. S./ Gowing, J. G. (eds.). Water and the Environment. Innovative issues in irrigation and drainage, London: E/ FN Spon, an imprint of Routledge, 308-317.

Barr, J. (ed.) (2000): Final Technical Report for Project No. R 6756, Investigation of livelihood strategies and resource use patterns in floodplain production systems in Bangladesh: Submitted to DfID's Natural Resources Systems Programme.

Boyce, J.K. (1990): Birth of a megaproject: political economy of flood control in Bangladesh. Environmental Management, 14: 419-428.

Brammer, H. (1996): The Geography of the Soils of Bangladesh, Dhaka: University Press.

Brammer, H. (2004): Can Bangladesh be protected from floods? Dhaka: University Press.

Carney, D. (ed.) (1998): Sustainable Rural Livelihoods. What contribution can we make? London: Department for International Development.

Castro, A.P./Nielsen, E. (2001): Indigenous People and Co-Management: Implications for Conflict Management. Environmental Science and Policy, Vol. 4 (4-5), 229-239.

Cederlof, G./Sivaramakrishnanan, K. (2006): Ecological nationalisms: nature, livelihoods/ identities in South Asia, New Delhi: Permanent Black.

Chowdhury, J.U. (1996): Flood Control in a Floodplain Country: Experiences of Bangladesh, Dhaka: IFCDR.

Clement, A./Chadwick, M.T./ Barr, J.F. (eds) (2000): People's livelihoods at the land-water interface: Emerging perspectives on interactions between people and the floodplain environment. Proceedings of Symposium held at LGED Bhaban, Agargaon, Dhaka.

Conway, G. R./Barbier, E. B. (1990): After the green revolution: sustainable agriculture for development, Earthscan, London.

Cook, B.R. (2010): Knowledges, controversies and floods: national-scale flood management in Bangladesh, Unpub. PhD thesis: University of Durham (http://etheses.dur.ac.uk/371/).

Crouch, B.R. (1991): The Problem Census: Farmer-Centred Problem Identification, In: Haverkort, B./ van der Kamp, J. /Waters-Bayer, A. (eds.): Joining Farmers Experiments. ILEIA Readings in Sustainable Agriculture, London: Intermediate Technology Publications,171-182.

Crow, B./Lindquist, A./Wilson, D. (1995): Sharing the Ganges: the politics and technology of river development, New Delhi; London: Sage Publications in association with the Book Review Literary Trust.

Dasgupta, A. (1998): Growth with equity: the new technology and agrarian change in Bengal, New Delhi: Manohar Publishers/Distributors.

Doha, S. (1973): Fishes of the districts of Mymensingh and Tangail. Bangladesh Journal of Zoology 1 (1): 1-10.

Elahi, K.M./Rogge, J.R. (1990): Riverbank erosion, flood and population displacement in Bangladesh: a report on the Riverbank Erosion Impact Study. Dhaka: Jahangirnagar University REIS.

FAP 16 (1993): Effects of flood protection on the fertility of soils at the Chandpur Irrigation Project, Dhaka: FAP 16 Environmental Study – Special Studies Program.

FAP 20 (1994): Special Fisheries Study. Tangail Compartmentalization Pilot Project, Dhaka: FAP 20 Final Report.

Griffin, K. (1979): The political economy of agrarian change: an essay on the green revolution. London: Macmillan.

Hofer, T./ Messerli, B. (2006): Floods in Bangladesh: history, dynamics, and rethinking the role of the Himalayas, Japan: United Nations University Press.

Hossain, M. (1989): Green revolution in Bangladesh: impact on growth and distribution of income, Dhaka: University Press Ltd.

Hossain, M. (1991): Agriculture in Bangladesh: Performance, problems and prospects, Dhaka: University Press Limited.

Huq, S./Rahman, A.A. (1994): An environmental profile of Bangladesh. In: Rahman, A. A./ Haider, R./ Huq, S./ Jansen, E. G. (eds): Environment and Development (Chapter 2), Dhaka: University of Dhaka Press.

Huq, S.M.I./Kamal, G.M. (1993): Characteristics and dynamics of wetland soils. In: Nishat, A./ Hossain, Z./ Roy, M.l K./ Karim, A. (eds.): Freshwater wetlands in Bangladesh: Issues and approaches for management (Ch. 4). Gland: The World Conservation Union, IUCN.

Islam, A.K.A. (1974): A Bangladesh village: conflict and cohesion: an anthropological study of politics, Cambridge, Mass: Schenkman Pub. Co.

Islam, A.K.M.N. (1993): Limnology and pollution of wetlands. In: Nishat, A./Hossain, Z./Roy, M.K./Karim A (eds.) Freshwater wetlands in Bangladesh: Issues and approaches for management (Ch. 8). Gland: The World Conservation Union, IUCN.

Islam, M.R. (1987): The Ganges water dispute: international legal aspects. Dhaka: University Press Limited.

Jansen, E.G. (1990): Rural Bangladesh: Competition for scarce resources. Dhaka: University Press Limited.

Joshi M.V. (1999): Green revolution and its impacts. Delhi: A.P.H. Publishing.

Khan, Asadullah M. (2009): Coping with Aila devastation. The Daily Star, June 6. (http://www.thedailystar.net/newDesign/news-details.php?nid=91358).

Karim, A. (1993): Plant diversity and their conservation in freshwater wetlands. In: Nishat, A./ Hossain, Z./ Roy, M. K./ Karim, A. (eds.) Freshwater wetlands in Bangladesh: Issues and approaches for management (Ch. 6). Gland: The World Conservation Union, IUCN.

Karim, K./Rahman, A. (1995): Bangladesh: assessment of the vulnerability of coastal areas to climate change and sea-level rise; a pilot study of Bangladesh. Proceedings of World Coast. Ministry of Transport, Public Works and Water Management, The Netherlands, 469-487.

Laird, S. (ed.) (2002): Biodiversity and traditional knowledge: equitable partnerships in practice, London: Earthscan (People and Plants Conservation Series).

Lewins, R. (2004): Integrated floodplain management – institutional environments and participatory methods. Project No. R8195 Final Technical Report for DFID Natural Resources System Programme.

Lewis, D.J./ Wood, G./Gregory, D. (1996): Trading the silver seed: Local knowledge and market mortalities in aquacultural development, Dhaka: University Press Limited.

Mamun, M.Z. (1996): Awareness, preparedness and adjustment measures of riverbank erosion-prone people: A case study. Disasters 20 (1): 68-74.

Matiru, V./Hart, N./ Castro, P. (eds) (2000): Conflict and Natural Resource Management. Rome: Food and Agriculture Organization of the United Nations (FAO), 20 pp. (Online: http://www.fao.org/forestry/foris/pdf /conflict/conf-e.pdf.}.

Ministry of Food and Relief Division (2010): National Plan for Disaster Management (2010-2015), Dhaka: Disaster Management Bureau, Bangladesh.

Minkin, S.F./Boyce, J.K. (1994): 'Development' drains the fisheries of Bangladesh. The Amicus Journal Fall 1994,.36-40.

Mokhlesur, R.M. (1995): Wetlands and biodiversity: A case study of common property resources in Bangladesh. Unpublished paper presented at the 5th International Association for the Study of Common Property Conference, Bodo, Norway.

Muhammad, A. (2004): Waterlogged again: why control measures have not worked. Economic and Political Weekly, 39 (31) (Jul. 31-Aug. 6, 2004), 3447-3449.

Naseem, S. B./Sillitoe, P. /Khan, A. /Alam M./Rahman, K./Barr, J. (2001): A study of people's livelihoods affected by prolonged water congestion: changing scenarios. Grassroots Voice 3 (3): 28-41.

Orlove, B. (2002): Lines in the water: nature and culture at Lake Titicaca. Berkeley, Calif.: University of California Press.

Paul, B.K. (1995): Farmers' responses to the Flood Action Plan (FAP) of Bangladesh: An empirical study. World Development 23 (2): 299-309.

Posey, D.A. (ed.) (1999): Cultural and spiritual values of biodiversity: a complementary contribution to the global biodiversity assessment, London: Intermediate Technology Publications (for the U.N. Environment Programme).

Potrykus, I. (2001): Golden Rice and Beyond. Plant Physiology 125: 1157-1161.

Rahman, A. (1995): Beel Dakatia: the environmental consequences of a development disaster, Dhaka: University Press.

Rahman, M.M. (1986): Small-scale fisheries in Bangladesh: some socioeconomic problems and issues. Bangladesh Journal of Agricultural Economics 9 (2): 97-110.

Rasid, H./ Mallik, A. (1995): Flood Adaptations in Bangladesh. Is the compartmentalization scheme compatible with indigenous adjustments of rice cropping to flood regimes? Applied Geography 15 (1): 3-17.

RDRS (2009): Improving community coping mechanisms to adapt to climate
change, Northwest Bangladesh: Rangpur Dinajpur Rural Service (local
NGO) project report, funded by Norwegian Church Aid.

Sadeque, M.D. (1990): Survival pattern of the rural poor: a case study of a village in Bangladesh, New Delhi: Northern Book Centre.

Schmuck-Widmann, H. (1996): Living with flood: Survival strategies of char-
dwellers in Bangladesh, Berlin: FDCL.

Schmuck-Widmann, H. (2002): Facing the Jamuna River: Indigenous and Engineering Knowledge in Bangladesh. Berlin: Metropol Formularende.

Schmuck-Widmann, H. (2001): Facing the Jamuna River: indigenous and engineering knowledge in Bangladesh, Dhaka: Bangladesh Resource Centre for
Indigenous Knowledge.

Scoones, I. (1995): Investigating difference: Applications of wealth ranking and
household survey approaches among farming households in southern Zimbabwe. Development & Change 26, 67-88.

Scoones, I./Thompson, J. (2011): The politics of seed in Africa's green revolution, Sussex University Institute of Development Studies Bulletin 42.4.

Shiva, V. (ed.) (1992): Biodiversity: Social and Ecological Perspective, London:
Zed Press.

Shiva, V. (1993): Monocultures of the Mind: Biodiversity, Biotechnology and
Agriculture, London: Zed Press.

Shiva, V. (2000): Stolen Harvest: The Hijacking of the Global Food Supply,
Cambridge Massachusetts: South End Press.

Sillitoe, P. (1998): The development of indigenous knowledge: a new applied
anthropology, Current Anthropology 39 (2): 223-252.

Sillitoe, P. (ed.) (2000): Indigenous knowledge development in Bangladesh:
Present and future, London: Intermediate Technology Publications/ Dhaka:
University Press.

Sillitoe, P./ Bicker, A./ Pottier, J. (eds.) (2002): Participating In Development:
Approaches To Indigenous Knowledge, London: Routledge (ASA Monograph Series No. 39).

Sillitoe, P./ Dixon, P./Barr, J. (2005): Indigenous knowledge inquiries: a methodologies manual for development, London: Intermediate Technology Publications.

Stepp, J.R./ Wyndham, F.S./ Zarger, R.K. (eds.) (2002): Ethnobiology and biocultural diversity, Athens: University of Georgia Press.

Subedi, S.P. (ed.) (2005): International watercourses law for the 21st century:
the case of the river Ganges basin, Aldershot: Ashgate.

Swain, A. (1996): Displacing the conflict: environmental destruction in Bangladesh and ethnic conflict in India. Journal of Peace Research 33 (2) 189-204.

Tsai, C.F.A./Ali, M.Y. (1997): Open water fisheries of Bangladesh. Dhaka: University Press Limited.

Ullah, M. (1996): Land, livelihood and change in rural Bangladesh, Dhaka: University Press Limited.

Warner, M./Jones, P. (1998): Assessing the need to manage conflict in community-based natural resource projects, London: ODI (Natural Resources Perspectives No. 35).

Warner, M. (2001): Complex problems, negotiated solutions, London: Intermediate Technology Publications.

Yu, W./Mozaharul A./Hassan, A./Khan, A. S. /Ruane, A./Rosenzweig, C./Major,
D./Thurlow, J. (2010): Climate Change Risks and Food Security in Bangladesh, London: Earthscan.

World Bank (1990): Flood control in Bangladesh: a plan for action, Dhaka:
World Bank.

Ye X./Al-Babili, S./Klöti, A./Zhang, J./Lucca, P./Beyer, P./Potrykus, I. (2000):
Engineering the Provitamin A (β-Carotene) Biosynthetic Pathway into (Ca-
rotenoid-Free) Rice Endosperm. Science 287:303-305.

Hattori, Y./ Nagai, K./ Furukawa, S./ Song, X-J./ Kawano, R./ Sakakibara, H./
Wu, J./ Matsumoto, T./ Yoshimura, A./ Kitano, H./ Matsuoka, M./ Mori, H./
Ashikari, M. (2009): The ethylene response factors SNORKEL1 and
SNORKEL2 allow rice to adapt to deep water. Nature 460, 1026-1030.

Yu, W./Mozaharul, A./Hassan, A. (2010): Climate Change Risks and Food Security in Bangladesh. London: Earthscan (Earthscan Climate).

Managing Fire Risk in Indonesia's Peatlands[1]

VIOLA BIZARD

INTRODUCTION

Fires have always formed part of Indonesia's tropical landscapes, as an agricultural means and for ensuing land management, as an instrument in social conflicts, or as an unintended consequence of human actions (Brookfield et al. 1995: 158-178).[2] Yet, with growing concern about global climate change, fires, particularly in the country's peatlands, have increasingly been considered a "problem, or even, disaster" (Murdiyarso/Lebel 2007: 28).

Peatlands not only play an essential role in local livelihood support, biodiversity conservation, and the hydrological regulation of a region, but they are also particularly important for carbon storage (Rieley/Page 2005: 33-51).[3] Since the 1970s, however, Indonesia's peatlands have been deforested and drained, due to rapidly increasing demand for timber and farmland. Land use change followed by drainage has ruined the natural hydrology of the peat swamp forest ecosystem, and this now causes flooding in the wet season and water shortages during the dry season, thus making peatland extremely prone to recurrent fires.

---

1 A similar version of this article has been published in the International Quarterly for Asian Studies (cf. Bizard 2011a). The papers are based on the author's M.A. thesis (Bizard 2011b).

2 I would like to thank Anna-Katharina Hornidge and Christoph Antweiler for their comments.

3 Indonesia contains the largest area of peatland in the tropical zone. Estimates range from 16 to 27 million hectares (Mha). Most of these peatlands are located on the islands of West Papua (4.6 Mha), Kalimantan (6.8 Mha), and Sumatra (8.3 Mha) (Page et al. 1999: 1885).

In 1997-1998, fires in Indonesia's peatlands, particularly in the province of Central Kalimantan, represented 60 to 90 per cent of the country's carbon emissions, resulting in a dense smoke haze and releasing vast amounts of carbon dioxide into the atmosphere (Tacconi 2003: 5).

Without doubt, peat fires have not only been a calamity for forests, ecosystems, and global climate, but also an economic and social disaster, devastating health, livelihoods, and property (Mayer 2005: 202f.). Harwell (2000) reminds us that the perception and evaluation of the fires still depends on the observer's position. The disaster assessment of international and national agencies has foremost been centered on national economic and environmental costs (Tacconi 2003: 5), and there has hardly been "any systematic field data of impacts on local communities" (Harwell 2000: 324) or their experience and perception of the fires.[4] Yet, as Erikson (1994, cited in Harwell 2000) argues, the overlooked definition of disaster lies in the experience of the victims, meaning that "local voices need to be heard" (Harwell 2000: 334).

The paper at hand is thus an empirical account seeking to expose the stories and experiences of those living with recurrent fires in their environment. How do affected people explain, perceive, and manage fires? On what premise is their perception of fire built? How is the performance of their management strategies embedded into the regulatory customary law (*adat*) framework? And what constraints do people face in their mitigating and coping practices?

While community vulnerabilities to hazards are real, so are their abilities to act (Flint/Luloff 2005: 400). Hence, instead of an a priori victimization of the affected people, which exhibits an incomplete understanding of community life, it shall be addressed how people engage actively with and understand the fire risk that they voluntarily or involuntarily experience in their life (cf. Clay/Olson 2008: 146). For, as Bankoff argues, "populations at risk are populations actively engaged in making themselves [at least from an etic perspective] more vulnerable and who live in communities whose cultures are themselves increasingly shaped by hazard" (2003: 183, addition by VB).

Against these premises, it will be shown that, for those living with fire risk, fires do not solely imply disastrous impacts. Rather, according to Rosa, who defined risk as "an event or situation where something of human value has been put at stake and the outcome is uncertain" (1998: 28), fire is perceived as a phenomenon of ambivalent character with the potential to both entail benefits and

---

4   Though fire causes and impacts on communities have been investigated (e.g. Dennis et al. 2005; Mayer 2005; Chokkalingam et al. 2006), only a few works (Gönner 1999; Harwell 2000; Colfer 2002) refer to people's fire experiences in line with emic explanations and perceptions of fire (cf. Carmenta et al. 2011).

create loss. The residents of the researched sites are aware that fire forms a possible threat to something that is of value to them; the outcome, however, i.e. the desirable and undesirable effects of fire, is not predetermined but probabilistic and therefore embedded in uncertainty.

RESEARCH SITES

The findings are based on anthropological fieldwork conducted in communities living on the boundaries of the tropical peat swamp forest of Sebangau in Central Kalimantan in 2009 (cf. map 1).[5] Sebangau is Borneo's largest remaining connected peat swamp forest (Siegert/Boehm 2001: 4), experiencing extensive fires in recent years.[6] The respective field sites were selected according to the occurrence of fires, ethnic background, community size, and the willingness of the villagers to accommodate and accept the presence of an outsider and researcher in their community. In order to allow for comparison, two villages of different ethnographic background were chosen.[7]

---

5   The time frame for data collection was 15 weeks, with a total of 11 weeks of permanent residence in the field sites. The main methods applied were structured interviews (n=25 respectively n= 45) with members of randomly selected households, 36 qualitative interviews with 41 subject samples and participant observation.

6   Because of its high biodiversity value, Sebangau was designated as a national park with an area of 568,700 ha² in 2004 (Forestry Minister Decree No. 423/Menhut-II/2004).

7   Though I permanently resided in these two sites, neighboring communities were frequently visited, allowing for a general overview of the area.

Map 1: Thickness of peatland in Central Kalimantan

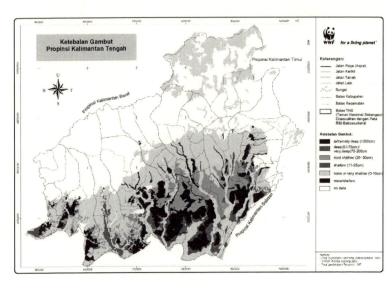

Source: WWF Indonesia 2009.

Located along the Katingan River and home to 374 residents (April 2009), the Ngaju Dayak village of Tumbang Lewu is relatively small.[8] Though inhabitants avow themselves to Islam, their worldview and daily practices reveal many elements of the *adat* found among the Ngaju Dayak in Central Kalimantan.[9] In the past, people lived on swidden agriculture, fishing, and the collection of rattan and latex *jelutong* (*Dyera* sp.). Like most Dayak groups on Borneo, people used the shallow peat areas near to the river banks for agricultural purposes.

Yet, with the (legal and illegal) logging boom in the mid-1980s, local livelihood patterns changed drastically. The extraction of timber remained the major income source for the next 25 years, while fishing, the collection of rattan, and swiddening functioned as supplements. In 2006, however, the logging op-

---

8   All names of the villages and informants have been anonymized.

9   Ngaju Dayak is the largest ethnic category in Central Kalimantan and refers to swidden cultivators living along the middle and lower reaches of many waterways. People in Tumbang Lewu, however, explicitly claim to be Kapuas Dayak (referring to their dialect and the origin of their ancestors) and dissociate themselves from 'being Ngaju'. 'Njagu' is associated with the indigenous Hindu Kaharingan religion that is rejected mainly for its assumed 'primitive' secondary burial of the dead (tiwah). For details on the Kaharingan belief see, for example, Schiller (1997).

erations closed down, causing local livelihoods to decline dramatically. Since then, people have largely depended on fishing, and vegetable cultivation, rattan, and rubber play a secondary role. Still, people in Tumbang Lewu could switch back to some of their former livelihood sources and thus, in contrast to inhabitants of Hidup Baru, buffer the adverse impacts of the end of logging on their livelihoods.

Hidup Baru, developed as part of Indonesia's former transmigration program in 1985-1986, is inhabited by people from multiple ethnic and religious (Muslim, Christian, Kaharingan) backgrounds. Though almost 90 per cent of the population are Javanese, Dayak from adjacent settlements and other parts of Kalimantan, Banjarese, and Batak have migrated spontaneously to the area.

Soon after their arrival, most people began to extract timber or work as wage laborers in one of the countless sawmills located around the village. During the logging boom (beginning of the 1990s until 2006), about 1,500 people lived in Hidup Baru. Yet, since the logging operations closed, the population has shrunk to around 900 people (June 2009). In particular, many young men left in order to try to make a living as wage laborers in the palm oil industry. The remaining residents sustain livelihoods by investing in paddy and vegetable cultivation. Compared to the era of timber, when Hidup Baru was filled with life, today many houses are uninhabited and a strange, almost desperate, atmosphere prevails.

FIRE RECORD OF TUMBANG LEWU AND HIDUP BARU

Vegetation and land fires are not new phenomena in the area. According to informants in Tumbang Lewu, fire incidences occurred during the time of their ancestors. In the past, however, fires happened less frequently and were not as large in scale, usually far from the settlement, and only noticed because of the rising smoke. The earliest fires that an elder could remember took place in the late 1950s, followed by fire events in the mid-1960s, in 1969-1970, 1972, and 1977. In recent years, however, fires "have already become a tradition" (Am I, April 27, 2009), with larger blazes occurring in 1997, 2005, 2006-2007, and 2009.

The fire record of Hidup Baru is, in line with its history, comparatively young. Though a Dayak elder of a nearby village reported that in former times small fires were also common, the worst fires that happened since Hidup Baru came into existence took place in 1997, 2003-2004, and 2005-2006. Additionally, smaller fires take place on a regular basis, as repeatedly confirmed by my informants with the words, "Here, there are definitely fires every year" (Field note [FN], June 08, 2009).

In both villages, it was difficult for people to specify the scale of these fire events, resulting in them being generally described as "extensive." A few respondents, though, gave more detailed information on the burnt vegetation. In Tumbang Lewu, informants spoke of up to "500 to 600 ha in 1997" (Nur I, May 01, 2009). In Hidup Baru, the fires of that year apparently had destroyed "thousands of hectare of jungle" (survey note; [S] April 2009) and "seemed the most extensive fires here" that had ever happened "since the village came into existence" (Agu II, June 26, 2009). In 2003-2004, more than 1,000 ha were said to have been burnt down, and in 2005-2006, many different fire hotspots destroyed between 5,000 and 10,000 ha, particularly in the Sebangau National Park. Similar to this account, a WWF staff member assessed the recently burnt vegetation of the area at about 10,000 ha (cf. map 2). Around Tumbang Lewu, he estimated 600 ha to have been destroyed by the latest fires (cf. map 3).[10]

Map 2: Burnt vegetation in the area of Hidup Baru (dark gray)

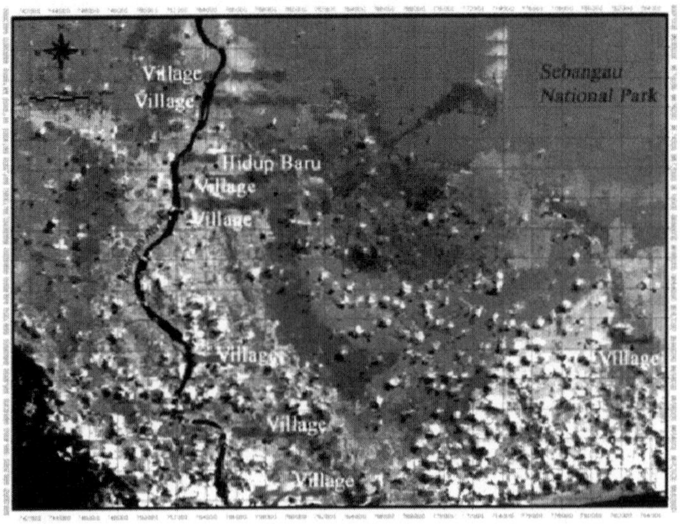

Source: WWF Indonesia 2009, modified.

---

10 However, at the date of writing no official data on administrative boundaries existed, which made it impossible to quantify exactly the real extent of burnt vegetation, especially since shrubs and small trees have repopulated the area.

Map 3: Burnt vegetation in the area of Tumbang Lewu (dark gray)

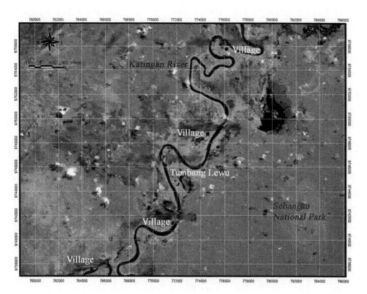

Source: WWF Indonesia 2009, modified.

In Tumbang Lewu most fires occurred across the Katingan River. The fact that the river thus functions as a natural firebreak seems to bestow a sense of security on most people, as almost all the interview participants considered the fires to be far away. In some parts of Hidup Baru, by contrast, fires have come as close as 15 m to people's homes. Accordingly, inhabitants of this area considered the fires to be "very close," whereas residents in the 'safe' parts of the village usually perceived the fires to be "far away in the forest" (S, April 2009). Obviously, past experience, disaster potential, and possible personal involvement are decisive factors influencing the evaluation of fire risk (cf. Smith/Petley (2009[2001]: 64f.).

Hence, in both villages, vegetation and land fires are not utterly new phenomena. Yet, whereas in the past fires were lower in scale and frequency, in recent decades they have recurred on a regular basis and, partly, at an alarming rate. How can these changes in fire frequency and intensity be explained?

"Why did things change in such a way that large fires occur as we have them now? Even though in the past, there were also often long droughts. Why did fires like that still not happen? Following my own observation, who also used to work in the forest, the basis for the fires actually were laid by the problem of wood, the logging." (Ra II, June 25, 2009)

THE SOCIAL AND ENVIRONMENTAL EFFECTS OF LOGGING

Indeed, the era of timber has entailed major socio-cultural and environmental changes (cf. Bizard 2011b). Most remarkable is the influx of people from all over Indonesia, and even from abroad, which has not only altered the social fabric and population density, but also led to conflicts over resources, reflected in ethnic stereotyping and, in Hidup Baru, frequent burglary and an atmosphere of rivalry, most evident in the malicious destruction and arson of gardens and logs.

Informants further cited gambling, prostitution (in the area of Hidup Baru), alcohol consumption, and a focus on money accompanied by a prodigal lifestyle impacting adversely on the local culture. Apparently, hardly anybody diversified livelihoods and saved money for future needs. Understandably, many residents viewed the final closure of the logging operation in 2006 as traumatic: "After the logging [operation] closed, people here were like chickens that had been given drugs" (FN, June 27, 2009).

Though people in Tumbang Lewu can cope better with the challenges brought on by the end of logging, they face the environmental effects of previous and continuing (upriver) deforestation. People have had to move their fields to higher – less fertile – areas, as due to the deforestation affecting soil erosion and recurrent floods they can no longer practice swiddening along the river. Also, it is no longer feasible to predict climatic conditions by means of knowledge drawn from ancestors:

Pak[11] Jusuf: "But if we observe the state of nature as it is now [...], there are many more floods than droughts. Why? Because it is very different...In the past, we could forecast the weather by looking at the wind, west-wind or the moon. If the moon leans to the north it means, like people in the past said in the local language *suruk ampah*, that it might rain...But now, no...We can no longer read it. Like the moon now, as I observed it when it appeared yesterday, indeed, it leans a bit to the west, meaning rain...but if we look now..."

V.B.: "Where is the rain?"

Pak Jusuf: "Yes, there is a drought." (Ju I, May 09, 2009)

In addition, the residents state that "when the logging began, the relationship with the environment changed drastically" (FN, June 12, 2009). Certainly influenced by the prevailing competition for forest resources, particularly in the Hidup Baru, people apparently "took what was in the forest" (Agu II, June 26,

---

11 Term to address male interlocutors in a respectful manner.

2009). Against local wisdom, trees of 15-20 cm in diameter were cut down, accelerating deforestation. Furthermore, logging entailed the construction of countless ditches to extract the logs, which altered the hydrology of the peat swamp forest, so "after the logging opened [...], what else would one expect? In the forest it was dry and it would always burn" (Sha, June 26, 2009).

Interestingly though, for some Dayak elders the ecological changes were not caused by the logging per se. As it is a common feature of such cognitive processes (cf. Douglas 1985), people related the responsibility for these adverse developments to logging practices that had ignored ancestors' wisdom used to manage natural resources as well as violated social norms and religious duties, i.e. the disregard of ancestral advice not to cut any young trees and the practice of permission rituals (*ngariau*), as well as the violation of culture-specific restrictions (*pantangan*) and taboos (encroachment into holy forest sites [*pahewan*]).

Hence, some respondents observe the environmental and socio-cultural changes that the era of logging entailed, accompanied by altered living conditions and a changed value and belief system. Nevertheless, few inhabitants consider their own logging activities to have contributed to these processes and the formation of "ecological and social landscapes vulnerable to fire" (Harwell 2000: 314). Rather, the majority of people attribute deforestation to either logging concessionaires (*Hak Pengusahan Hutan,* HPH) and immigrants or forest fires, regardless of the fact that logging and subsequent deforestation in reality set the stage for the latter. Thus, the era of timber is usually not mentioned as an underlying cause of fires, which are attributed to other reasons.

EMIC EXPLANATIONS OF POTENTIAL FIRE SOURCES

If, in the past, fires were out of human reach and just noted because of the presence of ascending smoke, how did the ancestors reason their origin? Kaharingan Pak Joko recalls an old legend that serves as explanation by assigning the fires to some supernatural agency:

"It is true that there is often a fire, of which we don't know the origin. [...] It can inflame by itself. There is nobody igniting it. People refer to it as spirit of fire. There is a legend. [...] In former times, it was said that there was an old person who was walking around in the evening and carried a small fireplace with smoke. But the people here, the people from this hamlet did not know this very old person. That's what they called spirit of fire. It can inflame people's house or inflame the forest." (Jk, July 12, 2009)

According to other villagers, however, their ancestors explained the fires as the result of a long drought accompanied by heat and the rubbing of tree limbs in the wind. While the cosmological explanation thus seems to have vanished, the use of 'nature' to explain the latest extensive fires, and consequently to construct them as isolated events outside of human agency, is very much alive. These explanations notwithstanding, diverse individuals have nevertheless stated that "Fire ignition is primarily caused by humans" (Hri, April 27, 2009). "In fact, there cannot be any fire without humans lighting it" (Jo, June 24, 2009), one person equally concludes. How do residents of Tumbang Lewu and Hidup Baru then explain ignition caused by humans?

At both sites, many villagers assigned ignition to people who had, while working in the forest, carelessly thrown away cigarettes or left a cooking fire unattended to ward off the cold and insects (cf. Colfer 2002; Chokkalingam et al. 2005; Vayda 2011), therefore unwittingly starting a fire.[12] Most respondents transferred the responsibility for such carelessness to people outside their direct social environment ("those hunting"/"those fishing", i.e. people from adjacent villages). In Hidup Baru, many people moreover reported that accidental fires resulted from careless fire use in land preparation:

"In 2003-2004, there was a fire here, more than 1000 ha burnt down. [...] The person who burnt his field didn't inform the people owning the adjoining gardens and also didn't make a firebreak. In the end the fire broke out and the gardens burnt down." (FN, June 10, 2009)

Although in Tumbang Lewu most people said that fires for land clearing were controlled by traditional fire management methods (see below), others still reported fire incidences following from fire use in land preparation (attested during the fieldwork). Colfer (2002) proposed that such carelessness results from the fact that people's fire use has evolved in a very humid tropical rainforest context in which ecological conditions a priori limit the spread of fire and, consequently, people's concerns about wildfires. Perhaps this might also explain why people set fires for their enjoyment, without concern or being aware about the potential consequences of their actions: "It's just like a hobby, I am happy to see the fire" (FN, July 08, 2009) or "Formerly, I really enjoyed burning, above all when very deep in there [pointing to the forest]" (Ped II, July 11, 2009). These statements were definitely not related to a 'perfect burn' (*kebakaran sempur-*

12 However, Vayda (2011) notes that no reliable studies exist identifying cigarette butts as ignition sources for actual forest fires either in Indonesia or anywhere else.

na) in the context of swiddening.[13] Therefore, it can only be concluded that, in the formerly humid landscape, 'playing' with fire, driven by "the thrill and intrinsic enjoyment it brings" (Rosa 1998: 28), might have been without severe ecological consequences. Yet, with a significantly drier environment than before, such actions might now become a source of accidental fires, too.

That said, the research disclosed that further potential sources of fire need to be taken into account, as residents of Tumbang Lewu and Hidup Baru have long used it in diverse contexts.

MANAGING LIVELIHOODS WITH FIRE

Fire is not just commonly used for daily purposes, but also serves people while working or camping in the forest. Most importantly, however, it is an essential agricultural tool in land preparation. Logically, local people unanimously stressed that fire is indispensable when preparing fields. Although some residents were aware that repeated burning decreases soil fertility, no other agricultural tools as efficient as fire were available. In Tumbang Lewu, most of the land cleared is secondary forest. In Hidup Baru, by contrast, slashed and burnt vegetation mainly comprises annual weeds and *imperata cylindrica*, as extensive fires in 2003-2004 destroyed the remaining forest.

However, given pressing livelihood needs, and with the incidence of a drought, the land cover of grassland seems also to offer an opportunity to intentionally set uncontrolled fires on empty land: "There are still ignorant people who don't slash, since it looks dry and all these kind of things... Well, thank God if [the conditions] are good, we plant paddy!'" (Ln, June 20, 2009). Similarly, residents of Hidup Baru appear to have profited from fires in the surrounding forests. Although nobody admitted to having set fires purposely – though some villagers considered this very likely – many people stated that they 'welcome' such fires, as they provide an opportunity to plant rice:

"Actually, the residents here are pleased if there is a fire. They just seek the easy way, are lazy to slash and wait until a fire comes." (FN, July 01, 2009)

"I am happy if there is a fire, because we can plant paddy." (S, June 2009)

---

13 A lecturer at the local university insisted that "fire only makes people happy if they practice swiddening, because a big fire means a 'perfect burn', meaning that the land is 'perfectly' cleaned" (FN June 02, 2009). Though I share his interpretation (I made similar observations during burning for land preparation), none of the recounted stories about people's 'fire play' referred to burning for land preparation.

Besides, people in both villages mentioned the expansion of their fishing grounds as another positive effect of extensive fires, as reported for other peat areas, too (cf. Chokkalingam et al. 2005). In Tumbang Lewu, people have a long tradition of using peat swamp forest and barren peat floodplains for harvesting fish (formerly also turtles). In this regard, fire serves as a means of expanding and accessing fishing grounds, to provide flushes of nutrients and to clear dried weeds, which makes it easier to access and locate fish in the remaining water pools (*luhak*):[14]

"In the dry-season people come and look for fish in the luhak because you know the water is scarce. Because there are a lot of weeds that are high, it is practical to burn them, [...] so that we can easily see the *luhak*. Fishermen try their luck." (Hj, July 12, 2009)

Uncontrolled fire is also frequently used at both sites to clear scrubby vegetation along channels, rivers, roads, and footpaths leading into the forest or to fields (cf. Chokkalingam et al. 2005). Moreover, in Tumbang Lewu, the respondents stated that people benefited from fires insofar as they facilitated locating and accessing game, a phenomenon noted in East Kalimantan, too (cf. Gönner 1999). Likewise, during the era of logging, extensive fires allowed people to extract fire-resistant and commercially valuable Borneo ironwood trees following a fire (cf. Vayda 2011). In Hidup Baru, informants further reported that previously, when people used to raise cattle, the uncontrolled burning of *imperata* served to generate fresh grass (cf. Colfer 2002; Chokkalingam et al. 2005). And following the cessation of logging, many people in this area coped with the subsequent economic changes by collecting iron left over in sawmills and along the formerly established logging rails, as well as burning.

Besides controlled and (intentionally or unintentionally) uncontrolled burning for livelihood support, fire was said to have also been used commonly in arson attacks driven by psychological motives, mainly during and after logging (cf. Vayda 2011).[15] Particularly in Hidup Baru, people apparently deliberately

---

14 The flushes of nutrients stimulate algal growth and therewith maintain high levels of fish populations.

15 Elsewhere, arson has been used in land use conflicts between communities and plantation companies (e.g. Colfer 2002; Dennis et al. 2005; Vayda 2011). Vayda (2011) furthermore notes that there have been plausible, even if unproved reports of arson being committed in logged forest areas by agents of timber concessions or plantation companies seeking government approval either for converting the areas to plantations or for moving on to new areas for timber harvesting. Also, there have been reports of

set fire to forest plots for which they competed with rivals. After the closing of logging operations, "people deliberately set fires because they were angry with the government that they could no longer benefit from the forest" (FN, April 24, 2009). In addition to arson related to the logging context and motivated by feelings of injustice or inequity, informants at the trans-migrant site, where social ties and thus feelings of respect, affection, and trust appear to be less close than in Tumbang Lewu, suggested that people intentionally set light to gardens because of jealousy (cf. Colfer 2002).

The listed contexts describe ignition events which, according to the locals, have been real and potential sources of widespread fires. However, we need to keep in mind that these possible sources of fire ignition do not necessarily explain the spread of fire or even forest fires, as Vayda (2006) warns. In order to attest to this point, further "studies of fire use in or near forests during times of drought specifically; fine-grained research on fire behavior and fire susceptibility under varying conditions of fuel availability and moisture; and systematic research on human actions affecting those conditions" (ibid: 631) are needed.

Albeit, the foregoing paragraphs make clear that controlled and uncontrolled fire is a vital livelihood management tool for people living in peatlands. The range of positive livelihood benefits notwithstanding, vegetation and land fires in Hidup Baru and Tumbang Lewu, however, have entailed adverse effects as well.

THE SEASON OF THE SMOKE HAZE – ADVERSE FIRE IMPACTS

Residents from each village named the dense smoke haze blanketing their environment as the most obvious impact of the fires. Yet, their overall assessments of the season of the smoke haze differed considerably. Some villagers laughed at the question about how they had experienced the smoke and commented "According to me, there is no adverse effect" (Jo, June 24, 2009). It is unclear whether these people did not really feel any negative impacts such as health problems or economic impairment, or whether these negations resemble a wise means of adapting to the "objectively extant dangers" imposed by fire risk (Hoffman/Oliver-Smith 1999: 8f.). Still, the majority of people indicated that they been hindered in their activities.

Many residents reported to have suffered from acute medical impacts including asthma, bronchitis, acute respiratory infection, and skin and eye irritations.

---

arson by illegal loggers for the purpose of either destroying evidence of their activities or diverting attention therefrom.

Except for one elder, who evidently suffered from the long-term effects of air pollution, nobody else mentioned having used or possessed a mask. While one person reasoned this was due to people's lack of awareness about the perilous long-term effects of the smoke haze, another voice raised the question: "In villages like this one, where do you get masks from?" (Am III, July 12, 2009), demonstrating that the use of masks also depends on people's material capital.

In addition, the smoke haze constrains transportation. With visibility being down to only a few meters during the first few hours of the day, people cannot follow their usual activities. Particularly in Tumbang Lewu, where people depend on river transportation to carry out fishing or to reach gardens, the smoke impacts negatively on livelihoods. Sometimes, the fires and smoke are so heavy that the fishermen do not dare to look for fish at all:

> "There's a lot of loss. [...] You well know, we all engage in fishing, [but] because of the smoke haze we don't dare, because the fire spreads, you know. So we don't dare to go anywhere for catching fish, because, if we aren't alert, the fire can surround us." (Ju I, May 09, 2009)

The worst and most long-term loss is considered to be caused by the fires themselves by degrading soil fertility and wiping out agricultural crops and, hence, livelihoods: "Just imagine if one productive rubber garden with, for example, 500 trees has been burnt down, how much is that already? That, we can't imagine" (Is, May 09, 2009).

The previous extensive fires in Tumbang Lewu primarily destroyed rubber and rattan gardens, while in Hidup Baru, mainly orchards fell victim to the flames. Noticeable, however, were the differences in loss assessment, particularly in Hidup Baru. Those residents whose gardens had ever been affected by fire were greatly aware of adverse fire effects, but numerous other respondents seemed less concerned. Surprisingly, they stated that in their village – that can be walked across in 15 minutes – fires had never destroyed any gardens. While this appraisal seems incomprehensible, it underscores both (a) that damage is often unevenly spread within a community and (b) that past experience and potential personal concerns govern judgements about the fire risk. And evidently, social ties do not appear to be as close in Hidup Baru, also mirrored in 'unsocial' – as in uncontrolled – burning for land preparation. A few times already, such burning practices are said to have destroyed adjacent gardens and thus provoked disputes about compensation.

Some villagers mentioned forest degradation accompanied by a decline of forest resources, thus resulting in fewer livelihood options being another adverse fire impact. Mainly in Tumbang Lewu, where livelihoods had previously depended on the surrounding forest, people read the changes in their natural environment:

"Now, there are fewer animals. Why? Maybe because of the fires." (Ilh, May 06, 2009)

"In the past, before there were fires, there was a lot of wood in the forest that was very benefiting." (Al, May 06, 2009)

"The people can no longer work there to look for their needs, to look for fish. That's already an impact. In the past, before the fires, they could catch fish there." (Is, May 09, 2009)

Apart from the decrease in fish stocks (which fires indeed also destroy), villagers were primarily concerned about wood degradation, as it was difficult to find construction material.[16] The decline of the other resources was seldom perceived as harmful, which might be due to the fact that Dayak livelihoods became less dependent on the use of forest products during logging operations, while migrants never made use of forest resources anyway (except for timber).

The observation that many villagers may currently not perceive any adverse effects from forest degradation is affirmed insofar as numerous people made comments like, "If the fire is in the forest, admittedly we don't care" (S, June 2009) or "If it is in the forest, never mind whether the forest is gone or not" (S, June 2009). During the era of logging, people apparently were more concerned about fires, as they "were afraid to lose the wood" (Jo, June 24, 2009). With changed livelihood patterns, people today seem rather to perceive livelihood benefits resulting from fires, underlining that the evaluation of fire effects is dynamic.

Informants justified their attitudes and present disinterest by pointing to absent profits due to a lack of rights to utilization, namely property rights, reflecting the aforementioned frustration, despair, and anger about denied access to timber, enacted through the end of logging and the establishment of the National Park:

---

16 Decreasing fish stocks were said to also result from overfishing and failed irrigation channels set up by the government. Furthermore, the use of electrical current and chemicals that have become a common 'fishing technique' in the area – stricter law enforcement in recent years notwithstanding – certainly have contributed to the decline.

"If the forest is burnt down, the people care less. There are no benefits for them." (FN, May 01, 2009)

"If the fire is in the forest, the government is responsible and experiences the loss. The people don't possess any single tree there." (S, June 2009)

"The people depended too much on the logging and since there are no profits anymore from the forest, 'Just leave it, if the forest burns down'." (FN, June 16, 2009)

Accordingly, the respondents summarized people's consciousness about fire effects as follows, for instance: "They just care if there are gardens" (FN, July 08, 2009). Although the forest is of symbolic meaning, mainly for the Dayak, there appears to be the tendency among residents to be chiefly concerned about fire damage to people's property rather than to something considered of value. While the frustration about the closing logging operations certainly is an explanatory variable, a consideration of people's strategies when managing fires, as well as of *adat* regulations framing fire management, may provide additional insights.

LOCAL CAPACITIES IN FIRE MANAGEMENT

In order to manage fire, people in Tumbang Lewu and Hidup Baru rely on a set of different strategies that are largely based on measures used to manage fire in the context of swidden cultivation. Although from an etic perspective this knowledge exhibits a hybrid character, for it "represents a confluence of local and extra-local experience" (Dove 2000: 238), Dayak people refer to these strategies as "local knowledge" (*kearifan lokal*). By means of this knowledge, residents seek both to promote the positive effects and to mitigate and respectively cope with the adverse effects of fire risk.

A good burn is central to swiddening. Its success, however, requires not only suitable climatic conditions, as well as slashing and burning, but also, traditionally, before land clearing, people perform *ngariau*. With the provision of an offering (*ancak*), villagers seek "to ask permission from the spirits [...] so that there are no calamities [in the shape of] sorts of disasters that exist, and that people's work can bring about good yields" (Jk, July 12, 2009). If people prepare fields without providing an *ancak*, "they can become possessed by a spirit, sick, like that. [...] Also, the paddy can't be used, it's empty [...] so it doesn't have any content, already eaten by someone. Here are many challenges" (Ped II, July 11, 2009). Thus, *ngariau*, like agricultural ritual in general, can be interpreted as a means of boosting the likelihood of a successful swidden cycle, and equally as a means of reducing the likelihood to experiencing harm in an uncertain environmental context (cf. Dove 1996).

Besides, like other Dayak groups in Borneo, Dayak informants are said to have previously oriented their swidden cycle and thus time burning to the constellation of Orion (*patendu*). Yet, due to climatic changes, this knowledge no longer guarantees validity, and people no longer dare to rely entirely on their stellar lore.

Other important variables for a successful burn are the time of day, wind strength, and wind direction. In order to ensure a fast and strong burn, people in Tumbang Lewu mentioned that they "call the winds", "*Kuuuuuuuris*" (Ju I, May 9, 2009). Also, to avoid the accidental firing of a neighboring farm, the prevailing wind direction determines which edge of the field is set on fire first.

Further protective measures include the making of firebreaks (*landa*) around the swidden that will be burnt and the digging of ditches (*parit*). While firebreaks are most commonly applied (as probably all over Borneo and elsewhere), only a few people use ditches because their construction is time- and labor-intensive. In order to enhance protection, ditches may be filled with water, which makes sense because underground fires in peatland are common. Another strategy that some respondents, foremost in Tumbang Lewu, apply is to sprinkle firebreaks with water, i.e. to make a water strip (*jalur air*).

Dayak informants know a number of other methods to prevent fire spread, including the distribution of salt around the farm, the use of fire-resistant woods, and the application of specific knowledge (*ilmu*) by a ritual expert called a *pawang api*. Yet, in the researched villages, we met only one Dayak elder who was said to possess the skills required to anticipate fire spread by using such *ilmu* (cf. Bizard 2011b).

Hence, residents of Tumbang Lewu and Hidup Baru are aware of diverse strategies to manage fire, of which the consideration of wind direction, information from neighbors, collective protection during burning, and the making of firebreaks and ditches are most frequently applied. Nevertheless, despite this knowledge, and pursuant to our informants, these strategies have not always been applied with care.

As mentioned above and exemplified by these statements, in Hidup Baru it has apparently been common practice to burn swiddens in a rather uncontrolled manner:

"When people want to burn their farms, do they make firebreaks?" – "No, no one is making a firebreak. At the most people consult each other." (FN, June 11, 2009)

"They don't know where the wind direction goes. This isn't considered. The important thing is to set fire. That's what can spread to other people's fields." (Res, June 29, 2009)

Consequently, it transpired that people did not know by whom their fields had been burnt, indicating a rather low social awareness: "They don't consider the interest of people in a wider scope; whether with this fire someone will be aggrieved or not" (Adi I, June 23, 2009). Most clearly, however, this attitude is reflected in the deliberate burning of fields motivated by jealousy. This attitude also conforms to the noted disinterest about fire spreading to the adjacent forest. As one person reasons, "... there is no importance for them. For instance, if it's their field that burns down, maybe yes. But because it's forest, thus, there is no care" (Agu II, June 26, 2009). A similar attitude seems to prevail in Tumbang Lewu, though social awareness appears to be higher there. Usually, people inform the owners of adjoining farms, consider the wind direction, and apply firebreaks at edges where their swidden borders a neighboring farm (cf. King 1996):

"Firebreaks are made when, well, if there are gardens, if there is something, if there is land that is of benefit to people. If there are no benefits, it's just left." (Hri, April 27, 2009)

The principle to protect only what is considered of value and of direct or potential benefit seems also to hold true for the application of fire coping mechanisms, as argued by diverse inhabitants in both villages:

"Nobody helped to extinguish these fires. So it (the fire) was just left, it blazed. Well, the thing is that it was outside of people's farms. Only if it had actually been their farm, they would have tried to extinguish [the fire]. [...] For example, last year, not a single resident went there to extinguish [the fire], but it was just left. And also one thing, if they want to extinguish, actually the capacities are lacking, because for extinguishing you need to use water. [But] there is no water." (Jo, June 24, 2009)

Obviously, for people in Hidup Baru and Tumbang Lewu it is not worthwhile to invest in the control of fires occurring outside of personal property that is not of direct benefit (cf. Dennis et al. 2005). Given the frustration about the end of logging, as well as the diverse benefits that fires indeed can entail for livelihoods, this attitude is plausible. Yet, as the statement above indicates, even if people try to extinguish fires, they are hardly capable of doing so, as diverse constraints hamper fire control.

"JUST WAIT FOR RAIN..." – CONSTRAINTS FACED IN FIRE MANAGEMENT

If a fire is detected, the first thing that the villagers do is to "return to the hamlet" and "inform the people there is a fire." Then, "all residents go to the field, go to the site where the fire is occurring" and try to cope with the fire by "making emergency firebreaks, so that the fire doesn't enter the gardens." "Many people carried water," "every person, one by one, carried buckets [...]; this was spurt, sprayed." Moreover, "people brought wet branches" or "used banana leaves in order to beat the fire." They also "hoed the soil" to extinguish the fire and "dug ditches" to prevent the fire from entering gardens. In Tumbang Lewu, people spontaneously started a burn opposite to the ongoing fire (Adi I, June 23, 2009; Am I, April 27, 2009; Et, June 20, 2009; Ha, July 01, 2009; Hri, April 27, 2009; Tu, June 29, 2009; Wa, July 01, 2009).

Nonetheless, these efforts notwithstanding, and given people's deficient fire fighting equipment, large fires are virtually uncontrollable. Respondents particularly criticized the government for never having provided any support in the form of equipment or fire-fighting training.[17] However, one voice in Hidup Baru aptly asked the question: "Even if there was [adequate] fire equipment, where do you get the water from?" (Ln, June 20, 2009).

The major obstacle to fighting fires is water shortages during the dry season. In Hidup Baru, all small irrigation channels are dry and people have to wait for a high tide on the Java Sea to push water from the Katingan into the main irrigation channels. In Tumbang Lewu, the Katingan River is the only available water source during the dry season. At sites where people's gardens are located and fires usually occur, "it's already dry, there is no water anymore" (Is, May 09, 2009). However, due to a distance of roughly 3km, with shrubs and roots further hindering movement, carrying water from the river, and thus damming up the fire, is actually impossible.

Moreover, the prevailing soil structure of peat constrains fire fighting. Due to the extremely low water table during the dry season, peatland is prone to underground fires, additionally complicating fire control, not to mention that fire fighting itself poses a threat to the people involved. If people get close to the fire, they "have to be careful, [as] in the dense forest, as trees can topple" (Am I, April 27, 2009). Under conditions of dense smoke haze, extreme heat, and being badly equipped, it is therefore extremely dangerous to approach fires. Thus, "it's

---

17 Tumbang Lewu has recently been provided with fire-fighting equipment and training facilitated by WWF.

indeed difficult, difficult to cope or to control fire" (ibid) and all that people sometimes can do is "just wait for rain" (Arif, May 10, 2009).

Hence, people in Hidup Baru and Tumbang Lewu actually experience diverse constraints in anticipating and controlling fire risk. Albeit, in both villages some informants noted people's awareness to hinder fire control:

"So we already try to fight the fire, but we are not capable, if the fire has already eaten the soil. But people's awareness is very low. [...] The people don't care, 'The important thing is that what I own is not affected'. In general, people's attitude is like that." (Ra II, June 25, 2009)

Against these premises, it seems that people's fire evaluation, and therefore fire management, is based on a certain rationale: Fire is primarily of concern, if it might cause damage to personal property or to something that is considered of value. Nevertheless, this principle did not evolve in a social vacuum; rather, it appears to be built on what is conventionally accepted in Hidup Baru and Tumbang Lewu as valid and customary, mirroring itself in *adat* regulations framing sanctions for fire mismanagement.

ADAT – REGULATORY FRAMEWORK OF FIRE MANAGEMENT

With some local variation, the Ngaju Dayak share a common *adat* that was first codified in 1894 (Schiller 1997: 185). Accordingly, the regulations for fire management found in the area of Tumbang Lewu and the area of Hidup Baru, located six hours by speedboat away from each other, are the same. Compared to the past, however, the *adat*, its implementation, and thus its relevance seem to have experienced a transformation, at least in regards to regulations for fire management in the context of agriculture (see also Bizard 2011b).

Although, theoretically, in both villages the *adat* prescribes that people who want to burn their swidden have to inform the owners of adjoining farms and make firebreaks, this does not seem always to be the case. In the past, people mismanaging fires, and thus causing damage to neighboring fields, had to pay a fine to the local *adat* community. Nowadays, defaulters just have to compensate the loss of the aggrieved party (*ganti rugi*) (cf. van Noordwijk 2008). Furthermore, the *adat* in both sites stipulates that if the defaulter is not capable of compensating for the loss with money, his land can be claimed by the aggrieved party.

While in Hidup Baru there had been rare cases in which people had been forced to hand over their land, inhabitants of Tumbang Lewu said that such conflict situations would be solved "in a manner of kinship" (Nur II, July 10, 2009). So, due to social conventions, the foreseen *adat* sanctions are usually open to negotiation (cf. Suyanto et al. 2004). Some people, though, perceive kinship relations to impact on the negotiation process more in the form of unfavorable social pressure:

"We asked for compensation, [but] in what manner among what you still call kin? In the end we asked as little as possible. We asked for 10 litres pesticide. But the reality is that we got 5 litres, pseudo pesticide that doesn't kill [the weeds]." (Ra II, June 25, 2009)

In most cases, however, the aggrieved party cannot hope for compensation. Either the person mismanaging the fire is not in the economic position to pay the aggrieved party off (with money or land), or, as is most frequently the case, *ganti rugi* cannot be enforced, as "it is difficult to know who the perpetrator of the particular fire is" (Fi, July 01, 2009). Besides, in Hidup Baru, *ganti rugi* includes a regulation stating that, in the case of fire spread, the defaulter still has to compensate for the loss, but only if the destroyed garden had been properly tended.

Obviously, the present *adat* regulations are primarily geared to regulate potential social conflicts arising from fire mismanagement rather than uncontrolled fire use per se. This assumption is underscored insofar as the *adat* in any of the field sites does not dictate any sanctions, if fire spreads to (forest) land that is not under personal property. Corresponding to the present assessment of the forest outlined above, this regulation may additionally explain why residents solely apply firebreaks where their farms border with personal property.

Hence, apart from possible social scandal and personal shame, *ganti rugi* within the context of agriculture is currently the only *adat* sanction about which the inhabitants have to worry. Other situations, in which fire is used, are not incorporated in the *adat* framework. The same holds true for the recently passed provincial bylaw (Reg. 52/2008 CK), seeking to regulate the fire use of smallholders in land clearing. Although the bylaw was revoked when extensive fires plagued the province in August and September 2009, its announcement still seemed to influence people's evaluations of fire.[18]

---

18 The bylaw was passed to counter the province's declining rice production that had steadily decreased following the national government's "Zero Burning Policy" (Government Regulation 4/2001) being strictly enforced.

Changing Fire Evaluation?

Although prior to 2008 diverse regulations concerning fire (mis)use existed, people's statements suggest that these did not really affect local fire management practices:

"In the past, to burn the forest and so on was prosecuted with fines and so on. Just why didn't it work? Because there was little socialization about these regulations, then little awareness of people to obey this regulation, and it was made worse with weak enforcement. If there was an incidence, case, [the authorities] did not immediately act but kept silent." (Agu II, June 26, 2009)

Given these political conditions, it is understandable why many informants stated made comments such as "Just recently there was a program [stating] that you were not allowed to burn" (Ped II, July 11, 2009). Now, with the bylaw, depending on the size of field that will be burnt, people need permission from the village head (till 0.5 ha) or the sub-district head (from 0.5 to 2.5 ha) (Reg. 52/2008 CK).[19] The application involves a range of bureaucratic steps, such as submitting a copy of the land certificate or an identity card, which are just not feasible to accomplish.[20]

Apart from these technical aspects, the new regulation above all caused a great deal of concern regarding annual land preparation procedures, especially in Hidup Baru. Most frequently, people worried about how they would make a living without being able to burn, the related costs, and the whole procedure in general, which still appeared to be rather unclear. The statements of residents and village administrators were often contradictory and confusion prevailed. Given these circumstances, the implementation, and consequently overall effectiveness, of the new regulation remained doubtful.[21]

Nevertheless, the announcement of the bylaw by Hidup Baru's administration seemed to affect people's evaluations of potential fire effects, underlining that processes of communication influence fire risk perception, too. Often, in-

---

19 The regulation applies to the first year only. In subsequent years, the land officially can no longer be prepared by burning.

20 E.g. the closest copying machine from Tumbang Lewu is six hours away by speedboat, not to mention that in Hidup Baru many residents do not possess an identity card.

21 How matters were solved in the end is unclear. During my stay, I never observed that anybody went through all the formalities, but the residents quickly informed the village head and left for burning.

formants expressed the fear of possible sanctions imposed as a result of fire misuse:

"Now, one has to ask for permission if one wants to burn, and one can be sent to jail if one destroys somebody else's garden. Uuuuuiiiii, in the past, one directly burnt, the fire spread to everywhere. Now, it's dangerous." (FN, June 23, 2009)

"Now, one has to report [...], if one wants to burn. If the fire spreads, one can be sent to jail, if one doesn't have the money for ganti rugi and the owner of the adjoining field is bull-headed and keeps on claiming 10 million. Where do I have 10 million? That makes it difficult for us, to alarm us like that." (FN, June 22, 2009)

Although such conversations dealt with potential scenarios, people's fears about possible future fines were very real. However, other than the risk of being forced to compensate for damage or face judicial sanctions, these concerns need to be understood with due consideration of the current livelihood context. At the end of logging, in both villages, people had to set up gardens that, in the long-term, would serve as primary income sources. Given the altered importance of gardens securing livelihood needs, it is likely that their destruction has also been re-evaluated, meaning that the aggrieved party will more likely strive for compensation than previously.

While these changed land use patterns might indeed evoke an altered perception of fire, particularly its potential adverse effects, it remains to be seen how the people of Tumbang Lewu and Hidup Baru will actually evaluate fires in the future. When asked how villagers would manage fires in the upcoming months, the reactions reminded the researcher of the principle guiding fire management in previous years:

V.B.:	"For instance, if this year fires happen across the village, will people busily extinguish?"
Pak Pedi:	"No."
Pak Amir:	"We observe the condition, whether people's gardens [are affected] or not. If not, the fire will be left."
V.B.:	"Although there is the government regulation and equipment?"
Pak Amir:	"Yes. [...] It's just tiring. What for, Viola?" (Am III/Ped II, July 11, 2009)

Thus, a few months after the fieldwork was completed, the residents of Tumbang Lewu sent the following information via e-mail: "It feels that there are fires around, but [we; VB] don't know where the fires are" (e-mail, September 27, 2009). "Well, that's how it is here: every time there is a drought, there is definitely a fire..." (e-mail, September 29, 2009).

CONCLUDING REMARKS

Based on the empirical account outlined above, a few main types of fire – as perceived and managed by people in Tumbang Lewu and Hidup Baru – can be identified. While fire as the result of some supernatural agency no longer seems valid, it is generally portrayed as the outcome of pure bio-physical processes, and thus out of human responsibility, as a consequence of human agency, or as resulting from the combination of ecological and human factors.

Human-induced fires comprise accidental fire, fire used for livelihood support, and fire as arson, driven by psychological motives. Accidental fire is usually assigned to "any people's" carelessness while working in the forest and to careless fire use in land preparation, but it is also attributed to people's "fire play." Fire used for livelihood management is both of a controlled and an uncontrolled nature. Arson has been related to rivalry and feelings of jealousy and injustice, particularly during and after the logging era.

In due consideration of the emic explanations given for potential ignition sources, people's livelihood management by fire, the potential adverse fire impacts perceived, and people's strategies to manage fire, it seems that villagers in Tumbang Lewu and Hidup Baru perceive fire as a phenomenon of ambivalent character. Corresponding to the risk concept advanced by Rosa (1998), fire constitutes a situation where something of human value has been put at stake and the outcome is uncertain. The residents are aware that fire forms a possible threat to something that is of value to them, but the outcome is not predetermined but probabilistic, and therefore embedded with uncertainty: "Sometimes there are benefits from fires, sometimes they cause loss" (FN, April 24, 2009).

The variety of possible desirable fire impacts brought about by controlled and (intentionally or unintentionally) uncontrolled fire that the villagers perceive ranges beyond the daily purposes of the household economy and important livelihood services (e.g. land preparation, warding off insects and cold while staying in the forest, the extension of fishing grounds, open access to locate and access fish and game, clean channels and paths to forests and fields, the uncovering of iron along logging rails) to short mental relief (arson driven by rivalry and feelings of jealousy and injustice), and thrill and intrinsic enjoyment. On the other hand, people perceive (intentionally or unintentionally) uncontrolled fire to entail potentially diverse negative effects, including smoke haze accompanied by adverse health effects, damage to livelihoods due to the impediment of transport and daily activities, soil degradation, the destruction of agricultural property, social conflicts, political sanctions, social scandal, shame, and declining forest resources.

However, people's assessment of fire impacts is diverse, dynamic, and depends on multiple factors. Just as with past experience, the disastrous potential of the fire event, social awareness and potential personal involvement affect fire risk perception and communication processes, and livelihood context also impacts on how people perceive and evaluate fire effects. Within the scope of these interdependencies a general pattern of fire perception seems to prevail. While fire generally is perceived to entail possibly diverse positive livelihood impacts, its potential adverse impacts appear to be a factor of concern, but only if personal property or something considered of value is at stake.

According to this perception, and embedded in the local *adat* framework, people in Hidup Baru and Tumbang Lewu manage fire. (Dayak) villagers apply diverse measures to promote positive fire effects and thus to boost the likelihood of a successful swidden cycle. Concrete protective measures, however, seem to be primarily undertaken if damage to personal property, and thus social conflicts and political sanctions, are feared. As a rule, it is not worthwhile investing in the control of fire occurring outside of personal property (cf. Dennis et al. 2005). The principle only to protect what is considered of potential benefit seems also to hold true for the performance of fire coping mechanisms. Despite these premises, we should nevertheless keep in mind that people experience a vast range of constraints in their efforts to anticipate and cope with fire risk, raising doubts about the success of any real or potential efforts to control fire.

Against the background of empirical accounts, we see that, just as fires "have always been a part of the natural environment in Borneo, at least for the last several thousand years" (Brookfield et al. 1995: 177), vegetation and land fires are not new phenomena in the areas of Tumbang Lewu and Hidup Baru. Rather, for the (Dayak) residents, fire has always been an integral part of life. Not only has it always been an essential means to secure livelihoods, as seen across the length and breadth of Borneo, but also, analogous to the considerations of Bankoff (2003) regarding the Philippines, the cultures *in situ* have themselves been shaped by fire hazards. These have equally created a general source of danger to people's welfare, as reflected in the Dayak tenet "Small fire becomes your friend, big fire becomes your enemy." While humans' use of fire has modified the natural landscape, people have likewise developed fire management practices and adapted their social institutions, as well as belief systems, to fire, thus establishing that society and nature are reciprocally constitutive (cf. Ingold 1992).

This case study may indeed solely exhibit a partial understanding of the fire risk in Indonesia's peatlands, as counter-narratives of fire experience and respectively the evaluation of fire certainly exist. Moreover, the outlined accounts do not explain the spread of fire or even forest fires (cf. above). Additionally, it is important to stress that the findings should not be read as a counter-example to the obvious sustainability of swidden agriculture (e.g., Conklin 1957; Dove 1983), and the fire risk perception presented primarily builds on people's experiences and behavior during past fire events or potential future fire scenarios. Therefore, in order to assess how people living with fires in their surroundings evaluate these blazes, and therefore decide how to manage fire risk, further in situ research during times of fire events (cf. Vayda 1996) is needed.[22]

REFERENCES

Bankoff, G. (2003): Cultures of Disaster. Society and Natural Hazard in the Philippines, London and New York: Routledge.

Bizard, V. (2011a): Living with the risk of fire in Indonesia's peatlands. International Quarterly for Asian Studies 42/3-4.

Bizard, V. (2011b): Beyond vulnerability – managing the fire risk in peatlands. Fires and people in Central Kalimantan, Indonesia. Anthropological perspectives, Working Paper No. 17, Institute of Social Anthropology, University of Freiburg.

Brookfield, H. C./Potter, L./Byron, Y. (1995): In Place of the Forest. Environmental and Socioeconomic Transformation in Borneo and the Eastern Malay Peninsula, Tokyo, New York and Paris: United Nations University Press.

Carmenta, R./Parry, L./Blackburn, A./Vermeylen, S./Barlow, J. (2011): Understanding Human-Fire Interactions in Tropical Forest Regions: a Case for Interdisciplinary Research across the Natural and Social Sciences. Ecology and Society 16/1.

Chokkalingam, U./Suyanto/Permana, R. P. /Kurniawan, I./Mannes, J./Darmawan, A./Khusussyiah, N./Susanto, R. H. (2005): Community fire use, resource change, and livelihood impacts: The downward spiral in the wetlands of southern Sumatra. In: Mitigation and Adaptation Strategies for Global Change 12/1, 75-100.

Clay, P. M./Olson, J. (2008): Defining "Fishing Communities: Vulnerability and the Magnuson-Stevens Fishery Conservation and Management Act." In: Human Ecology Review 15/2, 143-160.

---

22 I only witnessed a comparatively small fire and only once experienced slight smoke haze.

Colfer, C. J. P. (2002): Ten Propositions to Explain Kalimantan's Fires. In: Colfer C. J. P./Resosudarmo, I. A. P. (eds.), Which Way Forward? People, Forests, and Policymaking in Indonesia, Washington, D.C.: Resources for the Future Press, 309-324.

Conklin, H. C. (1957): Hanunóo Agriculture: A Report on an Integral System of Shifting Culti-vation in the Philippines. Rome: FAO.

Dennis, R. A./Mayer, J./Applegate, G./Chokkalingam, U./Colfer, C. J. P./Kurniawan, I./Lachowski, H./Maus, P./Permana, R. P./ Ruchiat, Y./Stolle, F./Tomich, T. P. (2005): Fire, People, and Pixels: Linking Social Science and Remote Sensing to Understand Underlying Causes and Impacts of Fires in Indonesia. Human Ecology 33/4, 465-504.

Douglas, M. (1985): Risk acceptability according to the social sciences, London: Routledge and Kegan Paul.

Dove, M. R. (1983): Theories of Swidden Agriculture and the Political Economy of Ignorance. Agroforestry Systems 1, 85-99.

Dove, M. R. (1996): Process versus product in Bornean augury: a traditional knowledge system's solution to the problem of knowing. In: Ellen, R./ Fukui, K. (eds.), Redefining Nature: Ecology, Culture and Domestication, Oxford and Washington, D.C.: Berg, 557-596.

Dove, M. R. (2000): The Life-Cycle of Indigenous Knowledge, and the Case of Natural Rubber Production. In: Elle,n R./Parkes, P./ Bicker, A. (eds.), Indigenous Environmental Knowledge and its Transformations. Critical Anthropological Perspectives, Amsterdam: Harwood Academic Publishers, 213-252.

Erikson, K. (1994): A New Species of Trouble: The Human Experience of Modern Disaster, New York: Norton.

Flint, C./Luloff, A. E. (2005): Natural Resource-Based Communities, Risk, and Disaster: An Intersection of Theories. Society and Natural Resources 18/5, 399-412.

Gönner, C. (1999): Causes and effects of forest fires: A case study from a Sub-District in East Kalimantan, Indonesia, Paper presented on the ICRAF workshop on Environmental Services and Land-Use Change. Bridging the Gap between Policy and Research in Southeast Asia. 30 May to 2 June 1999, Chiang Mai, Thailand.

Harwell, E. E. (2000): Remote Sensibilities: Discourses of Technology and the Making of Indonesia's Natural Disaster. Development and Change 31/1, pp. 307-340.

Hoffman, S. F./Oliver-Smith, A. (1999): Anthropology and the angry earth: an overview. In: Oliver-Smith, A. / Hoffman, S. F. (eds.), The angry earth: disaster in anthropological perspective, New York and London: Routledge, 1-16.

Ingold, T. (1992): Culture and the perception of the environment. In: Croll, E./ Parkin, D. (eds.), Bush base: forest farm. Culture, environment and development, London and New York: Routledge, 39-56.

King, V. T. (1996): Environmental Change in Malaysian Borneo. Fire, Drought, and Rain. In: Parnwell, M. J.G./ Bryant, R. L. (eds.), Environmental Change in Southeast-Asia. People, Politics and Sustainable Development. London and New York: Routledge, 165-189.

Mayer, J. (2005): Transboundary Perspectives on Managing Indonesia's Fires. The Journal of Environment & Development 15/2, 202-223.

Murdiyarso, D./Lebel, L. (2007): Southeast Asian forest and land fires: how can vulnerable ecosystems and peoples adapt to changing climate and fire regimes? iLEAPS Newsletter 4, 28-29.

Noordwijk, M. v./Mulyoutami, E./Sakuntaladewi, N./Agus, F. (2008): Swiddens in transition: shifted perceptions on shifting cultivators in Indonesia, Occasional Paper No. 9, Bogor: World Agroforestry Centre.

Page, S. E./Rieley, J. O./Shotyk, W./Weiss, D. (1999): Interdependence of peat and vegetation in a tropical peat swamp forest. Philosophical Transactions of the Royal Society: Biological Sciences 354/1391, 1885-1897.

Rieley, J. O./Page S. E. (2005): Wise Use of Tropical Peatlands: Focus on Southeast Asia, Wageningen: ALTERRA.

Rosa, E. A. (1998): Metatheoretical foundations for post-normal risk. Journal of Risk Research 1/1, 15-44.

Schiller, A. L. (1997): Religion and Identity in Central Kalimantan: The Case of the Ngaju Dayak. In: Winzeler, R. L. (ed.), Indigenous People and the State: Politics, Land, and Ethnicity in the Malayan Peninsula and Borneo, New Haven: Yale University Southeast Asia Studies, 180-200.

Smith, K./Petley, D. N. (2009[1991]): Environmental hazards. Assessing risk and reducing disaster, London and New York: Routledge.

Suyanto/Applegate, G./Permana, R. P./Khususiyah, N./Kurniawan, I. (2004): The role of fire in changing land use and livelihoods in Riau-Sumatra. Ecology and Society 9/1.

Tacconi, L. (2003): Fires in Indonesia: Causes, Costs and Policy Implications, Bogor, Indonesia: CIFOR.

Vayda, A. P. (1996): Methods and Explanations in the Study of Human Actions and their Environmental Effects, CIFOR/WWF Special Publication. Bogor and Jakarta: CIFOR and WWF.

Vayda, A. P. (2006): Causal Explanation of the Indonesian Forest Fires: Concepts, Applications and Research Priorities. Human Ecology 34/5, 615-635.

Vayda, A. P. (2011): Dos and Don'ts in Interdisciplinary Research on Causes of Fires in Tropical Moist Forests: Examples from Indonesia. In: Vayda, A. P. / Walters, B. B. (eds.), Causal Explanations for Social Scientists: A Reader, Lanham, MD: AltaMira Press, 287-304.

Cassava Diversity and Toxicity in Relation to Environmental Degradation
A Feature of Food Security in the Moluccas, Indonesia

ROY ELLEN AND HERMIEN L. SOSELISA

INTRODUCTION

This chapter reports in a summary and provisional fashion on a comparative study of cassava (*Manihot esculenta*) diversity, local knowledge, and management practices in two contrasting eastern Indonesian populations that differ both ecologically and socioculturally.[1] We focus on the situation in the Nuaulu village of Rouhua on the island of Seram as it existed in 2009, and then in Debut on the Kei archipelago, both in the province of Maluku (the Moluccas). Using these data, we examine the significance of cassava toxicity in relation to a history of environmental change in the region since late colonial times, and in relation to how cassava toxicity features as both benefit and hazard in the context of overall patterns of agriculture, nutritional health, and population adaptation. We suggest that although in the Nuaulu case cassava is an increasingly important crop, its main role here is as a secondary 'fallback' food and that the local microclimate and ecology are consistent with a focus on a narrow range of mostly sweet cassava folk varieties. By contrast, in the Kei Islands a heavy reliance on bitter cassava is a strategy for ensuring food security in the context of a history of sago palm depletion, deforestation, and replacement with a more arid woodland savanna environment. In this case, the diversity of cassava folk varieties is a response to farming uncertainty under changing conditions.

---

1   For basic data on the underlying biology of Manihot esculenta relevant to this discussion, see Veltkamp/de Bruijn (1996) and Hillocks et al. (2002).

In terms of the corpus of work on cassava worldwide, we can see that there now exists considerable anthropological and ethnobotanical output, which largely focuses on South America and on the issues of diversity and domestication. A good summary of this subject is found in Rival and McKey (2008), but see also, for example – and especially – a series of justifiably influential papers by Boster (1983, 1984a, 1984b, 1985, 1986) and more recent papers by the Montpelier Group (Rival et al. 2000; Elias et al. 2000; Elias et al. 2001a; Elias et al. 2001b). By contrast, most of what we know of cassava in the diaspora – that is exists in those areas that adopted the crop following what Crosby (1972) called "the Columbian exchange" – relates to pragmatic agronomic issues and the problem of toxicity, particularly in relation to Africa (e.g. Rosling 2003; Oluwolea et al. 2007), where it has proved to be a major health problem. Although cassava has been of increasing importance in Southeast Asia since the late 19th century, its biocultural dynamics are less well understood. As such, and given the contrasting geographic, ecological, and sociocultural contexts of cassava in South America and the rest of the world, we might reasonably ask whether the socio-ecological dynamics of this cultigen in the diaspora are different from its area of endemism.

Cassava in Island Southeast Asia and in the Moluccas

On the basis of present linguistic and historical evidence, cassava possibly arrived in island Southeast Asia by two main routes: with the Portuguese across the Indian Ocean and with the Spanish across the Pacific. Cassava is noted (though not clearly locally reported) by the Dutch naturalist Rumphius (de Wit 1959: 386), although it remained quite unimportant until the 19th century. During the early 20th century it became increasingly significant in Indonesia (Boomgaard 1989; van der Eng 1998), and by 1970 it had eclipsed many traditional starch staples (yams, taro, millet, sago) in the Moluccas, especially in areas of low rainfall and poor soils. In some areas the growing and processing of toxic or "bitter" cultivars[2] had by this time become strongly associated with cer-

---

2   The description of sub-specific crop types has resulted in some confusion in the literature, preferred terms varying with disciplinary and professional specialism, as between botanists, agriculturalists, and ethnobotanists. The designations 'landrace' and 'cultivar' are widely found, though neither of these must be understood as 'variety' in the strict taxonomic sense. Neither do these terms necessarily nor adequately capture the qualities of terms and categories as perceived, organized, and used by local farmers who seek to conceptualize and describe the variation they encounter in

tain ethnic groups, such as the Butonese (originally from southeast Sulawesi), and with Kei islanders. Cassava is now widely found both as a staple of first choice and as a main buffer crop (Hill 2004), and it has been integrated into the subsistence and economic patterns of local populations through numerous food products.

We here compare two populations: people of Nuaulu ethnicity living in Rouhua village on the island of Seram, and the people of Debut village on the island of Kei Kecil (Figure 1). Ellen has conducted ethnographic and ethnobiological fieldwork amongst the Nuaulu over a period of some 40 years. The data reported here build on this accumulated experience, supplemented by a specific field visit of two weeks in August 2009 to conduct the tests that we describe below. Nuaulu speakers numbered 1,686 in 2001, of which the Rouhua group in 2009 constituted 402 individuals. In contrast, Debut had a recorded population in 2009 of 2,628. Both populations are linguistically related within the Ambon-Timor group of the Austronesian family (Collins 1984). However, Nuaulu remains largely animist in terms of religious practices, living at low density on the margins of mature forest, with a mode of subsistence largely focused on swiddening, hunting, sago extraction, and forest collecting. By contrast, Debut has been a mainly Catholic community for about 100 years, and it is more densely inhabited and more integrated into both the state and the market. Although swiddening is important, Debut relies more heavily on fixed forms of agriculture, cash cropping, some agroforestry, and fishing. Our fieldwork in Debut was conducted jointly during the second half of August 2009. In both locations we adopted similar procedures of data elicitation: ethnographic interviews with farmers in agricultural plots and in household settings, freelisting techniques, plot surveys, ranking exercises, and participant observation of processing methods. In addition, we conducted toxicity tests and collected leaf specimens for later DNA analysis.

their own crop species. In an attempt to minimize this confusion we describe the (emic) categories identified by the subjects of our research as 'folk varieties' and use the term 'varietal' when referring to the local names. The term 'varietal' has some authority, having been first defined by Berlin (Berlin, Breedlove, and Raven 1973; but see also Berlin 1992) as part of his widely adopted system of ethnobiological nomenclature and classificatory ranks. We use the term 'cultivar' to refer to the (etic) distinctions between sub-specific types when judged by scientific experts of whatever background. Also, as there is no settled popular English name for Manihot esculenta, we use the name 'cassava' rather than 'manioc', as this is the predominant term in the technical literature and in the literature on Southeast Asia.

Figure 1: The Moluccan islands of Indonesia, illustrating the geographic relationship between the populations studied.

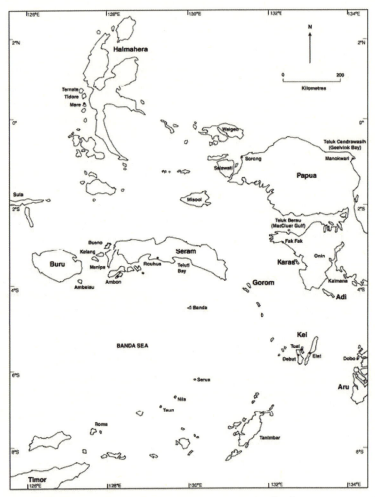

Source: Adapted from Figure 1.2 in Ellen 2004 by Kent Design Studio.

NUAULU KNOWLEDGE AND MANAGEMENT OF CASSAVA DIVERSITY

For the Nuaulu, cassava is currently the most important root crop grown in otherwise high diversity swiddens, and it is second only to sago (*Metroxylon sagu*) as the most important form of dietary starch (Ellen 1978, 2006). In Rouhua we recorded 13 widely shared and terminologically distinct varietals for cassava (excluding synonyms). These labeled folk varieties were perceived to differ from each other according to a range of morphological features, for example the color and texture of root parenchyma, the color of tuber periderm and cortex, color of petiole and stem, leaf shape, length of maturation, productivity, and toxicity. Only one varietal (*paru*) is flagged as 'bitter' and is always processed by grating the roots and then pressing to remove toxic cyanogenic glucosides. How the various folk varieties are perceived as relating to each other is shown in an indicative consensus folk classification of the Nuaulu category *kasipii* (figure 2). Note that the species *Manihot glaziolii* is also included in the category. This has an independent biocultural history in Southeast Asia, and although it is not a source of edible starch it is harvested for its edible leaves as well as serving as a village shade plant. All cassava diversity in Nuaulu swiddens is due to clonal selection, and plants rarely flower or fruit.

Figure 2: Indicative folk classification of Nuaulu category kasipii.

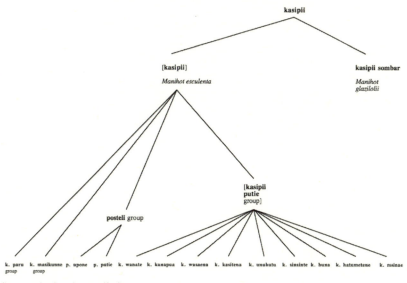

Source: Authors' compilation.

Management strategies (planting techniques and patterns, tending, harvesting, and germplasm exchange) are limited compared with what we found for Debut farmers (Figure 3). A planting preference survey flagged *masikunne, paru, wasaena,* and *putie* as those folk varieties most frequently planted, though preferences for different folk varieties in terms of taste were regarded as being less important. Although influenced by consumption factors (such as cooking), in a survey of 12 subjects there was an overall taste preference for *wasaena* and *masikunne* equally. *Paru* was consistently ranked lower, although Nuaulu tended to be relaxed about the side-effects of cassava toxicity and there was little clinical evidence of poisoning. Although it is not on the whole either encouraged or common, raw cassava will occasionally be eaten.

Figure 3: Nuaulu cassava management, August 2009

Explanatory Note: (left) Massive lignified cassava stems in a swidden belonging to Son Matoke, river Mon. Note the angle of slope and minimal management typical of Nuaulu forest-fallow agriculture. Such swiddens are generally protected with a close tree canopy cover that helps to retain moisture.

Explanatory note: (right) Heunaka Neipane planting cassava stem cuttings in a new swidden near the Upa River. Source: Roy Ellen, 2009.

CASSAVA KNOWLEDGE AND MANAGING DIVERSITY IN THE KEI ISLANDS

If we now turn to Debut, we are dealing with the coastal margin of a predominantly dry, deforested woodland savanna area in which cassava is grown in a mixture of swiddens, other kinds of dry field (home gardens) nearby the village, and in a government-sponsored agricultural project zone. Compared with the Nuaulu situation described above, in Debut we found a far larger number of folk varieties. Some of the more widely shared varietals for which we have good data are listed in Table 1, adjusted for synonyms and where we also provide some selected characters that mark them out as distinct. It should be noted that the stability of the names used varies between both contexts and individuals, depending on the frequency with which the varietal is found and the opportunities for arriving at consensus. Although the names as given to us were sometimes in a mixture of Kei language and Malay (which we believe anyway to be common usage), we have standardized names here to the Kei language alternatives wherever possible.[3] As in the case of the Nuaulu, although many additional characters

---

3 The orthography for Kei words mainly follows that adopted by Ed Travis in his 'Draft Kei-English dictionary – 28 Jan 2011', and we thank him for his permission to access this unpublished manuscript. We have departed from this standard in particular cases, where advised to do so by authoritative local speakers and writers of the language.

– such as root parenchyma texture, productivity, maturation period, and leaf shape (to which we will return later) – are additionally important when farmers make decisions about planting and consumption, we have listed here just five simplified morphological characters based on color. When combined, these characters contribute to the perceptual distinctiveness of each folk variety and make recognition, and therefore management decisions, easier.

Table 1: Cassava varietals in Debut, 2009: names (excluding synonyms) and selected, simplified morphological characters based on colour

No.	Name	Root parenchyma	Periderm	Cortex	Petiole	Stem
	Enbal					
1	enbal lislis ngain ngangiar	w	b	w	r	w
2	enbal lislis ngain ngametan	w	b	w	r	b
3	enbal ngangiar ulin ma'afa	w	b	w	w	w
4	enbal ngangiar har'u	w	b	w	w	w
5	enbal hukun hail	w	b	r	w	w
6	enbal ngangiar vaar vulvul	w	b	w	r	w
7	enbal waleu	w	b	w	w	b
8	enbal Tayad	w	b	w	w/y	b
9	enbal tepong/Namar	w	w	w	w	w
10	enbal tom har'u	y	b	w	r	r
11	enbal ngangiar tom	y	b	w	w	w
12	enbal Loon roan ket	w	b	w	r	w
13	enbal Loon roan baloat	w	b	w	w	w
14	enbal paped	w	b	w	w	b
15	enbal tom	y	-	-	-	w
16	enbal Ngabub	-	-	w	b	b
	Kasbi					
17	kasbi nas putih	w	b	w	r	w
18	kasbi nas bakayu/nafai	w	b	w	r	r
19	kasbi nas	w	b	w	r	r
20	kasbi nas daun bulat pendek	w	b	w	r	w
21	kasbi mabut/Tepa	w	b	r	r	w
22	kasbi ngangiar	w	w	w	w	w
23	kasbi tom	y	b	w	r	w

24	kasbi tom har'u	y	b	w	r	r/w
25	kasbi tom mas	y	b	y	y	w/y
26	kasbi tom faar vulvul	y	b	w	r	w
27	kasbi tom/Namar	y	b	w	r	w
28	kasbi Ambon	w	b	r	r	r
29	kasbi presiden [1]	w	b	r	r	w
30	kasbi presiden [2]	w	w	w	w	w
31	kasbi enbal	r/w	b	w	r	w
32	kasbi kapas	w	w	w	r	r/w
33	kasbi Passo	y	w	w	r	w

Key: w = white, b = black, r = red, y = yellow, r/w = reddish white, w/y = whitish yellow

Source: Authors' compilation.

The local inhabitants (like – we infer – most rural Kei islanders) describe bitter folk varieties as *enbal* and sweet folk varieties as *kasbi* (figure 4). We collected at least 22 distinct varietals for the former, and upwards of a further 22 distinct varietals for the latter. *Enbal* grows better on drier and poorer soils and is more resistant to pig depredations. The subjects insisted on separate preference rankings for *kasbi* and *enbal*, but (as with the Nuaulu) management factors were rated more important than taste, although taste was relatively more important for *kasbi* than for *enbal*. In contrast to the position we found on Seram, all Debut cultivars frequently flower and fruit, though similarly virtually all planting is through clonal selection (figure 5). F1 hybrids dispersed via the cockatoo *Cacatua moluccensis* (*enbal kanar tean*, literally 'cockatoo faeces enbal') are said not to produce good roots and are therefore not deliberately used for breeding. Debut farmers are aware that toxicity is variable genetically and heavily micro-environmental. All *enbal* is detoxified through grating, pressing, drying, and cooking (figure 7), and few deaths or long-term ill-effects are reported.

Figure 4: Cassava folk varieties in Debut, Kei Kecil, August 2009

Explanatory note: (left) *Kasbi tom*, a common sweet folk-variety; (right) Distinctive leaf form and red petioles of *enbal lislis*, amongst the most toxic of folk varieties.

Source: Hermien L. Soselisa, 2009.

Figure 5: Cassava management in Debut, Kei Kecil, August 2009

Explanatory Note: (left) Exposed flat dry field mono-cultured with cassava. Note the absence of significant tree cover, encouraging rapid moisture evaporation and soil deterioration; (right) Cassava in flower.

Source: Hermien L. Soselisa, 2009.   Source: Roy Ellen, 2009.

*Figure 6: Indirect lever beam press (gepe enbal) being used
to process bitter cassava.*

Source: Hermien L. Soselisa, 2009.

TOXICITY AND FOLK CLASSIFICATION

We wished to test the extent to which the distribution of cyanogenic glucoside toxicity was reflected in folk classifications, and to see what different patterns we might find when comparing Rouhua with Debut. Relatively little work has been undertaken on cassava toxicity in Indonesia (although see Hidayat et al. 2000) and even less on how toxicity management is situated in local knowledge systems. Using 'Bradbury' picrate tests (Bradbury, Egan and Bradbury 1999; see also Wilson et al. 2000 and O'Brien et al. 2007) on portions of cassava root medulla, we found that for nine Nuaulu varietals (Table 2) mean toxicity was 151 ppm (range = 10-300) and for 23 Kei varietals (Table 3) 290 ppm (range = 20-800). As demonstrated in Figure 7, there was a considerable amount of overlap between folk varieties designated *kasipii* (all Nuaulu), *kasbi* ('sweet' Debut), and *enbal* ('bitter' Debut), although *kasbi* folk varieties showed a mean of 206 and *enbal* a mean of 360. The one Nuaulu folk variety marked out as 'bitter', *kasipii paru* (that had come from Buton), yielded a toxicity score of 200-300.

Table 2: Results of toxicity ('Bradbury') tests on root samples: Rouhua, August 2009

No	Nuaulu varietal	Score
1	kasipii masikunne	100
2	kasipii paru	200
3	kasipii wasaena	50
4	kasipii kanapua	10
5	kasipii masikunne hata ikine	100
6	kasipii putie hata metene	200
7	kasipii paru	300
8	kasipii watane	200
9	kasipii watane	200

m = 151

Source: Authors' compilation.

Table 3: Results of toxicity ('Bradbury') tests on root samples measured as total cyanide ppm: Debut, August 2009

Kei varietal	Score	Kei varietal term	Score
1. kasbi ngangiar	100	9. enbal Tayad	100
2. kasbi enbal	400-800	10. enbal Namar	100
3. kasbi tom	20	11. enbal waleu	100
4. kasbi presiden	200	12. enbal tepong	800
5. kasbi nas	200-400	13. enbal ngangiar ulin ma'afa	400
6. kasbi Ambon	200	14. enbal tom har'u	400
7. kasbi tom mas	30	15. enbal hukun hail	200+
8. kasbi mabut	200	16. enbal Loon roan ket	200-400
		17. enbal Loon roan baloat	400
		18. enbal ngangiar tom	200
		19. enbal Tayad	400-800
		20. enbal ngangiar faar vulvul	400
		21. enbal lislis ngain ngametan	800
		22. enbal lislis ngain ngangiar	200-400
		23. enbal ngangiar har'u	200-400

n (kasbi) = 8   n (enbal) = 15
m = 206   m = 360

Source: Authors' compilation.

Figure 7: Overlap in toxicity ranges for the Nuaulu category kasipii, and the Debut categories kasbi and enbal. (-100), (100-300), (400-600) and (800) refer to ppm (parts per milligram) ranges for varietals in the indicated sectors of the diagram.

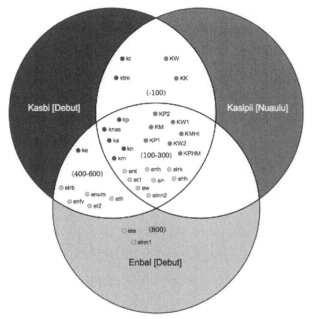

Key: Kasipii [Nuaulu]: KK, kasipii kanapua; KM, kasipii masikunne; KMHI, kasipii masikunne hata ikine; KP1, KP2, kasipii paru; KW1, KW2, kasipii watane; KPHM, kasipii putie hata metene; KW, kasipii wasaena; Kasbi [Debut]: ka, kasbi Ambon; ke, kasbi enbal; km, kasbi mabut; knas, kasbi nas; kn, kasbi ngangiar; kp, kasbi presiden; kt, kasbi tom; ktm, kasbi tom mas; Enbal [Debut]: ehh, enbal hukum hail; elnn1, enbal lislis ngaen ngametan; elnn2, enbal lislis ngaen ngangiar; elrb, enbal Loon roan baloat; elrk, enbal Loon roan ket; en, enbal Namar; enh, enbal ngai ngiar har'u; enfv, enbal ngai ngiar faar vulvul; ent, enbal ngai ngiar tom; enum, enbal ngangiar ulin ma'afa; et1, et2, enbal Tayad; ete, enbal tepong; eth, enbal tom har'u; ew, enbal waleu.

Source: Authors' compilation.

Finally, we undertook a DNA analysis (Figure 8) of 32 leaf specimens for different folk varieties collected in Rouhua and Debut, in order to explore whether toxicity associated with different varietals might be reflected in the genetic profiles of groups of cultivars. This analysis was conducted in Bandung by Dr. Asri Peni Walandiri. We found a weak correlation between genetic relatedness and toxicity and perceptions of toxicity, suggesting that toxicity is largely phenotypic and micro-environmental. This much is widely established in the literature, though our own data seemed to be suggesting that, as a trait, toxicity repeatedly and rapidly reappears in new and different habitats, depending on local conditions, where it is also deliberately selected by farmers. Similarly, farmer evidence for the geographic provenance of individual folk varieties does not correlate well with genetic relatedness, suggesting here that naming follows phenotypic resemblance rather than firm evidence based on traceable germplasm. On the other hand, the DNA evidence shows close genetic relatedness between most of the larger number of Debut varietals and a distant genetic relatedness between all of the smaller number of Rouhua varietals, strongly suggesting that farmers in Debut are much more active in manipulating propagative material than the Nuaulu.

Figure 8: Phylogenetic tree based on DNA collected from leaf samples of Manihot esculenta from different named folk varieties in Rouhua (R) and Debut

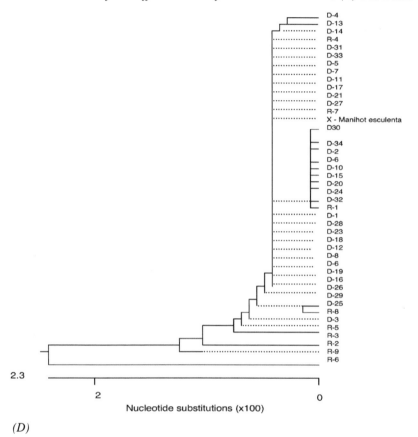

(D)

Explanatory note: The tree was determined using the Clustal method, based on an alignment of 1181-bp 18S rRNA for sample X.

Source: Asri Peni Walandiri (personal communication with the authors).

DISCUSSION

If we summarily compare the wider environment (Figure 9) and the ecology and management of *Manihot esculenta* among the Nuaulu and in Kei, we can see an interesting pattern of contrasts. Whereas the Nuaulu area has higher rainfall, greater forestation, higher soil fertility, lower human population density, high starchy root crop diversity in swiddens, and sago remains the primary source of starch (Ellen 2010), Kei has lower rainfall, is characterized by heavy deforestation, savanna, lower soil fertility, higher human population density, low starchy root crop diversity in swiddens, and sago is much depleted (Monk et al. 1997). In the Nuaulu case, the ecological profile appears to be correlated with low cassava diversity, a low proportion of bitter types, minimal management, little evidence of regular flowering and fruiting, and even less evidence of volunteer seedlings. Ellen reports a maximum of 17 consistently and widely distinguished varietals for Nuaulu, only one of which is flagged by the Nuaulu themselves as 'bitter'. By contrast, in Kei there is high cassava diversity, a high proportion of bitter types, extensive management, much regular flowering and fruiting, and some evidence of volunteer seedlings. Ellen and Soselisa between them report at least 44 varietals, approximately 22 each for *enbal* (bitter types) and for *kasbi* (sweet types). For the purposes of this chapter, we have erred on the cautious side and reduced this number to a core where we have reliable data, a subset of which we have used for the toxicity tests. This gives us 16 for *enbal* and 17 for *kasbi*. Nevertheless, given that we sampled a small part of the total number of households, home gardens, and swiddens, the actual number of folk varieties planted and in circulation is most likely to be higher than this figure.

Figure 9: (left) Upland rain forest in central Seram, looking north from the Trans-Seram Highway towards Mawoti (March 1996), compared with (right) degraded savanna woodland near Debut on Kei Kecil (August 2009)

Source: Roy Ellen 1996, 2009.

We believe this pattern of contrasts to be a result of environmental and subsistence change in Kei over a period of more than 100 years, and that this is reflected in a changing diet, food culture, and ethnic identity. As a category, *enbal* has a higher salience than *kasbi* and there is no evident cultural consensus about how all varietals of *Manihot esculenta* should be collectively described, whether as *kasbi* or as *enbal*. In general discourse concerning identity and food (including that of non-Kei Moluccans), and in evaluations of Kei as a 'cultural other' – such as those common amongst the demographically preponderant Ambonese – *enbal* is the term of pre-eminence, and which metanymically evokes an important difference between Kei Islanders and other Moluccans. And much like Laura Rival (2001: 62) has described for the Makushi of Guyana, sweet cassava is somehow less "real" than bitter cassava, and the two groups of folk varieties are treated as two distinct kinds of crop, despite their morphological similarities and the evidence for the continuous distribution of toxicity between the two extremes that they represent.

Despite these differences, the data from both research sites allows us to make some tentative observations regarding the emerging biocultural history of cassava diversity in eastern Indonesia. In both cases, folk classifications provide a framework for making sense of toxicity, a strong local correlation between leaf shape and perceived toxicity, and possible selection for perceptual distinctiveness (particularly evident in *enbal lislis*). Local differences in the numbers and types of folk variety recorded reflect ecology, environmental change, previous food histories, and human population movement. In the Nuaulu area, a wet micro-environment, low population density, extant lowland rainforest, and complex vegecultural swiddens favor low cassava diversity with few toxic folk varieties. In Debut, a drier micro-environment, higher population densities, deforestation, and the denudation of sago favor high diversity with a greater proportion of bitter folk varieties. This relationship is consistent with recent work on the chemical ecology of cassava, which shows that polymorphism for cyanogen levels facilitates the analysis of how costs and benefits of crop defenses vary between human populations with different management regimes. High cyanogen levels appear to confer important ecological advantages for the plants and agronomic advantages for farmers, as well as health costs and constraints linked to sociocultural factors, which necessitate effective detoxification or dietary buffers against high levels of toxicity (McKey and Beckerman 1993; McKey et al. 2010).

We conclude that there are significant differences between the two eastern Indonesian populations compared herein. In Debut and Kei generally, sago appears to have preceded cassava as the main starch staple.[4] And we can see in the processing and consumption patterns of *enbal* certain cultural continuities, such that the hard biscuits used in mortuary ceremonies and other ritual exchanges in parts of the Kei archipelago (Kaartinen 2007) resemble those made from sago of similar appearance that are important in ritual exchange elsewhere in the Moluccas, such as amongst the Nuaulu. In east Seram, and in other parts of the Moluccan region, such biscuits (both sago and cassava) were until quite recently widely traded and part of a regime of fish-for-starch barter (Ellen 2003: 215-19; Soselisa 2004: 97-100). We suspect this continues to be the case in some areas.

Although cassava may have been planted in the Moluccas much earlier, it was not widely planted until the end of the 19th century. We may presume that its earliest impact was in coastal areas and small islands (such as Ambon) where subsistence stress was at its greatest, and that it only arrived later in the large island interiors and uplands and among those populations who earlier inhabited these areas (such as the Nuaulu). By the mid-20th century, cassava had become a co-staple in many areas (along with sago, taro, and yams), but in others – such as the Kei islands – it entirely transformed agricultural and food culture through a process of rigorous farmer experimentation (compare e.g. Johnson 1972), utilizing inadvertent and deliberate clonal selection. Here, there developed a system dependent on the growing and consumption of bitter cassava and requiring processing to remove toxicity. Migration from South-eastern Sulawesi during the 20th century further encouraged the spread of bitter cassava in the Moluccas.

At the time of the visit of Alfred Russel Wallace to Kei in 1857, Kei Besar was covered in intact, mature, 'luxuriant' forest with tall trees, an "abundance of [...] magnificent timber" for boat-building, in which sago palms abounded, and which supplied "the main subsistence of the natives" (Wallace 1962: 320-1). Wallace also mentions "yams," and we know that Kei was exporting surplus sago to the Banda islands before this time (Ellen 1979: 68; Miller 1980). The situation was reportedly much the same running into the first decade of the 20th century (Riedel 1886: 215; Langen 1902: 12, 15-16, 63-4, 67; Merton 1910: 173-4), although by the 1970s, apart from a few patches of primary forest, Kei Kecil was reduced to savanna woodland and *Imperata* grassland (Effelsberg 1985: 24). This period of deforestation and, we might imagine, general ecological and micro-climatic modification saw the decline of sago as a starch staple, as well as the growth of cassava and, to a lesser extent, maize. In his literature review, Nutz (1959: 14, 19; see also Planten/Wertheim 1893: 285; Merton 1910:

---

4 Note, however, that in some areas, such as the small island of Kei-Tanimbar, foxtail millet (Setaria italica) was still being grown as a dominant crop in the 1980s (Barraud 1985).

196; Geurtjens 1921: 222-23, 229) characterizes the Kei islands at this time as emerging as an intermediate zone between Seram and Buru (with predominant dependence on sago) on the one hand, and Timor and Tanimbar (with predominant dependence on rice) on the other, and where various staples competed but cassava eventually prevailed.

CONCLUSION

In summary, we can see that the expansion of cassava growing in the Moluccas has been dramatic over the last 100 years, but the significance attached to it depends much on local environmental conditions, microclimates, population densities, and the overall spectrum of available subsistence strategies. Thus, the Nuaulu are at the extreme end of a group of more remote peoples living at low population densities and maintaining a wide array of subsistence strategies, who have added cassava to their subsistence repertoire because of its convenience and as a reserve in times of food shortage. Debut represents the opposite extreme: A larger group of populations in drier areas, with higher population densities, more market integration, greater deforestation, poorer soils, and where cassava has been a crucial part of a long-term strategy for adapting to these changing conditions. Ironically, the very biological features of cassava that allow them to do this – the way toxins are used by the plant to colonize otherwise difficult habitats, and how with no close genetic relatives outside of South America there are few evolved pathogens to check its fecundity – have resulted in a specialized food culture during the 20th century focused on the processing and consumption of bitter cassava. This appears not only to have been successful, in that it has compensated for the decline of the previous starch staple – sago – and for the decline of other more hydrophilic and risk-prone crops, but also the potential risks accompanying toxicity have been tolerably well-managed. This is certainly so compared with the experience of other arid zone populations where populations have become increasingly dependent upon cassava. Moreover, the *enbal* food complex has become something of a distinguishing cultural feature within wider Moluccan society, which is being promoted as a new income stream through the sale of packaged cassava-based food specialties. In the way *enbal* has become crucial to maintaining a particular set of interlinked, socioecological variables it might almost be described as a "cultural keystone species" (see e.g. Ellen 2006; also Nabhan and Carr 1994; Garibaldi and Turner 2004; Platten and Henfrey 2009).

Given the underlying environmental, climatic, and demographic trends reported for contemporary Southeast Asia, and the accompanying predictions (see also especially Sillitoe and Alam, and Deswandi et al. in this volume), this account might suggest that rural people will become more dependent on cassava in the immediate future, while those in the more resource-poor areas, such as Kei Kecil, will become even more dependent on cassava than they are at present. We detect an increase in the diversity of both *kasbi* (sweet) and *enbal* (bitter) folk varieties. The former arises partly through market-led demand in urban areas and partly through the movement of new folk varieties from Ambon and Seram, the selection of which has been influenced by the acquired taste preferences of migrant Kei-islanders, a trend particularly noticeable amongst those returning home due to community conflict between 1999 and 2001. Indeed, the trend towards increased cassava consumption in general can only be exacerbated by socially-induced environmental stress of this kind (e.g. Ellen 2004; Soselisa 2007). Local farmers in high stress areas can be seen to have developed knowledge of cassava diversity and clonal reproduction as a way of responding to and mitigating the consequences of environmental change over a period of more than 100 years. Present-day government and NGO recognition of the continuing important role of cassava is reflected in current agricultural development programs – such as *Pola Usaha Tani Berbasis Enbal* in Kei Kecil, a scheme for sustainable arid zone management through the companion planting of bitter cassava with ground nut (*Arachis hypogaea*) and other crops, to maintain soil quality and to yield a potential cash crop.

However, in contradiction to this underlying trend is a second trend driven by different consumption and market factors, as well as by Indonesian government policy, in which imported rice is replacing *enbal* in local diets. This development can only be effectively sustained if rural cash incomes through the sale of produce and off-farm employment continue as of present. Unfortunately, this trend is susceptible to local, national, and global economic downturns. For this reason, and also because of the increasing unpredictability of rainfall linked to the precursors of climate change and especially *El Niño Southern Oscillation (ENSO)* events (e.g. Brookfield 1997; Boomgaard 2007: 99-105), the maintenance of cassava diversity in general (and in particular the diversity of bitter cassava) and the farmer knowledge base that accompanies this is likely to become an increasingly important dietary and subsistence buffer against uncertainty in arid areas well into the future (Ellen 2007).

ACKNOWLEDGMENTS

The research findings reported here are the partial outcomes of a project funded by the British Academy (ASEASUK) South East Asia Research Committee. Fieldwork was conducted under the auspices of Pattimura University, Ambon, within the terms of a Memorandum of Understanding with the University of Kent. For their assistance with the research we would like to thank the following. In Ambon: Rosemary Bolton and Hunanatu Matoke (it is their orthography for Nuaulu words that we follow here), and Thomas Namsa and Gerardina Elsoin; in Canterbury: Graciela Alcantara-Salinas and Neil Hopkins (both for work on figure 3), Simon Platten, Paul Gilbert, Susan Goldsworthy and Rory McBurney; on Seram: Saete and Retaone Soumori, Anakota and Son Matoke, and Heunaka Neipane; on Kei: Karel Ohoiwutun (Bapa Sekretaris, Debut) and his wife Lina, Tante Agu, Agus Namsa and his wife (Tin), Alfons ("Menyala") Yamlean, Mama Biba Jamlean, John Letsoin, and Mama Lis. We would like also to thank Howard Bradbury and Gerard O'Brien for technical advice on the measurement of toxicity, and Dr. Asri Peni Walandiri and Shabarni Gaffar of Padjadjaran University Bandung for conducting the DNA analysis.

REFERENCES

Barraud, C. (1985): Some aspects of millet cultivation in Tanebar-Evav (Kei Islands). Unpublished paper delivered at Seminar Penelitian Indonesia Bagian Timur, 23-29 July 1985. Lembaga Ekonomi dan Kemasyarakatan Nasional-LIPI dan UNSRAT.

Berlin, B. (1992): Ethnobiological Classification: Principles of Categorization of Plants and Animals in Traditional Societies, Princeton, New Jersey: University Press.

Berlin, B.,/Breedlove, D. E., Raven, P. H.. (1973): General Principles of Classification and Nomenclature in Folk Biology. American Anthropologist 75, 214–242.

Boomgaard, P. (1989): Children of the Colonial State: Population Growth and Economic Development in Java, 1795-1880, Amsterdam: Free University Press.

Boomgaard, P. (2007): Southeast Asia: An Environmental History, Santa Barbara, Denver, Oxford: ABC-CLIO.

Boster, J. S. (1983): A Comparison of the Diversity of Jivaroan Gardens with that of the Tropical Forest. In: Human Ecology 11/1, 47-68.

Boster, J. S. (1984a): Classification, Cultivation, and Selection of Aguaruna Cultivars of Manihot esculenta (Euphorbiaceae). In: Advances in Economic Botany 1, 34–47.

Boster, J. S. (1984b): Inferring Decision-making from Preferences and Behavior: an Analysis of Aguaruna Jivaro Manioc Selection. Human Ecology 12, 343-58.

Boster, J. S. (1985): Selection for Perceptual Distinctiveness: Evidence from Aguaruna Cultivars of Manihot esculenta. Economic Botany 39, 310–325.

Boster, J. S. (1986): Exchange of Varieties and Information between Aguarana Manioc Cultivators. American Anthropologist 88, 428–436.

Bradbury, M. G./Egan, S. V./ Bradbury, J. H. (1999): Picrate Paper Kits for Determination of Total Cyanogens in Cassava Roots and All Forms of Cyanogens in Cassava Products. Journal of the Science of Food and Agriculture 79, 593-601.

Brookfield, H. (1997): Landscape History: Landscape Degradation in the Indonesian Region. In: Boomgaard, P./Colombijn, F./Henley, D. (eds.), Paper Landscapes: Explorations in the Environmental History of Indonesia. [Verhandelingen van het Koninklijk Instituut van Taal-, Land en Volkenkunde, 178] Leiden: KITLV Press, 27-59.

Collins, J.T. (1984): Linguistic Research in Maluku: A report on Recent Fieldwork. Oceanic Linguistics 21/1-2, 73-146.

Crosby, A. W. (1972): The Columbian Exchange: Biological and Cultural Consequences of 1492, Westport, Connecticut: Greenwood Press.

Effelsberg, W. (1985): Medizin und kultureller Wandel auf den Kei-Inseln, Gelsenkirchen: Verlag Andreas Müller.

Elias, M./ Panaud, O./Robert T. (2000): Perception and Management of Cassava (Manihot esculenta Crantz) Farming System Using AFLP Markers. Heredity 85, 219-230.

Elias, M./McKey, D./Panaud, O./ Anstett, M. C./ Penet, L./Robert, T. (2001a): Traditional Management of Cassava Morphological and Genetic Diversity by the Makushi Amerindians (Guyana, South America). Perspectives for On-farm Conservation of Genetic Resources 120, 143–157.

Elias, M./ Penet, L./ Vindry, P./ McKey, D./ Panaud, O./ Robert, T. (2001b): Unmanaged Sexual Reproduction and the Dynamics of Genetic Diversity of a Vegetatively Propagated Crop Plant, Cassava (Manihot esculenta Crantz), in a Traditional Farming System. Molecular Ecology 10/8, 1895–1907.

Ellen, R. F. (1978): Nuaulu Settlement and Ecology: The Environmental Relations of an Eastern Indonesian Community [Verhandelingen van het Koninklijk Instituut voor Taal-, Land- en Volkenkunde, 83], The Hague: Martinus Nijhoff.

Ellen, R. F. (1979): Sago Subsistence and the Trade in Spices: A Provisional Model of Ecological Succession and Imbalance in Moluccan History.l In: Burnham and, P./Ellen, R.F. (eds.), Social and Ecological Systems, [Association of Social Anthropologists Monograph, 18], London: Academic Press, 43-74.

Ellen, R. (2003): On the Edge of the Banda Zone: Past and Present in the Social Organization of a Moluccan Trading Network, Honolulu: University of Hawaii Press.

Ellen, R. (2004): Escalating Socio-environmental Stress and the Preconditions for Political Instability in South Seram: The Very Special Case of the Nuaulu. Cakalele: Maluku Research Journal 11, 41-64.

Ellen, R. (2006): Local Knowledge and Management of Sago Palm (Metroxylon sagu Rottboell) Diversity in South Central Seram, Maluku, Eastern Indonesia. Journal of Ethnobiology 26/2, 83-123.

Ellen, R. (2007): Introduction. In: Ellen, R. (ed.), Modern Crises and Traditional Strategies: Local Ecological Knowledge is Island Southeast Asia [Studies in Environmental Anthropology and Ethnobiology, 6], Oxford: Berghahn, 1-45.

Ellen, R. (2010): Why Aren't the Nuaulu like the Matsigenka? Knowledge and Categorization of Forest Diversity on Seram, Eastern Indonesia. In: Johnson, L. M./Hunn, E. S. (eds.), Landscape Ethnoecology: Concepts of Biotic and Physical Space, Oxford: Berghahn, 116-140.

Eng, P. van der (1998): Cassava in Indonesia: A Historical Re-appraisal of an Enigmatic Food Crop. Southeast Asian Studies 36/1, 3-31.

Garibaldi, A./Turner, N. J. (2004): Cultural Keystone Species: Implications for Ecological Conservation and Restoration. Ecology and Society 9/3: art. 1. http://www.ecologyandsociety.org/vol9/iss3/art1.

Geurtjens, H. (1921): Spraakleer der Keieesche Taal [Verhandelingen van het Bataviaasch Genootschap van Kunsten en Wetenschappen, 63/2], The Hague: Martinus Nijhoff.

Hidayat, A./Zuaraida, N./Hanarida, I./Damardjati, D. S. (2000): Cyanogenic Content of Cassava Root of 179 Cultivars Grown in Indonesia. Journal of Food Composition and Analysis 13, 71-82.

Hill, R. D. (2004): Towards a Model of the History of 'Traditional' Agriculture in Southeast Asia. In: Boomgaard, P./Henley, D. (eds), Smallholders and Stockbreeders: Histories of Foodcrop and Livestock Farming in Southeast Asia, Leiden: KITLV Press, 19-46.

Hillocks, R. J./Thresh, J. M./Bellotti, A. C. (eds.) (2002): Cassava: Biology, Production and Utilization, CABI: Wallingford, UK.

Johnson, A. W. (1972): Individuality and Experimentation in Traditional Agriculture. Human Ecology 1, 149–159.

Kaartinen, T. (2007): Nurturing Memories: The Cycle of Mortuary Meals in an East Indonesian Village. In: Janowski M./Kerlogue, F. (eds.), Kinship and Food in South East Asia [NIAS Studies in Asian Topics, 38], Copenhagen: NIAS Press, 149-169.

Langen, H. G. (1902): Die Key- oder Kii-Inseln des Ostindien Archipelago, Wien: Carl Gerold's Sohn.

McKey, D./Beckerman, S. (1993): Chemical Ecology, Plant Evolution and Traditional Manioc Cultivation Systems. In:. Hladik, C. M/ Hladik, A./ Linares, O. F./Pagezy, H./Semple, A./Hadley, M. (eds.), Tropical Forests, People and Food: Biocultural Interactions and Applications to Development. Paris: UNESCO, Parthenon, 83-112.

McKey, D./Cavagnaro, T. R./Cliff, J./Gleadow, R.. (2010): Chemical Ecology in Coupled Human and Natural Systems: People, Manioc, Multitrophic Interactions and Global Change. Chemoecology 20/2, 109-133.

Merton, H. (1910): Forschungsreise in den südöstlichen Molukken, Frankfurt am Main: Selbstverlag Senckenberg.

Miller, W. G. (1980): An Account of Trade Patterns in the Banda Sea in 1797, From an Unpublished Manuscript in the India Office Library. Indonesia Circle 23, 41-57.

Monk, K. A./de Fretes, Y./Reksodiharjo-Lilley, G. (1997): The Ecology of Nusa Tenggara and Maluku, Hong Kong: Periplus.

Nabhan, G. P./Carr, J. L. (eds.) (1994): Ironwood: An Ecological and Cultural Keystone of the Sonoran Desert [Conservation International Occasional Paper, 1], Washington DC: Conservation International.

Nutz, W. (1959): Eine Kulturanalyze von Kei: Beiträge zur vergleichenden Völkerkunde Ostindonesiens, Düsseldorf: Michael Triltsch Verlag.

O'Brien G. M./Chow, E. P. L./Price, R. K. (2007): Initial Evaluation of a Field-friendly Extraction Procedure for the Enzymatic Assay of Cassava Cyanogens." In: International Journal of Food Science and Technology 42, 999-1006.

Oluwolea, O. S. A./Onabolub, A. O./Mtundac, K./Mlingid, N. (2007): Characterization of Cassava (Manihot esculenta Crantz) Varieties in Nigeria and Tanzania, and Farmers' Perception of Toxicity of Cassava. Journal of Food Composition and Analysis 20, 559-567.

Planten, H. O. W./Wertheim, C. J. M. (1893): Verslagen van de Wetenschap-pelijke Opnemingen en Oder-zoekingen op de Key-Eilanden Gedurende de Jaren 1889 en 1890, Ingesteld door den Luitenant der Zee H. O. W. Planten en den Heer C. J. M. Wertheim, Leiden: Overdruk uit het Tijdschrift van het Aardrijkskundig Genootschap, 1892.

Platten, S./Henfrey, T. (2009): The Cultural Keystone Concept: Insights from Ecological Anthropology. Human Ecology 37/4, 491-500.

Riedel, J. G. F. (1886): De Sluik- en Kroesharige Rassen Tusschen Selebes en Papua, s'Gravenhage: Martinus Nijhoff.

Rival, L. (2001): Seed and Clone: A Preliminary Note on Manioc Domestica-tion, and its Implication for Symbolic and Social Analysis. Rival, L./Whitehead, N. (eds), Beyond the Visible and the Material: The Amerindi-anization of Society in the Work of Peter Rivière, Oxford: Oxford University Press, 57-79.

Rival, L./Elias, M./McKey, D. (2000): Perception and Management of Cassava (Manihot esculenta Crantz) Diversity Among Makushi Amerindians of Guy-ana (South America). Journal of Ethnobiology 20/2, 239-265.

Rival, L./ McKey, D. (2008): Domestication and Diversity in Manioc (Manihot esculenta Crantz ssp. Esculenta, Euphorbiaceae). Current Anthropology 49/6, 1119-1128.

Rosling. H. (2003): Classification of Cassava into 'bitter' and 'cool' in Malawi: From Farmers' Perceptions to Characterization by Molecular Markers. Eu-phytica 132, 7–22.

Soselisa, H. L. (2004): Fishers of Gorogos: Livelihood and Resource Manage-ment in a Maluku Island, Indonesia, Darwin: Charles Darwin University Press.

Soselisa, H. L. (2007): A Comparison of Traditional and Innovative Subsistence Strategies on Buano During Periods of Socio-environmental Stress, 1980-2003. In: Ellen, R. (ed.), Modern Crises and Traditional Strategies: Local Ecological Knowledge in Island Southeast Asia, Oxford: Berghahn, 143-165.

Veltkamp, H.J./de Bruijn, G.H. (1996): Manihot esculenta Crantz. In: Flach, M. Rumawas, F. (eds), Plant Resources of South-east Asia No. 9. Plants Yield-ing Non-seed Carbohydrates, Leiden: Backhuys, 107-113.

Wallace, A. R. (1962 [1869]): The Malay Archipelago, New York: Dover.

Wilson, W. M./Dufour, G. M. and D. L. (2000): Application of a Picrate Semi-quantitative Screening Assay for the Cynanogenic Potential of Cassava Roots at a Remote Field Site. Journal of the Science of Food and Agriculture 80, 590-594.

Wit, de, H. C. D. (1959): A Checklist to Rumphius's Herbarium Amboinense. In: de Wit, H. C. D. (ed.), Rumphius Memorial Volume, Baarn: Hollandia, 339-460.

What makes a Social System Resilient?

Two Fishing Communities in Indonesia

RIO DESWANDI, MARION GLASER AND SEBASTIAN FERSE

INTRODUCTION

Environmental changes create a situation whereby communities dependent on natural resources become increasingly vulnerable, especially in terms of food security (Fraser 2006; Osbahr et al. 2008). With co-evolving interactions between social and ecological systems, surprises (dissonances between ecosystem behavior and a priori expectations) are the rule (Gunderson 2003). Human communities therefore need to be able to adapt to these surprises. Unexpected events or developments pose uncertainty – a concept of which scientists do not have a common or shared understanding (Walker et al. 2003). Uncertainty is generated by inherent low predictability in human-nature interaction (Smith 2007), as well as our imperfect knowledge of the system (Brugnach et al. 2008).

There is always a difference between what actually happens and what is understood or perceived by humans. One reason for this is that most human observations are scale-specific (cf. Antweiler, this volume). Local knowledge, through which humans try to understand phenomena within their surroundings, is constructed through a subjective process of framing, by which ideas are organized and meanings inferred (Nisbet and Mooney 2007). Uncertainty rises as local events are increasingly influenced by global phenomena (i.e. climate change, global political and economic upheavals) which fall outside of the horizons of local observation. As a result, human and social adaptation and coping capacities are limited. Recent climate change-related research documents the 'local impacts' of climate change in particular social and ecological settings and extracts lessons learned on how communities cope with altered uncertainty and livelihood insecurity (cf. Ford et al. 2006; Paavola 2008; Hahn et al. 2009; Ford et al. 2010; Glaser et al. 2010a).

According to recently published data (World Bank 2010), 70 percent of the world's poor live in rural areas and derive their livelihoods from natural resources. Thus, for more than two-thirds of the earth's human population, unexpected environmental changes imply food and/or other livelihood insecurity. However, the level of insecurity experienced by particular human communities will be different in different social, economic, political, and ecological settings (cf. Daniel G 1996; Lindström et al. 2003; Huang et al. 2010; Dean and Sharkey 2011; Wills-Herrera et al. 2011).

The ongoing exploitation and degradation of natural resource systems cumulatively contribute to a situation of low community and household adaptability to environmental changes in the context of multiple uncertainties for coastal households. In Indonesia, 60 percent of the population live in coastal areas and derives their livelihoods from marine and coastal resources and terrestrial resources near the coastal area. According to the most recent data published, more than 38 percent of the population (the highest proportion) derive their livelihoods from resource-dependent sectors such as fisheries, agriculture, and forestry (BPS 2011).

Communities whose livelihoods rely directly on the extraction of natural resources experience a relatively higher level of livelihood uncertainty (CARE 2002) than those who can fall back on secondary and tertiary sector occupations. A national newspaper reported that, in February 2011, at least half a million fishermen in forty coastal regencies and cities in Indonesia were temporarily unable to fish due to out-of-season harsh weather conditions. This put about 2.5 million people at risk of food insecurity (Joewono 2011). Households that depend on fishing incomes might find themselves in this predicament for days or even weeks. The Ministry of Marine Affairs predicted that 13 tons of rice were needed to support those fishermen and their families for two weeks.

However, in most situations, coastal households in Indonesia rely mostly on their own capacities, since outside assistance from the state or other agents is rarely available. Such situations prevail in many coastal communities situated in geographically less accessible areas, for example small islands and other remote coastal areas. Effective and efficient local strategies for coping with environmental changes and associated livelihood uncertainties that characterize marine and coastal systems are thus needed – a need that is well-captured in the term 'social resilience' (Adger 2000).

The notion of resilience was classically defined by Holling as the ability of ecosystems to absorb change and disturbance and still maintain the same relationships between populations or state variables (1973: 4). More recently, social resilience, that is the ability of groups or communities to cope with external stresses and disturbances as a result of social, political, and environmental change (Adger 2000), has also become a central concept in community adaptability (cf. Walker et al. 2004). The resilience of a human community rests, to a great extent, in its adaptive capacity, a concept Carpenter and Brock (2008) define as the ability of a community to adjust responses to changing contexts generated by environmental changes, for example the depletion of natural resource systems or a disaster. Another central determinant of system resilience is the ability of systems to learn. Interdisciplinary research on resilience and resilience management practice has started to focus on social-ecological systems assessing closeness to dangerous thresholds, and on the need to destabilize degraded or otherwise undesirable systems (such as coral reef 'graveyards' or autocratic regimes) to prepare for transformation to more desirable system configurations (Walker et al. 2006; Carpenter et al. 2009).

The analysis of systemic self-organization, with a focus on the identification of positive and negative social-ecological feedback loops, has become central in resilience management analysis (Glaser et al. 2010b: 341). Transforming vulnerable systems to more resilient states is thus the objective, if one wishes to arrive at system states that are considered desirable. This paper contributes to social-ecological resilience analysis by identifying the main properties that, in the context of continuing environmental change, make a social system resilient against food insecurity. We propose that a major component of social resilience rests in a community's ability to cope with food insecurity. In order to identify the main characteristics of a social system that is resilient to food insecurity, we analyze two case studies of food security-related coping strategies employed by Indonesian fishing communities.

METHODOLOGY

This paper compares two communities located in different regions in Indonesia (Fig. 1). The first is Nagari Sungai Pisang, situated in Padang Municipality, West Sumatra, in the western part of Indonesia. We selected this village as a study site because, even though Sungai Pisang is situated relatively near to the municipality of Padang (30 km), this village suffers from limited accessibility via both land and sea routes, and this is especially pronounced during the rainy seasons. No public transportation directly from or to the municipal center is available to the approximately 1,700 village residents (BPS 2007). To reach this village over land, a 30-minute motorbike ride is the only current option (Fig. 2). This coastal village is rich in terms of landscape diversity (from low land tropical forests to costal water), which is different to the situation in the second study location.

The second case study concentrates on the Spermonde Archipelago in eastern Indonesia, consisting of six small islands of this reef island archipelago off the coast of South Sulawesi. The small islands Barrang Lompo, Barrang Caddi, Kodingareng Lompo, and Bonetambung were selected as study sites because they lack fishing grounds within their immediate surroundings and/or lack fresh water. Two further islands, Langkai and Lanyukang, were selected because although fresh water is abundant and they are surrounded by spacious fishing grounds, they are situated a relatively large distance away from the city (from where foods are imported).

Figure 1: Map of Indonesia with study locations indicated by arrows

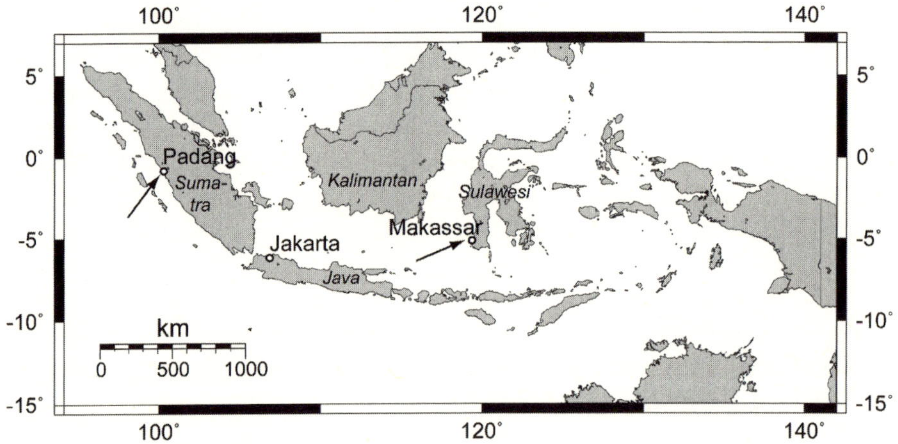

Source: Sebastian Ferse.

Each research study was carried out separately. In western Indonesia, field research was carried out between May and August 2007, while in Eastern Indonesia it was done between March 2008 and May 2010. Qualitative methods were employed in both locations. Semi-structured, in-depth individual and group in-depth interviews, participant observation, and some participatory tools (seasonal calendar, resources mapping, village transects, and focus group discussions) were the main data collection methods. On two of the small islands (Langkai and Barrang Caddi), a role-playing fishing game was conducted for collecting institutions in capture fisheries, especially those regulating interaction between fishermen. A survey for revealing kinship between households was implemented on Bonetambung Island. For this survey, all households were sampled.

Research informants were fishermen, middlemen (patrons who provide financial capital for fishermen), community leaders, and housewives. Informants were selected through a snowball strategy (cf. Stainback and Stainback 1988), which was relatively more complicated on the Spermonde Archipelago. Potential informants were geographically scattered on small islands, which are difficult to access during the northwest monsoon, and the prevailing illegal fishing methods in the region are still a sensitive issue not easily discussed with outsiders, including researchers.

The snowballing strategy employed on the Spermonde Archipelago was conducted by considering the patron-client networks of which the informants were part. The data therefore consists of interview transcriptions, data recorded by digital voice recorder, and pictures and flip chart sketches drawn during participatory data collection methods. These were converted into field notes for qualitative data analysis with ATLAS.ti (version 5.2.18). Genopro (version 2.0.1.4) was used to analyze data on social networks (i.e. kinship) which were collected in a survey.

Figure 2: Map of Sungai Pisang.

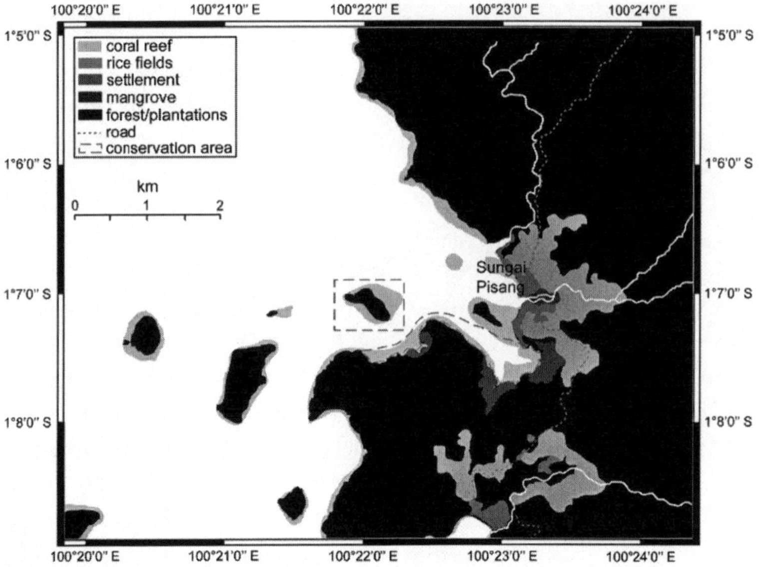

Source: Sebastian Ferse.

ENVIRONMENTAL CHANGES AND LIVELIHOOD VULNERABILITY

The northwest monsoon is the main constraint for the fishing communities in both locations. In the monsoon season, fishing is risky, sometimes fatal, and often impossible. The northwest monsoon season might last for four to five months, rendering the livelihoods of fishing households highly vulnerable. During the stormy monsoon period, fishermen's families cannot fully rely on marine and coastal resources. Their monsoon-related vulnerability is exacerbated by their more recent realization that the seasonality of the weather is becoming more unpredictable, displaying patterns that are out of sync with the experience and system knowledge they have acquired in the past. Fishermen in both study locations reported that the southeast and northwest monsoons have changed in terms of time of occurrence and of duration. Although they did not fully agree on how these changes had come about, they mostly agreed that the storm had become stronger as well as shorter in duration. Coastal erosion was reported to have become an increasingly serious threat in both locations. Fishermen also reported that the seasonal patterns of the occurrence of particular target fish had become irregular or unpredictable. Fishermen and other villagers/islanders did not understand how these environmental changes had come about, and they had little idea on how to cope with them. Fatalism, understanding all that happens as God's given destiny, appeared as the most frequently employed strategy to cope with mental stress in both communities, carrying the danger of communities simply surrendering to the increasingly felt livelihood vulnerability. The following statement made by a fisherman on the Spermonde Archipelago illustrated such fatalism:

"Fish are inexhaustible. [Their abundance] may decline, but [they] will never be exhausted [...] it is determined by God (tuhan) [...] it has nothing to do with [the activity of] humans. The amount of fish we can catch and our fortunes (rezki) have been determined by God..." (Edk , a handline fisherman from Barrang Lompo Island, April 12, 2008).

Both fishing communities in the study have experienced environmental changes, some of which have accumulated or fluctuated over time, while others have occurred abruptly. One of the abrupt changes which influenced fishermen's livelihoods in Sungai Pisang occurred by the end of the 1990s. Anchovy, which was the most important catch for the fishermen in Sungai Pisang, suddenly disappeared at that time. Previously, this target fish constituted the main source of income, not only for the fishermen, but also for the rest of the villagers, who took part in processing and trading activities. Capture fisheries were once the most important socioeconomic activity in the village, especially in terms of cash income. By the end of the 1990s, however, the anchovy "rush" stopped. According to the fishermen, the abundance of anchovy drastically declined soon after a substantial coral bleaching event in 1998: "I cannot remember the exact year, but I am sure it [coral bleaching] occurred after many reefs in Sungai Pisang became white," said Bsw, a senior fisherman (and an elder of the Caniago) in Sungai Pisang, who kept targeting this fish despite its declining abundance (May 25, 2007).

Coral bleaching in Sungai Pisang was part of the regional 1998 El-Niño effect in Southeast Asia (Hopley and Suharsono 2000; Chou et al. 2002). The disappearance of anchovy at the end of 1998 was a major shock to the socioeconomic vibrancy of Sungai Pisang village. In contrast, fishermen on the Spermonde Archipelago are exposed nowadays to more gradual change as a result of continuous fisheries exploitation in the region, especially through the extensive use of blast and cyanide fishing methods. However, fishermen, especially hand line fishermen, suppose that their catch continually decreases as a corollary of their fishing efforts. Cyanide fishing, which started in the context of the live reef food fishery (LRRF) boom sometime in the early 1990s, was especially singled out as a cause of livelihood insecurity: "[The abundance of] fish [in the surrounding of Langkai Island] has declined since cyanide fishing started fishing here…" (Btr, an ex-fisherman from Langkai Island, July 10, 2009).

Livelihood vulnerability in both fishing communities is also affected by their interactions with markets, as their fishing turns from mainly a subsistence activity to a commercially-oriented enterprise. This is especially clear among fishermen on the Spermonde Archipelago. When the Makassar Industrial Park (Kawasan Industri Makassar/KIMA) was established in the 1980s, fishermen started to export fish to faraway markets, for example Hong Kong (Bentley 1998). Until 2006, there were at least 12 companies registered in the industrial park that dealt with the export of various marine products (KIMA 2006). The Natural Resource Conservation Agency at Provincial Level (Balai Konservasi Sumber Daya Alam/BKSDA) issued 39 export licenses for various marine products in 2001, including three licenses to export Napoleon Wrasse (Cheilinus undulatus), a species listed as "endangered" on the International Union for Conservation of Nature (IUCN) (2011) red list, and live groupers (fish from the family Serranidae) (BKSDA 2007). On all researched islands, islanders no longer consume particular kinds of fish (i.e. narrow-barred mackerels, groupers, shrimps, squid, tuna, etc.), as these are all destined for export. Fishermen's households therefore rely on the by-catch or on food that is imported from the mainland, for example from city of Makassar. Hence, islanders' food self-sufficiency is severely reduced, as they become dependent on food supplies from the city. Their vulnerability to food insecurity is thus especially high during the increasingly unpredictable northwest monsoon, when access to the mainland is limited by harsh weather conditions.

COPING FOR FOOD SECURITY IN SUNGAI PISANG

The people that live in this village all belong to the same ethnic group of West Sumatra called the 'Minangkabau'. However, they divide into several different subgroups (locally called as suku), namely the Caniago, Jambak, Melayu, Koto Piliang, and Tanjuang. The Caniago constitute two-thirds of the total population of the community. Each group has a leader called a panghulu, who is responsible for managing social and economic matters within his (the panghulu is always male) group, for example solving conflicts regarding the distribution of inherited land. While the panghulu manages his group only, wider village matters are discussed and decided by a village council (badan musyawarah desa).

Figure 3: A village council meeting held in a mosque

Source: Deswandi, Sungai Pisang

Here, each group is represented by their panghulu and elders within the council and has equal rights, despite the dominancy of one group over others in terms of numbers of members (participant observation, May 2007). In Sungai Pisang, the village council has been politically important as the government's partner for the development of this area because all government programs for the village are discussed and decided through this council (interview with Lurah , May 2007).

The area is rich in terms of biological diversity (Figure 4). Sungai Pisang is supported by agriculture (especially paddy farming), household-scale livestock keeping, and capture fisheries. Fresh water and clean water are available in abundance, both from the continuous supply provided by the river and through some clean water facilities provided by a recent development project. Historical data collected from key informants shows that paddy farming and capture fisheries have been important for the villagers, with agriculture being their first activity when they started inhabiting Sungai Pisang in the 17th century. Some villagers soon learned how to operate capture fisheries.

The development of capture fisheries occurred as villagers interacted with outsiders who introduced them to new fishing technologies. Local coastal and marine ecosystems were once the backbone of local economic activity. Nowadays, after the collapse of anchovy stocks, over two-thirds of village households rely on paddy farming, while the other third depend on capture fisheries, with paddy farming a more recent alternative activity. Being exposed to growing livelihood uncertainties, fishermen have diversified their livelihood activities and coping strategies for both cash income and subsistence (i.e. paddy farming).

Figure 4: Landscape of Sungai Pisang

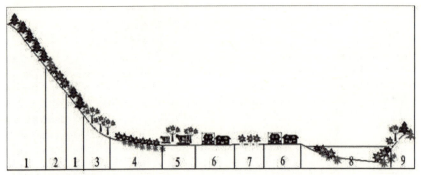

Explanatory Note: (1) Lowland forests; (2) Gambier (Uncaria gambir) plantations; (3) Perennial crops; (4) Rice fields (paddies); (5) Grazing land mixed with perennial crops; (6) Residential areas with public facilities; (7) Mangrove swamps; (8) Coral reefs and sea grass bed; (9) Coastal small islands.

Source: Modified from Deswandi 2007: 76.

During the northwest monsoon, when fishing activities are risky, Sungai Pisang people allocate most of their time to paddy farming or, for younger fishermen, to logging. While paddy cultivation mostly provides cultivators' households with rice for two to three months, logging provides cash income. During the southeast monsoon, when fishing activity is more intense, paddy farming activity continues. As fishermen allocate almost all of their time to fishing, some form working groups of three to five fishermen's families. Through these groups, they collectively work on all members' paddy fields rotationally. However, the most frequently encountered strategy employed to maintain farming during the southeast monsoon is to reduce the scale of paddy farming or for fishing households to pay other villagers to work on the paddy fields. The money paid to hired farmers is gained from capture fisheries. After the collapse of the anchovy, almost all fishermen began targeting mackerel (Rastelliger spec.), so they changed their fishing methods to suit the new target fish. Capture fisheries, paddy farming, and logging complemented each other, creating an optimum level of redundancy in Sungai Pisang's livelihood activities that subsequently increased the level and security of food availability (Deswandi 2007). Fishermen's wives also work and allocate more time to work on the paddy fields during the southeast monsoon. They are involved in planting, nurturing, and harvesting. During planting time, they go to the paddy fields at seven in the morning and return home at four in the evening (participant observation, June 2007).

In this context, the demand on land for paddy farming is increasing, and the conversion of land into paddy fields accelerates, both as new families engaged in paddy farming – and therefore established their fields – and as fishermen also seek to diversify into farming. Within only two years (from 2004 to 2006), 14 hectares of land were converted into paddy fields (Kelurahan Bungus Teluk Kabung Selatan 2006). Though many households seek more secure livelihoods from paddy farming, not all of the households have any land or their own fields. As the first group who arrived and established the village, the Caniago own most of the land, including paddy fields. The other groups (Jambak, Melayu, Koto Piliang, and Tanjuang) own little land, with many of the members of these groups not owning any paddy fields at all.

In Sungai Pisang, land is managed by customary institutions (locally called hukum adaik) under three different institutional arrangements: private property, tribal property, and village property. Private property (pusako randah or harato pancarian) is land that is owned and managed by individuals or families. Group property (ulayat kaum or pusako tinggi) is land that is owned by a group, with management rights granted to women belonging to that group. Women only have the rights to utilize the land, to use it for as long as they want, and to bequest the land to their daughters. They cannot transfer management rights (by leasing or selling the land) without approval from the panghulu of their groups. The last category, village property (ulayat nagari), refers to lands that are owned by the village. These can be utilized by any individual or family that lives in the village. Forests, coastal waters, rivers, and small islands are village property. These three different property rights arrangements are common institutions among the Minangkabau ethnicity in West Sumatra.

Very few paddy fields in Sungai Pisang are privately owned. Most of them are group property belonging to the Caniago. Under the matrilineal Minangkabau system, group property is inherited by females, so no adult male in the village owns land. Some adult fishermen farm paddy after marrying women, mostly in the Caniago ethnic group, who have inherited paddy fields. Others farm paddy under a customary profit-sharing arrangement (patigoan). Under this sharecropping arrangement, the owners of the land transfer cultivation rights of their paddy fields to another for an agreed time period in return for one-third of the harvest. Sharecropping increases the extent of land utilization for paddy by allocating otherwise uncultivated areas to otherwise landless cultivators (Deswandi 2007). The sharecropping rule is applied to group property and also to a few privately owned paddy fields.

With a growing number of villagers involved in paddy farming, the land available for paddy fields is likely to be insufficient in the longer term. In 2006, some fishermen started to cut down the forest to establish plantations of gambier (Uncaria gambir), a lucrative export commodity, on village property. Everyone is entitled to be granted the right to utilize village property, even if they do not belong to any of the subgroups in the village (they called them "outsiders" (orang luar) or are 'newcomers' (pendatang). They just need to have a permit from the panghulu from all subgroups and from the government representative in the village (the lurah). Utilization rights are granted for one hectare of land for a practically unlimited amount of time.

Customary institutions in Sungai Pisang are important, not only in redistributing access to land which concentrates on one group. They also ensure the availability of land as an important asset to support villagers' livelihoods (Deswandi 2007). Group property cannot, under any circumstances, be sold to outsiders (i.e. to individuals from other groups or persons that do not belong to any of the local ethnic groups). Selling group property is considered shameful and will denigrate the seller in the eyes of villagers. Shame has been an effective punishment for encouraging villager's compliance with customary institutions. In an urgent situation, villagers will thus borrow money from close relatives and use their land as informal collateral. This ensures that land, as an important group asset, does not fall into the hands of outsiders.

While paddy farming and gambier plantation require land, financial input, and maintenance, logging provides at least younger, physically fit fishermen who dare to break the law with "easy money." The forest surrounding the village, from which locals cut high-value trees such as mahogany, is a protected area according to national law. This overlap of institutions relating to the forest on the one hand, which, according to customary institutions, is village property, and on the other hand is protected area under Indonesian national law has been a crucial issue of debate between the locally elected village council and government representatives. When fieldwork was carried out in 2007, an "agreement" had been reached between villagers and government representatives (represented by the Lurah) whereby villagers could conduct logging to support their households' subsistence needs. This, however, is still illegal according to state law. The fact that many villagers are involved in logging activities (which financially benefits businessmen from the city rather than villagers engaged in logging) might cause more extensive deforestation in the future.

The management of village property (i.e. forests) is more flexible than that of group property in Sungai Pisang. Villagers may arrange the distribution of village lands to fit their needs, which means that, if needed, they can establish institutions to adjust to the prevailing environmental changes. The following are two current rules regarding the distribution and utilization of forests and forest land:

1. Each villager may utilize one hectare of forest area to establish gambier plantations for a period of one year. Utilization rights can be extended as long as they keep utilizing the land, or else they will lose this right.
2. For subsistence, villagers may do logging in the forest surrounding Sungai Pisang. Considering such activity is illegal according to national law, panghulu and the village council will not protect "law breakers" from possible legal consequences inherent in logging activities (for example, being arrested by the police or being sent to jail).

Previously, when capture fisheries still constituted the most important local socioeconomic activity for all villagers, the village council crafted institutions for managing the distribution of fishing rights in coastal waters in accordance with the fishing methods to be used. Through the village council, fishermen agreed that:

3. Larger-scale fishing methods for catching anchovy, stationary liftnet platforms (bagan pancang), and modern boat liftnets (bagan kapal) must be used only in the outer inshore area, while the nearer inshore area was allocated for smaller boats fishing with scoops (colok).

Flexibility in managing forest lands and coastal waters in Sungai Pisang is partly derived from the fact that the type of resources to be managed as village property is not specifically mentioned in the customary institutions. Customary institutions in West Sumatra, for example, do not specify how to manage marine and coastal resources. As a result, customary institutions still maintain room for creativity in coping with unexpected environmental changes.

COPING WITH FOOD SECURITY ON THE SPERMONDE ARCHIPELAGO

The Spermonde Archipelago is situated in the southern part of the Makassar Strait and on the western side of South Sulawesi. The coral archipelago consists of more than a hundred small islands, but local islanders call their area Sangkarang. Four of the researched islands can be reached by regular ferry from Makassar's harbour (Pelabuhan Kayu Bangkoa), the exceptions being the islands of Langkai and Lanyukang (Figure 5), where transportation to and from these islands relies on fishermen's boats. During the northwest monsoon, transportation to these islands is difficult and at times risky. At least three people died when a regular ferry sank on its way to Badi Island (situated in Pangkajene Kepulauan Regency) when a northwest monsoon storm occurred in 2010.

The Makassarese and Bugis constitute the dominant ethnic groups among islanders on the archipelago. Other ethnic groups are Mandar and Bajao. The social structure in this region is framed by non-symmetrical and stratified patron-client relationships (Pelras 2000). Within such relationships, patrons (punggawa) in general are obliged to provide economic and political protection for their clients (sawi), who will in return provide services, goods, and loyalty to their patron (Pelras 2000: 16; Glaser et al. 2010). The patron-client system thus extends to the economic sphere in which capture fishing is organized and managed as the main local livelihood activity.

Figure 5: The six Study Sites on the Spermonde Archipelago near Makassar, South Sulawesi

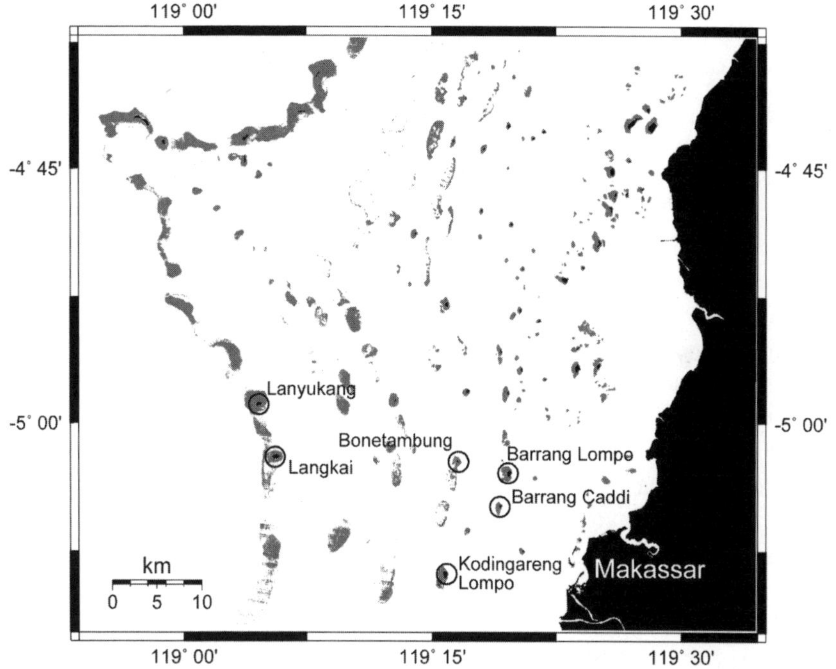

Source: Sebastian Ferse.

The ecosystem in the region supports mainly capture fisheries and, on some islands, household-scale poultry (chicken and ducks) and goat keeping. The availability of fresh water and soil fertility is a factor limiting the possibility of developing agriculture. Supplies of the main staple rice, vegetables, and drinking water during the dry southeast monsoon season come from the mainland. This is problematic during the northwest monsoon, especially for islands without regular ferry connections. Some annual and perennial trees (for example, cassava, some legumes, coconut, and bread fruit) are cultivated on the islands, providing households with limited vegetables and carbohydrates.

Marine and coastal products are the main resources for islanders. Relying on one type of resource, fishermen have to cope with the uncertainty associated with climatic features and changes and with the spatial and temporal variability of fishery resources. Local coping strategies involve foraging daily on different fishing grounds, migrating seasonally to remote fishing areas within or outside the Spermonde Archipelago, and seasonally changing fishing methods to adjust to changes in the availability of different target species or to respond to market demands. As a response to market demands, for example, fishermen adopted cyanide fishing when the live reef fish industry began on the Spermonde Archipelago. By providing credit in times of unfavorable weather conditions and by facilitating access to markets for a wide range of marine products, the links to patrons can also be understood as a kind of coping strategy in the face of highly fluctuating marine resources.

Recently, fishermen have had to sail further and further to find new fishing grounds, which indicates overfishing on the Spermonde Archipelago. From the middle of the 1980s, Makassar fisheries exports, including capture fisheries, started to expand. This motivated fishermen to allocate almost all of their fishing effort to fishing for sale, thus increasing islanders' dependence on food supplies from the mainland. With geographical and climatic constraints, this dependence on food supplies from the mainland has increased local livelihood vulnerability.

Capture fisheries on the Spermonde Archipelago have changed greatly since Indonesia's Blue Revolution started at the end of the 1960s. This era was marked by the introduction of new fishing technologies coupled with mechanization, as well as clear policy support for economic growth through export and foreign investments (BAPPENAS 2009). Mechanization and the adoption of new fishing technologies have altered fishermen's interactions and the way marine and coastal resources are allocated among them. Once a totally open access zone, fishing grounds on the Spermonde Archipelago nowadays fall under three institutional arrangements: open access zones, island-restricted zones (IRZ) managed by islanders (cf. Glaser et al. 2010), and narrower private-restricted zones (PRZ) managed by individuals or groups of fishermen (Deswandi 2012) (Figure 6). With the existence of these three institutional arrangements, access to the fishing grounds (fringing and patch reefs) is unevenly distributed among fishermen on the Spermonde Archipelago. Fishermen whose islands lack fishing grounds still can fish in the open access zone, and still may fish in IRZs or even PRZs, if they use certain fishing methods such as handlines.

Figure 6: Spatial Institutional Arrangements on the Spermonde Archipelago.

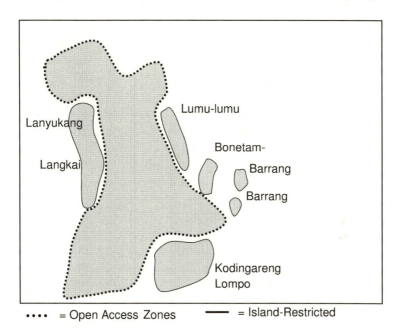

•••• = Open Access Zones ——— = Island-Restricted

Source: modified from Deswandi 2012.

IRZs emerged in early 2000 following serious conflicts between fishermen, which were driven mostly by technological externalities occurring between fishing methods. IRZs were fishermen's therefore solutions to coping with technological externalities. The existence of different institutional arrangements (open access zones, island-restricted zones, and private-restricted zones) effectively redistributes marine and coastal resources under changing technical and ecological conditions.

Institutions used to manage capture fisheries on the Spermonde Archipelago are diverse (consisting of conventions, norms, and rules). Starting with several simple conventions, rules have dynamically co-evolved with the ever-changing environment and the increasing complexity of fishing situations. Nowadays, besides some conventions that have managed to persist for generations, there are norms and rules that contain punishments for non-compliance. It is through the diversity of institutions that fishermen and other islanders are able to agree on how marine and coastal resources are allocated among them, how different types of complex situations should be handled, and how possible conflicts will be resolved.

The diversity of institutions and spatial institutional arrangements in this region provides fishermen with the flexibility to cope with the fact that marine and coastal resources, on which their livelihoods depend, are spatially and temporally highly heterogeneous. Local institutions still support daily foraging and fishing migrations, similar to the time when fishing on the Spermonde Archipelago was all open access; however, fishing is neither always successful nor reliable in supporting household livelihood security, and it is often unfeasible during the northwest monsoon. In such situations, fishing households require help from their fellows, neighbors, relatives, and patrons. Fishermen households on each small island relate to each other as kin, hence they traditionally try to help each other. A kinship survey on Bonetambung Island showed that, of the 272 households living on that island, only two households were not related to other households as kin.

If fellow fishermen, neighbors, and relatives are unable to provide help, the last resort lies with a fisherman's patron. Bound by unwritten rules, patrons are obliged to provide means of production, daily subsistence needs (i.e. food) and financial support for medical treatment for their clients and their families, as well as to protect their clients from social conflict and judicial prosecution. This social network provides the fishermen with insurance during harsh weather conditions in the west monsoon season or at other times when fishing fails to provide sufficient income. In return, clients provide their patrons with services (for example, paid and unpaid work and political support) and loyalty (Pelras 2000). As in many other places on earth where primary producers struggle with the vagaries of nature and markets (Foell et al. 1999; Wood 2003; Nelson and Finan 2009), Spermonde fishermen are obliged to show their loyalty by selling all or particular types of catch only to their patrons – and at considerably lower prices than those offered by markets.

Reciprocal obligations between patrons and their clients on the Spermonde Archipelago are institutionalized and continue to evolve over time. Any failure to fulfill obligations will result in exclusion from social networks, which is costly especially for the more vulnerable party, i.e. the fisherman. All financial support for clients and their families is considered as client debts. Considering that fishermen are always confronted with fishing uncertainty and that therefore most fishermen see this as a never-ending cycle of debts, none indicated wanting to detach himself from his patron. Fishermen considered their dependence on and loyalty to a patron as the only insurance available to them. Nevertheless, the fishermen acknowledged that entering a patron-client relationship is a dilemmatic option for them.

Reciprocal generosity through catch-sharing is commonly practiced in Spermonde Archipelago and is institutionalized as a convention. Fishermen and other islanders, for example, are free to collect catches from blast fishing, or to ask fishermen who fish with modern boat liftnets for a subsistence share. By sharing some of their catch to support the subsistence of less successful colleagues, fishermen are consciously investing in social capital, thus increasing their chances of receiving the help they themselves may need in the future.

INSTITUTIONAL ADAPTABILITY FOR A RESILIENT SOCIAL SYSTEM

Fishermen in Sungai Pisang cope with environmental changes by diversifying their livelihood activities, while fishermen on the Spermonde Archipelago cope by foraging daily in different fishing grounds, changing their fishing methods match seasonally available target species and/or market demand. The most important coping strategy in both research locations, however, appears to be the use of social networks (i.e. fishermen fellows, relatives, and patron-client networks) to fulfill the food subsistence needs of the concerned fishing households.

The coping strategies of fishers in Sungai Pisang and on the Spermonde Archipelago are supported by respective local institutional arrangements. In both locations, natural resources, as the most significant livelihood asset, are allocated so that everyone can access (although at different levels of accessibility) and utilize them accordingly. In both study locations, natural resources are managed under three distinct institutional arrangements: private property (i.e. pusako randah and PRZ), common property (i.e. group property/ulayat kaum and IRZ), and open access (i.e. ulayat nagari and open access zones). These different institutional arrangements have improved the opportunities of fishermen in Sungai Pisang to develop alternative livelihood options (i.e. paddy farming), even for those who do not own land. On the Spermonde Archipelago, fishermen who live on islands that are surrounded by fishing grounds with little (remaining) potential can still fish around other islands. This is important, since, for historical and geographical reasons, natural resources are unevenly distributed. Having developed and adapted to the context of day-to-day experience (Schlager and Ostrom 1999), local institutions in both study locations cope with the uncertainly and uneven distribution of the ecosystem resources upon which local livelihoods depend.

Institutions render the patterns of interaction among resource users, and between resource users and resources, more predictable (Jost 2005). The capacity to achieve exclusion (i.e. to implement effectively the decision about who may and may not utilize a local ecosystem's natural resources) (Quinn et al. 2007) to equitably distribute natural resources (Thorburn 2000) and to manage potential conflicts (Bennett et al. 2001) is also among the central functions of natural resources management institutions.

Local institutions can thus reduce environmental uncertainties, in particular for resource users, by increasing their ability to foresee actions or decisions that will be taken by others under particular circumstances. This potentially reduces conflict. Institutions also inform resource users about what action may (or may not) and must (or must not) be taken in relation to particularly important resource management questions. These local institution characteristics improve the coordination of behavior among resource users (Vatn 2005: 6), which in turn will improve the success of coping strategies. However, as the social-ecological system undergoes gradual, continuous, but fairly unpredictable changes as part of the dynamic interactions between social and ecological system components at and across multiple scales and levels, surprising system reactions might expose human communities to risky and unexpected developments. Successful institutions should have the capacity to co-evolve with and adapt to unpredictable environmental dynamics (Schlager and Ostrom 1999; Adger 2000). Successful institutions can enhance the capacity of ecosystem users to cope with environmental change (Colding et al. 2003). Bottom-up organization increases flexibility and provides room for creativity, change, and innovative responses to new conditions (Waldrop 1992: 280; Berkes et al. 2003: 22). Thus, our analysis supports the conclusion of Waldrop, who reasoned:

"Since it's effectively impossible to cover every conceivable situation, top-down systems are forever running into combinations of events they don't know how to handle. They tend to be touchy and fragile, and they all too often grind to a halt in a dither of indecision" (Waldrop 1992: 279).

We argue that local institutions in both research locations show such capacity to co-evolve with and adapt to environmental changes, but within different "ranges of flexibility" and through different processes. Institutional co-evolution and adaptation in Sungai Pisang have occurred only in institutions managing village property (i.e. forest lands and marine and coastal water), which are facilitated by the village council. The village council has never crafted new institutions for managing group property, and in fact they do not have the legitimacy to do so because they are constrained by customary institutions. As a well-established institution, hukum adaik appears to be a rigid association and resistant to change.

Institutional arrangements for managing private and group properties among the Minangkabau have existed and remained unchanged for generations.

"Institutions (aturan-aturan) for managing private property (pusako randah) and group property (pusako tinggi) have been managed by customary institutions (hukum adaik), since the time of our ancestors (jaman nenek-moyang). They cannot be changed, [if we changed them] we will be cursed (kutuak) [by our ancestors] by sumpah kawi." (Skm, panghulu of the Caniago, May 29, 2007)

In Sungai Pisang, the village council holds village meetings with representatives of all groups (suku) to identify how to move collectively towards the most desirable outcomes. Through village meetings (often held every Friday after Friday prayer), villagers create institutions known as 'village regulations' (peraturan desa). These are usually problem-specific and, in contrast to the existing customary institutions, often exist in written form. This village council and village meeting function of developing legitimate solutions to novel problems is crucial in Sungai Pisang.

The village council in Sungai Pisang is capable of providing legitimate and acceptable avenues for the fishing community to cope with environmental change and livelihood uncertainties. The process of constructing institutions is central in this instance. This type of central local coordinating and decision-making organization does not exist on the Spermonde Archipelago, where repetitive interactions (occurring under gradually changing environmental conditions) are the main basis from which institutions emerge (Jost 2005).

On the Spermonde Archipelago new institutions emerge, while previously crafted ones persist and change as fishermen rearrange the allocation of marine and coastal resources among resource users under changing circumstances. As fishermen's interaction became more complex with the "Blue Revolution" (i.e. the modernization and mechanization of capture fisheries) by the late 1960s (and the potential for conflict increased accordingly), a system capable of providing solutions to various complex situations, and storing flexibility to adapt to dynamically and unpredictably changing environments, was needed. Rather than trying to manage complex situations centrally, the collective actions of interacting fishermen, motivated by their interests, became the basis for addressing the increasing complexities of human-nature interactions in fisheries (Johnson 2009).

Through this repetitive interaction, every fisherman or groups of fishermen may challenge the previously crafted and agreed institutions and propose their own alternative, or even abandon them and craft new ones. Thus, from the 1960s to the present, institutions in capture fisheries (i.e. conventions, norms, and rules) have changed greatly. The absence of central local coordinating and decision-making organizations appears appropriate for coping with environmental change on the Spermonde Archipelago, where the geographical isolation of individual islands severely constrains interactions and communication between islands. Hypothetically speaking, a centralized system on the Spermonde Archipelago would put the whole system, including the livelihood system, at risk of failure, since communication is often hampered by geographical constraints and erratic environments. The absence of a central coordinating body in Spermonde has enabled the social system to respond to the unpredictably changing natural environment.

At both locations, compliance with institutions is the determining factor by which fishermen ensure that their coping strategies will work. Without particular mechanisms, compliance is barely performed. Compliance with institutions is partly achieved by punishments (cf. Henrich et al. 2006; Jaffe and Zaballa 2010), though, which is also the case for fishermen on the Spermonde Archipelago. Punishments range from public exposure, and thus guilt, to social exclusions for serious non-compliance with particular rules (Deswandi 2012). Compliance with institutions is also achieved by willingness to cooperate, motivated by social and cultural values and reciprocal generosity. In Sungai Pisang, the panghulu of each group or village council serves as a "third party" to ensure compliance with institutions at the group level and village level, respectively. However, cultural values (i.e. sumpah kawi) and the practice of reciprocal generosity also motivate compliance to institutions in Sungai Pisang.

CONCLUSION

Fisher households in Sungai Pisang, and on the small islands on the Spermonde Archipelago, are exposed to unexpected environmental changes. Such changes may gradually occur as the result of continuous fishery exploitation or abruptly as the impacts of increased hazards in the context of global environmental change. Hence, fishing is neither always successful nor reliable in terms of supporting household food security. In both of our study locations, local institutions were crucial in supporting successful livelihood and coping strategies, despite a range of limited options and limited accessibility to ecosystem resources. Through locally developed emergent institutions (Glaser et al. 2010) fishermen in both study locations have been able to secure their livelihoods – at least at the subsistence level.

Livelihood security at the household level is a central element of a resilient social system. However, as environments will always change, and mostly in an unpredictable manner, the most important property for local institutions is institutional adaptability, i.e. the capacity to (re)allocate natural resource use rights legitimately in a context of continuous environmental change. Such adaptability might take the form of modifying existing institutions or of constructing new institutions. A central function of institutional adaptability is to govern natural resource distribution, a major minefield in natural resource management. Adaptive local institutions in both study locations achieved a locally legitimate redistribution of resource access. Institutional adaptability to the ever-changing environment, in order to support the coping strategies of fishing households in the face of growing food insecurity, is thus the prominent property that contributes to a more resilient social system.

The ability and capacity of institutions to co-evolve and to adapt to ever-changing environments are inherent in the process through which institutions are crafted. Institutional adaptability can exist either as a coordinated process, as through the village council in Sungai Pisang, or as a self-organizing system which relies on repetitive interactions without any centralized coordination, as on the Spermonde Archipelago. The first option, a coordinated process, seems most suitable for communities that are homogenous in terms of culture, where the population resides in relatively clustered locations and where the managed natural resources are relatively near to resource users. The second option, a self-organizing process, seems to fit a culturally heterogeneous and geographically dispersed community, where the natural resources that need to be managed are spatially unevenly distributed and far from the resource users. Both centralized and non-centralized processes were found to be sensitive to the changing external and internal conditions in our study locations, and they were capable of providing legitimate and acceptable institutions to support the local development of coping strategies.

The vulnerability of natural resource-dependent communities to environmental changes, and hence to food insecurity, will continue to be affected by the increasing impacts of global change (e.g. climate change and international markets development). Such insecurity is further enhanced by the limited knowledge of respective global-local connectivity. On the other hand, scientists continue to document the specific impacts of local events on various social and ecological settings, and how communities manage to cope with the emerging vulnerability (cf. Kelkar et al. 2008; Hahn et al. 2009; Chikozho 2010). Knowledge exchange between resource users and scientists focusing on social-ecological system analysis is therefore increasingly crucial for both parties. For the community, this should enhance knowledge on prevailing environmental dynamics, especially global-local interactions, and help them to decide on the appropriate coping strategy that will not compromise their own livelihood system in the long run. For scientists and decision-makers, local knowledge is needed to plan the type of natural resources management that will contribute to more resilient social and ecological systems.

The prevalent coping strategies of the two studied communities entail unwanted impacts on exploited resource systems. Continuing fishing practices (including blast fishing, cyanide fishing, and ornamental coral collection) threaten the sustainability of the ecological system on the Spermonde Archipelago. Coral reef diversity and coverage in this region continue to decline year on year (cf. Jompa 1996; Knittweis 2008). In Sungai Pisang, 15 hectares of forest cover on the hill slope were cleared for gambier plantations only in 2006 (Yayasan Hayati Lestari 2006), a process that most likely continues. With continuing logging activities, forest clearing is likely to increase the vulnerability of Sungai Pisang villagers to landslides.

While there is a good deal of evidence that ecologically resilient systems support social resilience, there is less data on how social resilience may support the resilience of ecosystems (Adger 2000). Declining reef diversity and coverage on the Spermonde Archipelago, and continuing deforestation in Sungai Pisang, indicate an unbalanced relationship between ecological resilience and social resilience. This gap exists because the driving factors of social-ecological system dynamics in any particular locality originate at multiple spatial levels from the local to the global, and they are thus not always readily understood by local communities, or indeed by research, which still mostly focusses on a single system level. We hope that the empirical insight into the cases of Sungai Pisang and the Spermonde Archipelago offered here will contribute to closing this gap.

ACKNOWLEDGMENTS

Research in Sungai Pisang was carried out with financial support from the Ford Foundation, in collaboration with The Center for Irrigation, Land and Water Resource, and Development Studies, Andalas University and Asian Institute of Technology. Research on the Spermonde Archipelago was carried out within the frame of the bilateral Indonesian-German research program SPICE II (Science for the Protection of Indonesian Coastal Marine Ecosystems) sponsored by the German Federal Ministry of Education and Research (Grant No. 03F0474A), the Indonesian Ministry of Marine Affairs and Fisheries (DKP), and the Ministry for

Research and Technology (RISTEK), and it was supported by a scholarship from the Leibniz Center for Tropical Marine Ecology (ZMT), Bremen, Germany. We would like to thank the Center for Coral Reefs Research (CCRR) at Hasanuddin University for helping us to organize research on the Spermonde Archipelago. Muhammad Neil and the Student Association of the Anthropology Department of Hasanuddin University were very kind by providing us with data from a kinship survey on Bonetambung Island. We would also like to thank Kathleen Schwerdtner Máñez, who made valuable comments on the earlier version of this text.

REFERENCES

Adger, W. N. (2000): Social and Ecological Resilience: Are They related? Progress in Human Geography 24/3, 347-364.

Badan Perencanan dan Pembangunan Nasional (BAPPENAS) (2009): Repelita I Tahun 1969/70 – 1973/74, July 29th, 2010, accessible under: http://www.bappenas.go.id/node/42/1701/repelita-i-tahun-196970---197374/.

Badan Pusat Statistik (BPS) (2007): Jumlah Penduduk Kelurahan Teluk Kabung Selatan Menurut Kelompok Umur," September 30th, 2011, accessible under: http://www.padang.go.id/v2/content/view/2682/231/.

Badan Pusat Statistik (BPS) (2011): Data Strategis BPS, Jakarta: Badan Pusat Statistik.

Balai Konservasi Sumber Daya Alam (BKSDA) (2007): Izin Penangkar Tumbuhan dan Satwa Liar Balai Besar Konservasi Sumber Daya Alam Sulawesi Selatan Sampai Dengan Tahun 2007, June 10th, 2010, accessible under: http://www.dephut.go.id/files/statBKSDASulsel_07_KonservasiKeanekarag amanHayati.pdf.

Bennett, E./Neiland, A./Anang, E./Bannerman, P./Atiq Rahman, A./Huq, S./Bhuiya, S./Day, M./Fulford-Gardiner, M./Clerveaux, W. (2001): Towards a Better Understanding of Conflict Management in Tropical Fisheries: Evidence from Ghana, Bangladesh and the Caribbean. Marine Policy 25/5, 365-376.

Bentley, N. (1998): Fishing for Solutions: Can the Live Trade in Wild Groupers and Wrasses from Southeast Asia be Managed?, Selangor: TRAFFIC.

Berkes, F./Colding, J./Folke, C. (2003): Navigating Social-Ecological System: Building Resilience for Complexity and Change, Cambridge: Cambridge University Press.

Brugnach, M./Dewulf, A./Pahl-Wostl, C./Taillieu, T. (2008): Toward a Relational Concept of Uncertainty: About Knowing too Little, Knowing too Differently, and Accepting Not to Know. Ecology and Society 13/2, accessible under: http://www.ecologyandsociety.org/vol13/iss2/art30/.

Carpenter, S. R./Brock, W. A. (2008): Adaptive Capacity and Traps. Ecology and Society 13/2, accessible under: http://www.ecologyandsociety .org/vol13/iss2/art40/.

Carpenter, S. R./Mooney, H./Agard, J./Capistrano, D./DeFries, R. S./Diaz, S./Dietz, T./Duraiappah, A. K./Oteng-Yeboah, A./Pereira, H. M./Perrings, C./Reid, W. V./Sarukhan, J./Scholes, R. J./Whyte, A. (2009): Science for Managing Ecosystem Services: Beyond the Millenium Ecosystem Assessment. Proceedings of the National Academy of Sciences of the United States of America 106, 1305-1312.

Chikozho, C. (2010): Applied social research and action priorities for adaptation to climate change and rainfall variability in the rainfed agricultural sector of Zimbabwe. Physics and Chemistry of the Earth, Parts A/B/C 35/13-14, 780-790.

Chou, L. M./Tuan, V. S./Reefs, P./Yeemin, T./Cabanban, A./Suharsono/Kessna, I. (2002): Status of Southeast Asia Coral Reefs, Queensland: Australian Institute of Marine Science, accessible under: http://www.aims.gov.au /pages/research/coral-bleaching/scr2002/pdf/scr2002-07.pdf.

Colding, J./Elmqvist, T./Olsson, P. (2003): Living with Disturbance: Buiding Resilience in Social-Ecological Systems. In: Berkes, F./Colding, J./Folke, C. (eds.), Navigating Social-Ecological System: Building Resilience for Complexity and Change, Cambridge: Cambridge University Press, 163-188.

Cooperative for Assistance and Relief Everywhere (CARE) (2002): Household Livelihood Security Assessments: A Toolkit for Practitioners, Arizona: TANGO International Inc.

Daniel G. M. (1996): Measuring Food Insecurity: The Frequency and Severity of "Coping Strategies. Food Policy 21/3, 291-303.

Dean, W. R./Sharkey, J. R. (2011): Food Insecurity, Social Capital and Perceived Personal Disparity in A Predominantly Rural Region of Texas: An individual-level Analysis. In: Social Science & Medicine 72/9, 1454-1462.

Deswandi, R. (2007): Means Of Living: A Case Study Of Livelihood Strategies Of Fishermen in Kelurahan Bungus Teluk Kabung Selatan, Nagari Sungai Pisang, West Sumatra, Indonesia, Master Thesis. Department of Rural and Regional Development. Padang: Andalas University.

Deswandi, R. (2012): Understanding Institutional Dynamic: The Emergence, Persistence, and Change of Institutions in Fisheries in Spermonde Archipelago, South Sulawesi, Indonesia, PhD Thesis. Faculty of Social Sciences. Bremen: Bremen University.

Foell, J./Harrison, E./Stirrat, R. L. (1999): Participatory Approaches to Natural Resource Management: The Case of Coastal Zone Management in the Puttalam District, Brighton: University of Sussex.

Ford, J. D./Berrang-Ford, L./King, M./Furgal, C. (2010): Vulnerability of Aboriginal Health Systems in Canada to Climate Change. Global Environmental Change 20/4, 668-680.

Ford, J. D./Smit, B./Wandel, J. (2006): Vulnerability to Climate Change in the Arctic: A Case Study from Arctic Bay, Canada. Global Environmental Change 16/2, 145-160.

Fraser, E. D. G. (2006): Food System Vulnerability: Using Past Famines to Help Understand How Food Systems May Adapt to Climate Change. Ecological Complexity 3/4, 328-335.

Glaser, M./Baitoningsih, W./Ferse, S. C. A./Neil, M./Deswandi, R. (2010a): Whose Sustainability? Top-down Participation and Emergent Rules in Marine Protected Area Management in Indonesia. Marine Policy 34/6, 1215-1225.

Glaser, M./Krause, G./Oliveira, R. S./Herazo-Fontalvo, M. (2010b): Mangroves and People: A Social-Ecological System. In: Saint Paul, U./Schneider, H. (eds.), Mangrove dynamics and management in North Brazil, Berlin: Springer, 307-354.

Gunderson, L. H. (2003): Adaptive Dancing: Interaction between Social Resilience and Ecological Crises. In: Berkes, F./Colding, J./Folke, C. (eds.), Navigating Social-Ecological System: Building Resilience for Complexity and Change, Cambridge: Cambridge University Press, 33-52.

Hahn, M. B./Riederer, A. M./Foster, S. O. (2009): The Livelihood Vulnerability Index: A Pragmatic Approach to Assessing Risks from Climate Variability and Change--A Case Study in Mozambique. Global Environmental Change 19/1, 74-88.

Henrich, J./McElreath, R./Barr, A./Ensminger, J./Barrett, C./Bolyanatz, A./Cardenas, J. C./Gurven, M./Gwako, E./Henrich, N./Lesorogol, C./Marlowe, F./Tracer, D./Ziker, J. (2006): Costly Punishment Across Human Societies. Science 312/5781, 1767-1770.

Holling, C. S. (1973): Resilience and Stability of Ecological System. Annual Review of Ecology Systematics 4, 1-23.

Hopley, D./Suharsono (2000): The Status of Coral Reefs in Eastern Indonesia, Townsvile: Australian Institute of Marine Science.

Huang, J./Guo, B./Kim, Y. (2010): Food insecurity and disability: Do economic resources matter? Social Science Research 39/1, 111-124.

International Union for Conservation of Nature (IUCN) (2011): The IUCN Red List of Threatened Species, September 30th, 2011, accessible under: http://www.iucnredlist.org/apps/redlist/details/4592/0).

Jaffe, K./Zaballa, L. (2010): Cooperative Punishment Cements Social Cohesion. Journal of Artificial Societies and Social Simulation 13/3, 4.

Joewono, B. N. (2011): Cuaca Buruk: 473.000 Nelayan Tidak Bisa Melaut. Kompas February 15th, 2011, accessible under http://nasional.kompas .com/read/2011/02/15/18302243/473.000.Nelayan.Tidak.Bisa.Melaut.

Johnson, N. (2009): Simply Complexity: A Clear Guide to Complexity Theory, Oxford: Oneworld Publications.

Jompa, J. (1996): Monitoring and Assessment of Coral Reefs in Spermonde Archipelago, South Sulawesi, Master Thesis. Department of Biology. Hamilton: McMaster University.

Jost, J. (2005): Formal aspects of the emergence of institutions." In: Santa Fe Institute Working Paper, accessible under: http://www.santafe.edu /research/working-papers/05-05-018.pdf.

Kawasan Industri Makassar (KIMA) (2006): List of Company in Makassar Industrial Park, June 10th, 2010, accessible under: http://ptkima-makassar.co.id/index.php?option=com_content&task=category&sectionid=8 &id=26&Itemid=56).

Kelkar, U./Narula, K. K./Sharma, V. P./Chandna, U. (2008): Vulnerability and adaptation to climate variability and water stress in Uttarakhand State, India. Global Environmental Change 18/4, 564-574.

Kelurahan Bungus Teluk Kabung Selatan (2006): Monograf Nagari Sungai Pisang, Kecamatan Bungus Teluk Kabung Selatan, Padang.

Knittweis, L. (2008): Population Demographics and Life History Characteristics of Heliofungia actiniformis: A Fungiid Coral Species Exploitted for the Live Coral Aquarium Trade in the Spermonde Archipelago, Indonesia, PhD Thesis. Faculty of Biology. Bremen: University of Bremen.

Lindström, M./Merlo, J./Östergren, P.-O. (2003): Social capital and sense of insecurity in the neighborhood: a population-based multilevel analysis in Malmö, Sweden. Social Science & Medicine 56/5, 1111-1120.

Nelson, D. R./Finan, T. J. (2009): Praying for Drought: Persistent Vulnerability and the Politics of Patronage in Ceará, Northeast Brazil. American Anthropologist 111/3, 302-316.

Nisbet, M. C./Mooney, C. (2007): Science and Society: Framing Science. Science 316/5821, 56.

Osbahr, H./Twyman, C./Neil Adger, W./Thomas, D. S. G. (2008): Effective Livelihood Adaptation to Climate Change Disturbance: Scale Dimensions of Practice in Mozambique. Geoforum 39/6, 1951-1964.

Paavola, J. (2008): Livelihoods, vulnerability and adaptation to climate change in Morogoro, Tanzania. Environmental Science & Policy 11/7, 642-654.

Pelras, C. (2000): Patron-client Ties among the Bugis and Makassarese of South Sulawesi. Bijdragen tot de Taal-, Land- en Volkenkunde 156/3, 393-432.

Quinn, C. H./Huby, M./Kiwasila, H./Lovett, J. C. (2007): Design principles and Common Pool Resource Management: An Institutional Approach to Evaluating Community Management in Semi-arid Tanzania. Journal of Environmental Management 84/1, 100-113.

Schlager, E./Ostrom, E. (1999): Property Rights Regimes and Coastal Fisheries: An Empirical Analysis. In: McGinnis, M.D. (ed.), Polycentric Governance and Development: Readings from the Workshop in Political Theory and Policy Analysis, Michigan: The University of Michigan Press, 87-113.

Smith, L. A. (2007): Chaos: A Very Short Introduction, New York: Oxford University Press.

Stainback, S./Stainback, W. (1988): Understanding and Conducting Qualitative Research, Iowa: Kendall/Hunt Publishing Company.

Thorburn, C. C. (2000): Changing Customary Marine Resource Management Practice and Institutions: The Case of Sasi Lola in the Kei Islands, Indonesia. World Development 28/8, 1461-1479.

Vatn, A. (2005): Institutions and the Environment, Cheltenham: Edward Elgar Publishing.

Waldrop, M. M. (1992): Complexity: The Emerging Science at The Edge of Order and Chaos, New York: Simon & Schuster Paperbacks.

Walker, B./Gunderson, L./Kinzig, A. P./Folke, C./Carpenter, S./Schultz, L. (2006): A Handful of Heuristics and Some Propositions for Understanding Resilience in Social-ecological Systems. Ecology and Society 11/1, accessible under: http://www.ecologyandsociety.org/vol11/iss1/art13/.

Walker, B./Holling, C. S./Carpenter, S. R./Kinzig, A. (2004): Resilience, Adaptability and Transformability in Social-ecological Systems. Ecology and Society 9/2, accessible under http://www.ecologyandsociety.org/vol9/iss2/art5/.

Walker, W. E./Harremoës, P./Rotmans, J./van der Sluijs, J. P./van Asselt, M. B. A./Janssen, P./von Krauss, M. P. K. (2003): Defining Uncertainty: A Conceptual Basis for Uncertainty Management in Model-Based Decision Support. Integrated Assessment 4/1, 5 - 17.

Wills-Herrera, E./Orozco, L. E./Forero-Pineda, C./Pardo, O./Andonova, V. (2011): The relationship between perceptions of insecurity, social capital and subjective well-being: Empirical evidences from areas of rural conflict in Colombia. Journal of Socioeconomics 40/1, 88-96.

Wood, G. (2003): Staying Secure, Staying Poor: The "Faustian Bargain". World Development 31/3, 455-471.

World Bank (2010): Agriculture and Rural Development, July, 13th, 2010, accessible under: http://data.worldbank.org/topic/agriculture-and-rural-development.

Yayasan Hayati Lestari (2006): Rencana Strategis Pengelolaan Kawasan Pesisir dan Laut Sungai Pisang, Padang: Yayasan Hayati Lestari Foundation and Dinas Kelautan dan Perikanan Kota Padang.

Afterthoughts

Issues for an Anthropology of Knowledge and Development

FABIAN SCHOLTES

The editors have kindly invited me to contribute a short reflection on the different papers of this volume. Obviously, such reflection can come from different angles. There are two things that will probably influence the perspective I offer. On the one hand, I've been working for an aid agency until recently. Whether my interest in the practical importance of knowledge is a result of or rather a reason for doing so, it certainly influences my reading of the papers. On the other hand, I am interested in the present collection's topics as an academic. More specifically, my focus is on the many possible relations of knowledge and development, also in a conceptual sense. Given my background, environmental change in Southeast Asia is one empirical topic in which this more general issue appears.

My comments are therefore limited regarding regional studies, and they may involve some ambivalence between concerns of rigour, coherence, and the like and, on the other hand, practical utility. Of course, the fundamental question of whether the latter principally impedes the former is lurking here. However, rather than opening this can of worms, I hope this comment may actually gain from that double concern.

THE DEVELOPMENTAL KNOWLEDGE TURN

In my view, Hornidge's discussion of different knowledge discourses highlights two important factors. First, they are less distinct than the different catchwords suggest. At least the first three or four of them share the tendency that knowledge is primarily considered a resource, an instrument for technological change and growth, and that the kind of knowledge, knowledge production, and knowledge management of highly industrialized countries is reference. It does seem that, by and large, those who usually "name things" have successfully made their use of the interpretive space that the fuzzy concept of knowledge offers and inflicts.

This does not only mean that the topic has been captured to some extent, as some of its critical potential has also been taken away. This concerns development practice quite immediately. Agencies like the World Bank have been diagnosed as practising "repressive tolerance" (as Bierschenk 2008 p. 10 put it with reference to H. Marcuse), in that they tend to disarm critique by officially integrating the demands from critique into their repertory, appropriating the new issues and imperatives – such as equality or sustainability – without changing much their fundamentals such as growth. Similarly, the developmental knowledge turn seems to turn the concept of knowledge towards development practice rather than development practice towards knowledge, in a broader or critical sense. But the same practical reasoning that often emphasises a narrow instrumental importance of knowledge should also account for and make use of the potential of a critical approach. After all, development practice may only gain, in terms of effectiveness and legitimacy, from considering critical views that shed light on the incompatibilities of their approaches with local knowledge and practice or on implicit, deep-rooted assumptions of their work.

Agencies are of course not homogenous, but neither is their view on knowledge. You may not find many people with a decidedly critical view on knowledge and development. You may actually find quite a few without an elaborate viewpoint, because often enough programmatic publications calling for 'knowledge for development' have little to do with daily work. The point is that, based on their experience, many aid workers and bureaucrats are very well aware of knowledge involving much more than useful know-that and know-how. At the same time, few institutions phrase and acknowledge it this way.

WAYS OF KNOWING

So, we have what you may call a 'technical bias'. Moreover, and this is my second lesson from Hornidge's paper, there is also a bias towards content. As such, this picture is incomplete. As Fredrik Barth suggested in his outline of an Anthropology of Knowledge (2002), knowledge consists not only in a stock of knowledge (things that people know, be it know-that or know-how), but also in what have been termed "ways of knowing" (e.g. Harris 2007): something 'is known' by documentation, communication, it is distributed, employed, transmitted, etc., and there are ways as to how knowledge is validated as true, added to, and made coherent with previous knowledge. All these are ways of how something is known.

To date, knowledge has been mostly addressed under the question "What do you know?" (in terms of how the weather is changing, how to cope with changing weather, or where this change comes from). To understand other communities' knowledge more fully, the "How do you know?" question deserves more attention. As contributions to this volume underline, knowledge dynamics, contestation, and innovation in a broad sense matter greatly. These dynamics are certainly influenced by different ways of knowing and by the criteria for validity, coherence, etc. that people apply. Whether and how a Spermonde community develops new resource management institutions (Deswandi et al., this volume) most probably depends on the ways in which existing institutions are known as legitimate or how facts about resources are assembled and interpreted into a need for change.

This also matters a lot from a practitioner's point of view. Some aid agencies try to convey new knowledge via culturally established means of communication and related ways of knowing, for instance by putting legal information into the traditional medium of religious poetry. Often – also in this volume – there is a call for dialogue between climate science and local knowers, without which climate change adaptation measures seem doomed to be ineffective. This dialogue will probably have better prospects if Indonesian farmers not only come to know what science knows in terms of climate projections, and if scientists learn which repertory of adaptation measures these farmers already have, but also if awareness of how both sides know what they know enables actual compatibility of these different knowledge.

In the present volume, Ehlert is most explicit about these different ways of knowing, for instance when she presents proverbs as a mode of documenting local experience and of formulating laws of nature. This provides a useful basis for understanding how exactly the local stock of knowledge is (or, for that matter, can be) combined with new knowledge from science-based meteorology.

At the same time, it also shows how tricky – from a research point of view: worthwhile – it is to investigate the combination of distinct knowledge. The different concepts Ehlert refers to indicate the many possible ways available, and one should distinguish carefully if people substitute information from traditional indicators by that of science-based indicators, if they translate from one calendar to the other, if they intermingle different knowledge components, and if this is a loose co-existence of components, a functional 'division of labour' (e.g. traditional weather lore for short-term decisions, modern meteorology for long-term decisions) or indeed a hybridization resulting in new content or even a new form of knowledge.

Again, this is more than an academic exercise. It makes an important difference if people develop a way to take up meteorological information directly, such that this information turns out to be readily compatible and can be disseminated as it is, or if it requires – more or less reliable – translation into, for example, how the clouds to be expected will be formed.

TOWARDS A SYSTEMATIC APPROACH

While Hornidge shows how knowledge as a whole (albeit an incomplete, biased one) has figured in discourses of development, Antweiler offers a proposal for eliciting and analyzing (local) knowledge itself, for unpacking and going into it thoroughly. As part of his proposal, the aforementioned 'how' of knowing transpires as one of three "levels of thought" that prevail in any form of knowledge: ordering discontinuity and diversity. Local knowledge may be a patchwork rather than a fully organized, orderly system, but to 'knowing' there is always some ordering.

In his list of different levels of knowledge, one level concerns the knowledge of processes. Processes of knowledge, on the other hand, are only mentioned in a generic list of "interrelated qualities of local knowledge," e.g. as "informal learning" or as practicing "optimal ignorance." In my view a more general model, for which Antweiler offers a basis, should be more systematic about this 'how' of knowing. It may be worth exploring specific ways of knowing related to specific kinds of content. More generally, I wonder about the relations between the different qualities. Each quality, each of its aspects, may be inquired upon empirically. But to give orientation to research (however tentative and adaptable this orientation must be, given the slipperiness of the subject), it seems worth linking these qualities with models or concepts in a more narrow sense, such as the one given by Barth mentioned above, and to heuristically position and maybe categorize the listed aspects therein.

Thus, the debate may gain from a more systematic approach to knowledge, even if contributions do not aim at generalization as (rightly) advocated by Antweiler. I had some doubts about, or misunderstanding of, conclusions drawn by Reichel et al. (this volume) regarding the more persistent frames of reference of local knowledge that structure practice (is the fading of the religiously flanked 'open access' idea a cause or rather a result of the new profit maximization?). However, I did find it very helpful to see a systematic approach to how knowledge, politics of knowledge, practice, and reference frameworks are related.

LOCAL KNOWLEDGE?

Of course, any such approach needs an underlying idea of local knowledge. One thing to do is to suggest a heuristic concept of knowledge that 'only' serves the empirical purpose to collect and organize data, i.e. a concept according to which one looks at data as local knowledge. A different and more daring tactic is to go further and actually make propositions about what local knowledge actually is. Antweiler's idea of local knowledge being a specific, though universal, form of knowledge seems an attempt at this approach.

Unless 'local' is specified, the proverbial heretic would ask, "Which knowledge is not local?" After all, everything that is known is known by somebody who is always in a local context and who gives it a local meaning; otherwise, it would be mere information. Even 'global' knowledge such as projected climate change is known by people who refer to it quite differently. The question must therefore determine how and in which (in whatever sense, e.g. geographically) local interpretation something is known – and is thereby local knowledge.

So, how and how narrowly should local knowledge be specified? A common view seems to be that knowledge is local in that it is known by a limited group (also in some geographical sense – or would the knowledge of IPCC scientists worldwide figure as local knowledge?). In this case, local knowledge may encompass all that these local people know, or all that only they know. The first option may still be too broad, in that not all that local people know is something only they know; they know a lot of things other people know, too. Of course, the heretic will insist here that all is known in a local manner.

The second option is taken by Deswandi et al. (this volume) when they define local knowledge to be the knowledge of local people that concerns local phenomena. Consulting the heretic once again, he might hold here that few local phenomena are fully specific for one place. Cosmologies, for instance, may be locally specific explanations, but they are explanations of something rather global.

If I understand him correctly, Antweiler goes even further in that he limits local knowledge to action-oriented knowledge, and this together with other characteristics seems to make the specific form he suggests local knowledge to be. I wonder if this overshoots the target. Emic explanations of peatland fires (see Bizard, this volume) are certainly action-related, even if not necessarily action-oriented, but I have doubts as to whether cosmologies shared by local people, which are an important element of their knowledge, are action-oriented – unless one takes the pursuit of "ontological security" (Giddens) to be action.

The point is thus about exploring further definitions of local knowledge that dare to go beyond a case-specific heuristic device and allows us to think of more or less the same thing when we talk about local knowledge. I am by no means advocating some die-hard, strict blueprint definition or model to be applied regardless of context, as all the papers underlining that we must not essentialize local knowledge are right to do so. However, maybe a well-specified concept of local knowledge may indeed prevent local knowledge from being romanticized, reduced to folklore, exoticized, or the like.

KNWOLEDGE, UNCERTAINTY AND INNOVATION

Such a well-specified concept of knowledge may also provide orientation regarding whether or not local knowledge is actually the crucial factor or analytical entry point for understanding people's actions. While the question of the role of local knowledge naturally should figure in any analysis of local action, one should avoid the trap of the 'law of the instrument'. As Ehlert (this volume) rightly concludes, knowledge is only one element of coping with change. It may indeed be material constraints limiting the application of fire management knowledge, and rather than fire knowledge itself, the ambivalent evaluations of fire or the higher moral importance of fire damaging one's personal property, which allow for understanding how people in Tumbang Lewu and Hidup Baru deal with blazes (see Bizard, this volume).

Moreover, it may not be knowledge but rather the lack or loss thereof that is crucial, whether this is caused by environmental change or otherwise. Silitoe and Alam (this volume) translate the changing state of the environment into uncertainty. However, they do so in a varying sense. In the case of hydrological changes, uncertainty consists directly in unpredictability. In the case of "resource uncertainties" (fishing and others) or "economic uncertainties," uncertainty consists in uncertain livelihoods caused by decreases in resource availability or an increase in market dependency – which themselves are rather certain. There is a difference between not knowing what the (environmental) facts will look like and not knowing how to deal with them accordingly.

From an academic point of view, such different ways of viewing how uncertainty and knowledge are related may be explored more systematically. From a practitioner's point of view this matters, in that these ways call for different reactions. Climate change information may tame the uncertainty of facts such as the set-in of the rainy season; education and training may tame the uncertainty of how to deal with them suitably. In both cases, however, it is not only about the lack or loss of knowledge. It is also about which knowledge continues to matter. People who face uncertainty fall back to what they still know, in order to understand, manage, or even overcome uncertainty or a lack of knowledge.

This fallback could be substantial knowledge, such as "knowledge of cassava diversity and clonal" (Ellen and Soselisa, this volume p. 213). On a more fundamental level, it could indeed be the cultural frames of reference to which Reichel et al. (this volume) refer, or their cognitive ways of managing uncertainty, which allow people to understand and handle uncertainties. However, it could also be their ways of innovation, as a constructive element of their 'ways of knowing', as well as people's cultural attitudes towards knowledge and its dynamics and changing validity. Innovation and the uptake of knowledge and interventions do depend on attitudes such as what Ehlert, in her description of the Mekong Delta (this volume), calls pragmatism, a pragmatic 'what works' relationship rather than a cosmological relationship to knowledge and to the environment.

To me this seems to be a highly promising focus of micro-empirical research following up on the papers of this volume – again, from both an academic and a practical point of view. As mentioned before, some of the papers rightly underline the dynamics of knowledge. To understand how local knowledge changes more specifically, the ways, sources, and conditions of innovation and creativity are as crucial as the ways and causes of the loss of knowledge. The role of education, of material and environmental circumstances, of institutional space and flexibility, of innovation attitudes, and of pressure and leeway to innovate are obvious topics that are certainly worth exploring, and they would also help in linking the aspect of knowledge with the many other factors or aspects of how people live with, manage, and adapt to change.

Finally, regarding development practice, what could be more important to learn about than the ways in which people help themselves and bring about change? After all, decades of research and practice have shown again and again that any support from the outside is doomed to fail, if it does not rest upon what people on the inside know and do. Such learning will not only require many more resources and, in particular, time than is usually devoted to considering local practice and to adapting interventions. It will also require, for instance, a steadier and more interactive relationship with research, a much better defined and more realistic demand for research, more openness towards uncomfortable results, etc. – hence a paradigm of 'knowledge and development' that is very different from what Hornidge's paper shows to be dominating nowadays.

REFERENCES

Barth, Fredrik (2002): An Anthropology of Knowledge. Current Anthropology 43 (1), 1-11.

Bierschenk, Thomas (2008): Anthropology and Development. An historicizing and localizing approach. Working Paper no. 87, Department of Anthropology and African Studies, University of Mainz.

Harris, Mark (Ed.) (2007): Ways of Knowing: Anthropological Approaches To Crafting Experience And Knowledge, Chippenham.

Maslow, Abraham (1966): Psychology of Science. Harper & Row, New York.

Contributors

Alam, Mahbub is Assistant Professor of Social Science and Humanities in the School of Liberal Arts and Social Sciences at the Independent University, Bangladesh. He has been a visiting faculty member at BRAC University, Dhaka University, Uppsala University, and Gothenburg University, teaching on indigenous knowledge and natural resources management in Bangladesh. He has 18 years' experience working in the development sector in Bangladesh with NGOs, national and international research institutes, and UN organizations. He is affiliated with many national, regional, and global civil society forums. He has interests in the incorporation of indigenous knowledge, particularly of fisheries, into development programs.

Antweiler, Christoph studied Geology, Geography, and then Cultural Anthropology in Cologne, Germany, and obtained his PhD in Cultural Anthropology from the University of Cologne. From 1996 he was Professor of Cultural Anthropology in Trier and since 2008 heads the Southeast Asia Department at the Institute of Oriental and Asian Studies (IOA) in the University of Bonn, Germany. His research foci are cognition, decision-making, urbanity, natural resources, cultural evolution, and human universals. His regional focus is the Malay realm of Indonesia and Malaysia.

Bizard, Viola studied Social Anthropology and Political Science at Freiburg University, Germany. Since September 2011, she has been a PhD candidate in Environmental Anthropology at the School of Anthropology and Conservation at Kent University, Canterbury. Her research seeks to investigate the salience of the rattan domain in Katingan District, Central Kalimantan, within the context of dynamic socioeconomic and environmental variables and Indonesia's overall carbon emission reduction efforts.

Deswandi, Rio has worked in the Indonesian coastal zone on community-level institutional dynamics and volunteered in community-based disaster risk management in West Sumatra. Interested in complex systems, he is an alumnus of the Santa Fe Institute and PhD candidate in the Social-Ecological Systems Analysis Group at the Leibniz Center for Tropical Marine Ecology (ZMT), Bremen, Germany.

Ehlert, Judith studied Sociology in Germany and Ireland. She obtained her PhD in development research from the Center for Development Research, University of Bonn (Germany), where she currently works as senior researcher in the Department of Political and Cultural Change. Her PhD deals with environmental knowledge and agrarian change in the Mekong Delta, Vietnam. Based on her extensive field research she specializes in Southeast Asia and currently works on civil society and the political ecology of food and agriculture.

Ellen, Roy is Professor of Anthropology and Human Ecology, and Director of the Centre for Biocultural Diversity, at the University of Kent, Canterbury, UK. He has undertaken fieldwork mainly in the Moluccas and his books on Indonesia include The Cultural Relations of Classification: An Analysis of Nuaulu Animal Categories from Central Seram (1992) and On the Edge of the Banda Zone: Past and Present in the Social Organization of a Moluccan Trading Network (2003).

Ferse, Sebastian studied Biology and Marine Ecology in Bremen and Göttingen, Germany, and Santa Barbara, USA. He obtained an MSc and PhD in Coral Reef Ecology from Bremen University, Bremen. Since 2008, he has worked on marine resource use and coastal livelihoods in Indonesia within the social-ecological systems analysis group of the Leibniz Center for Tropical Marine Ecology (ZMT) in Bremen, Germany.

Glaser, Marion is an environmental sociologist and has worked in Asia and South and Central America. She is on the Scientific Steering Committee of the global LOICZ program, is Vice-President of the German Society for Human Ecology, and leads the Social-Ecological Systems Analysis Group at the Leibniz Center for Tropical Marine Ecology (ZMT), Bremen, Germany.

Harms, Arne holds a Master's degree with a background in Social Anthropology, Modern South Asian Studies, and Religious Studies. Arne has worked with coastal populations in South India, the Anglophone Caribbean, and Eastern India. While earlier research projects were centered on issues such as political conflict, migration, and popular religion, he is currently, in his PhD research, concentrating on natural hazards, forced migration, and social remembering among inhabitants of the Ganges delta.

Hornidge, Anna-Katharina studied Southeast Asian Studies, Indonesian and Sociology in Bonn, Germany and Singapore and obtained her PhD in the Sociology of Knowledge from the Technical University, Berlin. In 2006, she joined as Senior Researcher the Department of Social and Cultural Change at the Center for Development Research, University of Bonn, Germany. Here, she specializes in (local/national) knowledge and innovation systems in (natural) resources management under increasingly changing conditions in Southeast and Central Asia, as well as the accompanying global discourses.

Martens, Sofie Elena studied Social and Cultural Anthropology, Applied Botany, and Southeast Asian Studies at the University of Hamburg. Focussing on social-ecological systems, local ecological knowledge, cognitive ecological networks, and the social dimensions of natural disasters, she has worked with fishing communities in Indonesia. Currently, she is conducting participatory research on the spatial attribution of risk in urban environments at the Disaster Research Unit at the Freie Universität, Berlin.

Reichel, Christian holds a Master's degree in Social and Cultural Anthropology and Geography. His research and teaching focus on human-nature relations, local knowledge for the prediction, protection and adaptation to climate-related catastrophes, as well as ecosystem services and livelihood analysis. He has undertaken ethnographic fieldwork in Indonesia, Mongolia, and Romania. As part of his PhD, he conducts research on the mapping and visualization of local environmental knowledge about natural hazards in the Swiss, German, and Austrian Alps.

Scholtes, Fabian studied international economics in Tuebingen and Rio de Janeiro. In his PhD thesis (2006) he explored Amartya Sen's Capability Approach towards sustainability and intergenerational justice. After two years as a senior researcher at the Center for Development Research (University of Bonn) he joined the research cooperation division of the German development bank KfW in 2009. His research interests include critical development theory and the anthropology of organizations, knowledge, and technology. The points of view formulated in this paper are his personal ones.

Silitoe, Paul is Professor of Anthropology at Durham University and Shell Chair of Sustainable Development at Qatar University. His current research interests focus on local knowledge in tropical and sub-tropical natural resource management strategies, specializing in international development and social change, livelihood and technology, environment and conservation, political ecology and land issues, human ecology and ethnoscience. He has conducted extensive fieldwork in the Pacific region and is involved in projects in South Asia, and he is currently working in the Gulf region on conservation and sustainable development initiatives.

Soselisa, Hermien L. is a Lecturer in Cultural Anthropology at Pattimura University, Ambon, Indonesia. She has undertaken fieldwork on Buano (West Seram) and Garogos (East Seram), and is the author of Fishers of Garogos: Livelihood and Resource Management in a Maluku Island, Indonesia (2004).